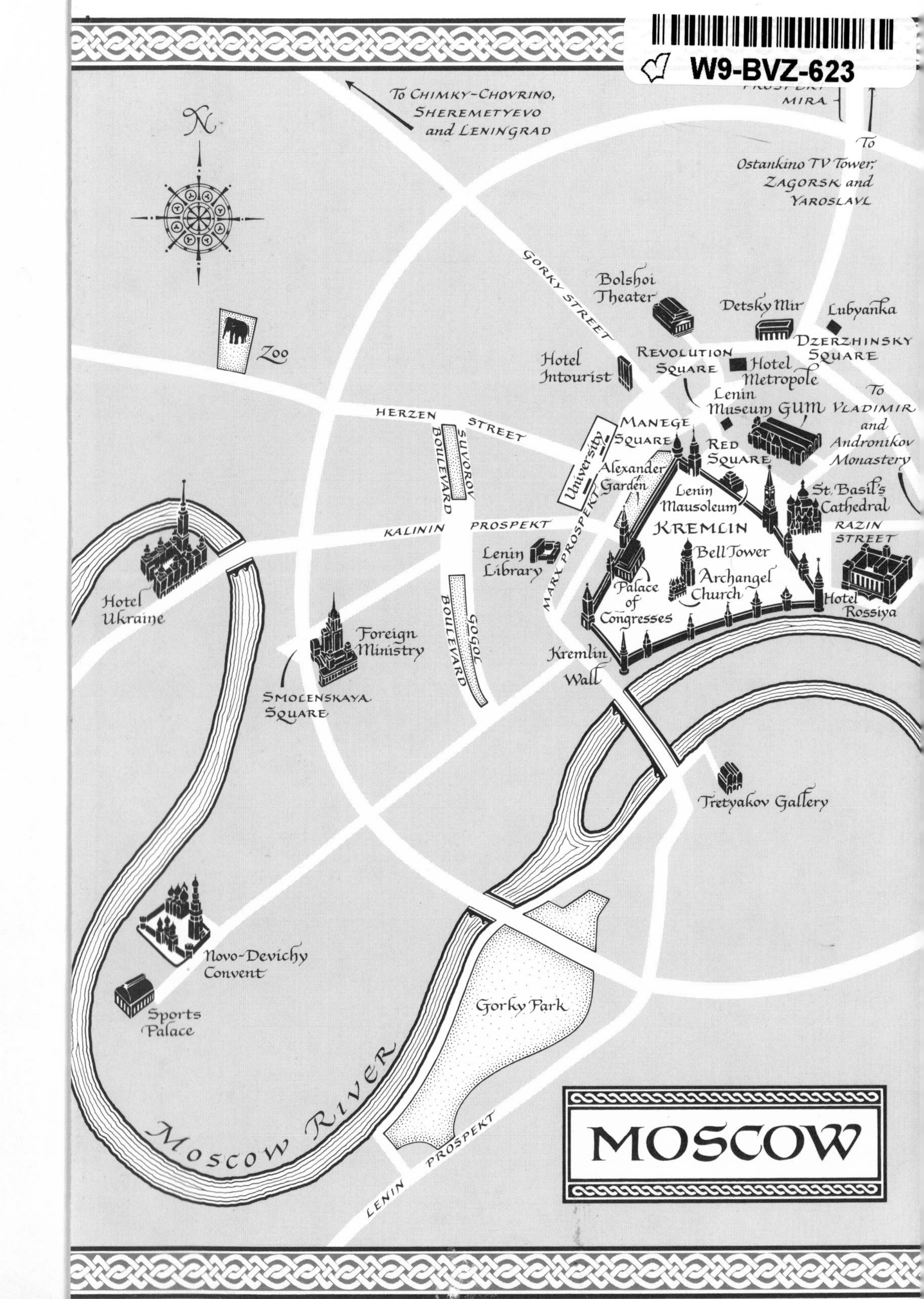

MOSCOW
To Chimky-Chovrino, Sheremetyevo and Leningrad
Prospekt Mira
To Ostankino TV Tower, Zagorsk and Yaroslavl
N
Gorky Street
Bolshoi Theater
Detsky Mir
Lubyanka
Dzerzhinsky Square
Revolution Square
Hotel Metropole
Hotel Intourist
Zoo
Herzen Street
Suvorov Boulevard
Lenin Museum
GUM
To Vladimir and Andronikov Monastery
Manege Square
University
Red Square
Alexander Garden
Lenin Mausoleum
St. Basil's Cathedral
Kremlin
Razin Street
Kalinin Prospekt
Marx Prospekt
Lenin Library
Bell Tower
Archangel Church
Palace of Congresses
Hotel Rossiya
Hotel Ukraine
Foreign Ministry
Gogol Boulevard
Smolenskaya Square
Kremlin Wall
Tretyakov Gallery
Novo-Devichy Convent
Sports Palace
Gorky Park
Moscow River
Lenin Prospekt

T

THR

ROM

ALSO BY RUSSELL FRASER

A Mingled Yarn: The Life of R. P. Blackmur

The Language of Adam

The Dark Ages and the Age of Gold

An Essential Shakespeare

The War Against Poetry

Shakespeare's Poetics

Russell Fraser

HARCOURT BRACE JOVANOVICH, PUBLISHERS

THE THREE ROMES

SAN DIEGO NEW YORK LONDON

HBJ

Library of Congress Cataloging in Publication Data
Fraser, Russell A.
The three Romes.
1. Moscow (R.S.F.S.R.)—Description. 2. Istanbul (Turkey)—Description. 3. Rome (Italy)—Description. 4. Fraser, Russell A. I. Title.
DK601.2.F7 1985 947'.312 84-12946
ISBN 0-15-190186-4

Designed by Dalia Hartman

Printed in the United States of America

First edition

A B C D E

CONTENTS

PREFACE

THE THREE ROMES are Moscow, Constantinople (now Istanbul), and Rome itself. Each of these cities, vitally alive in the present, is a magnet for tourists. Also, going back a long way, each lives in history. They have their points in common, each wanting to rule the world and establish the kingdom of heaven on earth. People, recognizing this, link them together as the Three Romes. They differ, though, in their understanding of man's nature and business. So the Three Romes are real places, also states of mind.

Rome, the City of the Seven Hills, became a great power in the centuries before Christ. This power was physical but appealed to moral sanctions, and Rome ruled the world by right as well as might. You could say the same for Constantinople, also for Moscow, yesterday and today. In 476 A.D. the last puppet emperor gave up his throne, but the First Rome had a sequel. This was Constantinople, renamed Istanbul in 1930. The Christian city, enduring for a thousand years, got its name from the Roman Emperor Constantine the Great. In 326 A.D. he refounded the old city of Byzas on the Golden Horn. The Byzantines called themselves Romans and they called their capital the Second Rome. In this New Rome, artists and statesmen tried to bring heaven to earth, sometimes succeeding. They taught us beauty—their art of icons, for instance—and how to set a drum on a rectangular surface. They gave the Pope his tiara, English kings the orb and scepter, the rest of us forks. Ingenious in cruelty, men of Constantinople were prototypically modern. They punished criminals by tying them up in a sack with a hog, cock, viper, and ape. Also they were "Byzantine," devious and ridden by symbols. Russians in the Third Rome followed their lead, refining on the cruelty, the symbolism too. In Moscow's Red Square, icons of national leaders are rank-ordered more precisely than they used to be in Constantinople.

Turks took Constantinople in 1453, and the metropolitan in Moscow mourned the fall of "the great Orthodoxy." But Moscow picked comfort from this fall and staked out its own claim to orthodoxy. The ruler in Moscow began to call himself the tsar. His new title harked back to the Caesars of old Rome. He traced his line to Augustus Caesar and his title to Constantinople. Philotheus, a monk of Pskov, wrote a letter to the tsar, saying how the First Rome had fallen, and the gates of the Second Rome had been hewn down by the axes of the infidel Turks. But the Third, New Rome shone in the universe "more resplendent than the sun." This was Moscow. The monk of Pskov ended his letter: "For two Romes have fallen, but the Third stands, and a Fourth shall never be."

Threes are important and lucky to some. For optimistic people, the Three Romes make a trinity that ascends to perfection. Marx, a millenarian thinker, sponsored a new trinity of thesis, antithesis, and synthesis. (Millenarian means never today, always tomorrow.) With the third term, real history was supposed to begin. Between the World Wars, followers of Marx, appealing to a new beginning, established the Comintern or Third International. Taking their cue from Moscow, they intended to redo the world.

Meanwhile the world kept going, always changing but still the same. In 49 B.C., a time of the breaking of nations, Caesar crossed the Rubicon, and Cicero, agitated, wrote to a friend: "The country people and farmers talk to me a great deal. All they care for is their lands, their little farms, their petty incomes." If Rome was falling, it was news to them. Also, even if you are partial to threes, you don't have to have an ax to grind. An old Roman poet, Ennius, knowing three languages, Greek, Oscan, and Latin, said he had three hearts or minds. They let him see into three different cultures, a good thing if you can do this.

Of the three languages spoken in my three cities, only Turkish gives trouble. Russian uses the Cyrillic alphabet, transliterated in English. Italian uses the Latin alphabet, and is more or less familiar. Modern Turkish, rejecting the Arabic alphabet, has replaced it with the Latin, but the look of words in Turkish is often at variance with pronunciation. In rendering Turkish words, I have spelled them the way they sound rather than the way they appear in the dictionary.

Telling the story of the Three Romes, I have had help from the Rackham School and Literary College of the University of Michigan. I thank my wife, Mary, an astute critic. Friends have helped me too, among them Deming Brown, Austin Warren, and principally Lincoln Faller. This book is for him, if he wants it.

Russell Fraser
Ann Arbor, 1984

MOSCOW

GOGOL'S TWO FACES

THEY WERE WAITING for us, three large men wearing white face masks, when we stepped down from the train. This was Leningrad in February, and if you opened your mouth to speak, your breath steamed in the air and hung before your face like those little balloons that tell you what people in the comic strips are saying. "Toot OH-chen HOH-lahd-nah!" it said in my balloon, but nobody needed a weather report. The Finland Station was an old cathedral of the Iron Age, steam from the locomotives censing the nave and rising to the tangle of girders in the dark above our heads, and only in some old churches have I ever been as cold.

It was going on midnight but trains were still coming into the station, huffing and puffing like our train from Helsinki. They weren't going out, though, or not that I could see. No exit, evidently, from Socialist Land. (VEE-khot nyet.) This spicing of melodrama warmed me a little.

Our welcoming committee had come forward to shake hands,

the head man of three holding out a bunch of carnations. Slavic noises rumbled in a cavernous chest. He was Akim Tamiroff in a movie about the partisans, rough-cut, bighearted, and not a man you'd want to cross. Only his eyes were visible and the bridge of his nose. Why was this?

The flu in Leningrad was very bad, said the head *partigiano*, rolling his r's, and no Russians were allowed to leave the city. Meanwhile his gauze face mask kept the germs in their place. Better be safe than sorry.

This was the moment when all my Berlitz lessons were going to cash. *"My zdorovye lyudi!"* I said. "We're a healthy people!" I meant this for a joke. It wasn't a joking matter to Tamiroff, however. *"My tozhe!"* he said severely, giving me a straight look. "We are too!"

Russia in the sixties, when I went there to help negotiate the academic exchange, was like Texas without money, all empty space, bragging rights to the universe, and a chip on every shoulder. They wanted their students to study science and technology in American schools, and if American students wanted to read Pushkin in Socialist schools that was all right with them. They thought they were Peter Minuit buying Manhattan Island from the redskins. Sharp traders, the redskins must have had a crystal ball. How sharp these Russians were is a question. I would rather read Pushkin than program the computer.

Getting out of Russia, when they signed the agreement and I got to go home again, was like getting out of Texas. I didn't suppose I would ever go back. It was Kraisky who changed my mind. This was fifteen years later. Things were different, he said. "You will see."

That bad first time around, Kraisky had functioned as my interpreter and cicerone-cum-watchdog. When he came to America I played this part for him. (I left out watching and warding.) *"Bosh-na-bosh,"* they call it, meaning sometimes "Scratch my back and I'll do the same for you," meaning also and frequently "An eye for an eye and a tooth for a tooth."

Kraisky was Secretary of the Faculty of Arts and Letters at Moscow University, the old branch downtown on Karl Marx Prospekt. His physical type was Slavic and uncomely, short, thick-set, fair thinning hair combed straight back from his forehead, a bulb of a nose flanked by high cheekbones. Some fashion models have their back teeth pulled out to narrow the face and heighten the cheekbones. This is thought to be beautiful. Kraisky, like most Marxists, believed that beauty was only skin deep. "I am a child of the Revolution," he said.

To his colleagues Kraisky presented one face and had another for people like me. "When I speak, let no dogs bark," his official manner said. He was the Inspector General in the Gogol play, a laugh every minute, and the eyes in his head ran around like little chickens. This good humor was specious, but Kraisky didn't lack for humor and did his best to smooth my way through the long and sometimes abrasive afternoons at the Ministry of Education on Zhdanova Street.

Rastaturov was spokesman for the ministry side, a seedy George Arliss with three gold teeth and a mouth like a mail slot. When he pulled his shapka over his ears and put on his getting-ready-for-the-great-outdoors face, he stood before you like a Mongol, one of Khan Mamay's soldiers from the days of the Golden Horde. A lot of Russians have this look of the East. "Yes," Blok says in one of his poems, "we are Asiatics, with our slanting and avid eyes."

At the ministry they spoke "from the chair," a custom that comes down from the old days. The tsar, in the old days, was "the only supporter of the true Orthodoxy," and when Stalin invaded Poland he said he had done this "to help the population of Poland to reorganize the conditions of its political existence." Things change and remain the same. "I shall help you, O Afghan!" reads a poem in the Moscow *News* by a Red Army soldier. "For a Russian it is the custom to help."

Rastaturov delighted in insult. Like Molotov negotiating with the affable Americans who thought that pressing flesh did the business, he made insult part of his technique. Once he turned the mail slot full in my face. "You are CIA," he said. Kraisky, standing behind his chief, translated word for word. Then, looking at me, he winked broadly. What was it with Rastaturov? "If you want to kill a moth," Kraisky told me later, "you light a candle."

Straight through these sessions in the drafty building across the street from the Lubyanka Prison, Kraisky chain-smoked cigarets, lighting one from the stub of another. I believe what they tell me about cigarets, and I consider them all equally pernicious. Some are more equal than others, however, e.g. the Russian variety known as *papirosy*, cardboard tubes loosely packed with pungent-smelling makhorka tobacco. Some days you saw Kraisky sucking on his *papirosy*. He preferred Kent filters, though, and went through them like tissues. How could he afford this? He got his American cigarets, he said, from the mission in New York, twice a month through the diplomatic pouch.

When I met him in New York a few years later, I took him for dinner to the Century Club and we had a beef Stroganoff that love or money couldn't buy where he came from. It made no difference to Kraisky. Food was food, he said, and like most Russians I have known he scorned the palate as a bourgeois affectation. Outside on Fifth Avenue, I suggested a present for his wife back in Moscow, maybe a nightgown or a filmy chemise? What was she like, I asked him. With his hands, Kraisky sketched a large rectangle in the air. Evidently not much palate here either. But on the way out to Newark and the airport, he lowered the car window and sniffed the hydrogen sulfide, taking in with approval the scaly horrors on both sides of the highway. "Ah, industry!" he said.

He had come to the States to visit with Russian students who were doing science and technology under the exchange. "So they won't get too homesick," he said. This piece of whimsy was an uncharacteristic blunder for him. Not often did he let you see the keen teeth behind the grin. But Kraisky wasn't a bad fellow, and in a way we were friends. He was, of course, KGB.

Brezhnev is out but Andropov is in. Long live the King and I have come back to Moscow. Kraisky arranges for me to lecture on Shakespeare and guarantees a full house. Shakespeare is a credentialed Marxist in this country where *Hamlet* is sometimes played as a cautionary fable of the indolent young man struggling pathetically against a better time to come, and Friar Laurence and his bromides take center stage in the story of Romeo and Juliet. "These violent delights have violent ends."

He has cleared the decks, Kraisky says, and the only thing on his agenda is seeing to it that I have a good time. My idea of a good time is exploring old churches. *"Bolshoi drap!"* Kraisky says, a favorite expression. Big deal! and he says it again. All the same, he thumps my shoulders and agrees to tag along. He takes me to the Kremlin and points out the churches in Red Square and Cathedral Square. About going inside them, he isn't so sure. "I am atheist," he says. Also he says that religion is the opium of the people. I agree that this is so. Russians, living on intimate terms with trouble, look to last things. Russia, said their monk Philotheus, was "the last earthly kingdom, after which comes the eternal kingdom of Christ," and the classless society and the withering away of the state. Kraisky laughs his merry laugh and says that I have a sense of humor.

We go together to the circus, where a casual word in the ticket-taker's ear bumps us to the head of the line. Bears are riding bicycles, there are dogs on roller skates, and agile men and women who catapult from springboards and somersault on stilts. They do it very well. Where the means are abundant, though, the ends are elusive. A good time is had by all, but not the time of your life. The audience takes its pleasure sedately, and the vigorous handclapping is rhythmic or ritual. Clap-pause-clap-pause. This might have been a political rally.

In the Kremlin Armory we admire the jeweled trains and the

Fabergé Easter eggs. On the iron doors of the armory I see the double eagle of the tsars and the Byzantines, the imperial seal of Constantinople. The guide tells me how after the fall of the city this seal came to Russia, and the tsar in Moscow made it his own seal. He called himself the new Constantine. In this gorgeous house of trophies the double eagle is everywhere, stitched on horse blankets and old military costumes, emblazoned on coaches and worked in filigree on their royal crowns. Alexander Herzen, a romantic exile, says in his memoirs how Russians were like this double eagle. "We looked in different directions, but the same heart throbbed within us."

Gogol, their greatest writer, is like the double eagle, and *The Inspector General* shows this. For the new production at the Stanislavsky Theater, they have boiled him down, however. This production is like the circus with words, the pathos all gone into high jinks. Gogol's scamp-hero is only a scamp and his victims are only victims. The colors are primary and the single-minded director lays them on with a trowel. His Gogol is only a comedian, and you don't need to take him seriously. "Who wants to take him seriously?" Kraisky inquires. "Life is serious." He means this for a reproach in which I am included, and he goes after me hammer and sickle. Why look on the dark side? It isn't a bed of roses we have here, he can tell me, and anyway who needs to be told.

"What about Socialist Realism?" I ask him. "The good are rewarded and the others get theirs. That is what Socialist Realism means." I remind him of *Dead Souls* and how Gogol pokes fun at the readers of his novel. *Readers of this book, none of you really care to see humanity revealed in its nakedness.* "I should go to the theater to see this?" Kraisky says. "When I go to the theater, I want to be entertained."

Gogol said his subject was life and nothing else. This didn't preclude entertainment. It argued a range of possibility, though. The one-dimensional reading collapses this range but makes life a lot simpler.

In Socialist Land, simple questions bristle with complexity. "Why can't you sell me any caviar today?" The clerk in Yeliseyevsky's rolls up his eyes. He doesn't have an answer. Complicated questions are another matter and get resolved without ado. If you want to know about life's purpose or the origin of evil, they don't leave you guessing. Their answers aren't tentative. Listening to their answers, I am back in Sunday school and I wriggle uncomfortably, feeling how the preacher has got hold of me by the lapels.

"As a matter of fact," Gogol says to a friend, "preaching is not my business. My business is to speak with living images and not with arguments." Enemies called him reactionary, but he wasn't reactionary and wasn't liberal either. It was only that he lacked point of view. Another way to put this is to say that he was endlessly accommodating. In Socialist Land, the accommodating instinct has gone the way of the vermiform appendix. Not that the tsars gave it much of a hearing. When this century was younger, different voices got a hearing, though, Symbolists, Acmeists, Futurists, Constructivists. They made a harmony too, and they looked in different directions but the same heart throbbed within them.

In this harmony beneath the skin, *Pravda*, the party paper, participates in spite of itself. "Pravda" means truth or law, as in laying down the law, and sometimes the law is remote from the truth. This is when it legislates a single point of view. The building the Constructivists intended for *Pravda* mixes different materials and different geometric forms. Mixing stone and plastic, circles and cubes, *Pravda* by design offers house room.

But ghosts have infiltrated the offices of *Pravda*, old Slavophiles from Dostoevsky's time and Old Believers from the time of Peter the Great. I meet them in Moscow when I pick up a copy of the English-language *News* or turn the radio to the English-language broadcast. Coming up from the pavement or coming out of the walls, they have stolen a march on this wide-awake city. Life for them is a struggle between the chaos of opinion and the orderly cosmos where truth is open and shut. Either them or us! is the watchword.

In *Anna Karenina* Levin's Pan-Slavic brother says how his compatriots, waking from deep sleep, are going to create a new epoch in history. There won't be any house room in the new epoch. Never mind what the others think, says Avvakum the Old Believer. "I wipe my arse with that." This angry old man is their first real Russian writer, and you can read him in English and see for yourself. He isn't an amiable writer, however, and life for Archpriest Avvakum was a fight to the death between Abel and Cain. They burned him at the stake three hundred years ago, but his single truth goes marching on. It isn't tentative, and boils down to either/or. "I believe in and serve my God, but the apostates I loathe and curse." The apostates are the ones who make the sign of the cross with three fingers.

Up-to-date custodians of the single truth have left off invoking God, and their notions of apostasy are different. But like the Slavophiles and Old Believers, they are Manichean in their deepest place and don't give or take quarter. Like the ancient Bogomils, Slavic heretics in the medieval time, they detest our world of shadows where clear-cut distinctions are blurred. The world they live in is black or white, or divided between East and West. If you aren't for us you're against us.

I tell Kraisky that in the bad old days before the Revolution, writers in his country liked to straddle both sides. This goes with being human. Kraisky says it goes with being dead, as when the man who walks down the middle of the road is run over by the oncoming traffic. Old Russian proverb, he tells me.

The Opposition, I tell him, isn't a monolith but breaks down to flesh and blood. "For us or against us," he mutters, and he recalls how Comrade Lenin likened party unity to the "apple of our eye." We talk about Lenin the benevolent man, and how he wanted to stroke the heads of the people. He wanted also to build the kingdom of heaven on earth. This meant that you had to crack heads. "Split them open ruthlessly," said Lenin to Gorky.

I have brought with me in my saddlebags Alexander Radishchev's account of his journey from Petersburg to Moscow two hundred years ago, and in the late evenings I read in this book. Radishchev thought that serfdom was wicked, and Catherine the Great packed him off to Siberia. The martyr to his opinions wasn't a man of the Enlightenment for nothing. "My opinion differs from yours," said Radishchev to the Opposition. He went on to say, however, that "your heart beats as one with mine." You see a plaque to Radishchev set into the wall as you go up from Revolution Square to the Kremlin, but this quotation isn't on it.

When you make a visit to Moscow, unless you are Sol Hurok or President Nixon they put you where they want to. They put me in the Metropole, and this suited me fine. The new hotels like the Cosmos are longer on comfort, but charm for Russians is a concept that went out with the Revolution. The Metropole dates from before the Revolution, and charm is what it has.

Partly this means dust collectors, a lot of glass and soiled gilt, cracked veneer on the doors, faded paper on the walls, tile missing here and there in the toilets. Palms and art nouveau lamps clutter the lobby and the alcoves as you go up the stairs. Nineteenth-century landscape paintings hang from gold tasseling. They go in for the sublime and are heavy on the varnish. Among the coyly erotic statues on mythological themes I recognize Cupid and Psyche. Electric lighting replaced the gas jets a long time ago. Even in bright sunshine the Metropole is a little sepulchral, however, as if they had taken out the gas jets and let the electricity go.

The old glaucous building fronts on Sverdlov Square and the statue of Marx, a benignant father figure. Up the road is the Lenin Museum. Before the Revolution the parliamentary Duma used to meet in this barn of a building. Marx on his pedestal is shedding disastrous twilight on all the nations, and you wouldn't care to spend a weekend in the Lenin Museum. They have had more time in London to hoard the dust of time, and maybe the Victoria and Albert Museum wins on points in the competition for Most Ho-Hums. But Red Square and the Kremlin are just around the corner. If the center of the web is where you want to be, the Metropole is the right place to stay.

Moscow is a spider's web, and all filaments lead from the Kremlin. Walk out of the Kremlin along Kalinin Prospekt and you come to the Arbat, the old trading quarter where Gogol flowed in high spirits and wrestled with his demons until they overcame him. The quarter as it used to be still lives in its unpretentious yellow buildings, dwelling places for the present. But the present has become the past, a little down at the heels, the high spirits have evaporated a long time ago, and nobody thinks twice about demons.

Prospekt Mira, running out of Dzerzhinsky and 25th October streets just north of the Kremlin, runs north and east out of town and brings you to Zagorsk where Sergius the monk preached salvation in Christ and holy war against the Mongols. He did this in 1380 when Khan Mamay and the Golden Horde marched against Moscow. Fierce for the Lord, Sergius sent two of his monks to lead the army of Grand Prince Dmitry. You can still see his inhospitable visage on an embroidered pall in the museum.

Dzerzhinsky Square marks the terminus of 25th October Street. In the center of the square is the statue of Felix Dzerzhinsky, thirty-six feet of him blotting the sky. "During the Revolution," says the guide from Intourist, "he helped Lenin out." This is true. He created the Cheka, "the sword of the Revolution."

They remember the master cop in the ordinary-looking building across the square. The Lubyanka Prison does not appear on my map. Color of mustard, white curtains at the windows, evidently an old apartment house but not a prime location, the Lubyanka is isolated from the buildings around it. Traffic hereabouts is noisy, and the windows are closed. To the left of the prison as you face it, the glass arches of Detsky Mir are winking in the sunshine. Detsky Mir is Children's World, and even in Moscow where consumer goods are hard to come by, this happy corner has everything to gladden the heart of a child.

Gorky Street is another filament running north and west from the center of the web, and Pushkin Square lies across it. Time collapses in Moscow, and sleigh bells or hoofbeats wouldn't come as a surprise, not even a troika drawing a sleigh. In the square, I hear the hoofbeats of the Bronze Horseman. The Horseman in Pushkin's poem is Peter the Great. His famous statue by Falconet stands in Leningrad on the Neva. But all Russia seems incarnate in the center of Moscow where past and present merge, and Stalin is the Horseman for me. He is harrying his people for benevolent reasons and other reasons that don't bear looking into. In this city where opposites confront one another, his equivocal presence is still vivid wherever I look.

Outside the Metropole, I catch a glimpse of the red brick wall that once encircled the Chinese quarter they call Kitay-Gorod. This is "Chinatown" where no Chinamen live. A glimpse is all you get. Stalin the master builder was a great destroyer too, like Baron Haussmann in Paris a hundred years ago or the master builders in New York. In the name of progress, he tore down the past. The old wall is mostly a sacrifice to progress. But a few sections of the swallow-tailed battlements still remain, and they provoke speculation.

The Mongol enclave butted on the Kremlin, and the conquerors and conquered swapped provisions and furs, black lamb and red fox, mink, sable, and marten. Also they swapped customs, and for Moscow this made a difference. Enter Fu Manchu and the inscrutable East, where people are a dime a dozen and if you know what's good for you, you do what you're told.

"We, the people of the North, are different," Glinka says. He was Stalin's favorite composer but not a bad composer, and he goes on to say how the gloomy song his people sing "was perhaps transmitted to us by the people of the East." If you know the melodies of Russian folk songs, Radishchev says, you will admit that "there is something in them which suggests spiritual sorrow." When I am down in the dumps, I see this gloomy strain as decisive for the future, and I shudder for the future where the rough beast is slouching towards Bethlehem to be born. Better gird up your loins while time serves, I tell myself. I am a Manichean. Either them or us.

Friends and some writers say how these dour Muscovites are full of the devil when you get to know them at home. It isn't easy for me to say how they are at home. Mostly, they don't ask you over. On the street, they endure. Their faces are shuttered and don't show curiosity or protest. Maybe the climate takes all their strength, or maybe coming to terms with the people who ride them and tell them what to do. Don't lean on the walls, don't open the windows or spit on the floor. When I make the expected pilgrimage to Lenin's Tomb in Red Square, a militiaman tells me to keep inside the white lines on the pavement. Toeing the line is second nature to Muscovites. He doesn't have to tell them. Eldritch old ladies at the ballet seize my coat when I enter and fling it back when I leave. "No smoking!" The attendant at the Beriozka store screams at me to put out my pipe. I am an ill-conducted little boy at the mercy of adults. But in this city they are all boys and girls. As they are done to, they do the same to you.

Flying into Sheremetyevo, I don't let Kraisky know the time of my arrival. This proves a mistake. No VIP treatment, and I shape up for Customs like everybody else. The militiaman who looks me over is all of nineteen, but already he has acquired the stony gravity of Brezhnev & Co. "Is this your picture?" he inquires, thumbing my passport. He knows it is my picture but isn't about to concede this. I was happy the day the picture was taken. I am not happy now. Nevertheless I grin foolishly, acting out the resemblance. Stony Face is not amused. I recognize the slanting and avid eyes. At last, however, he snaps the book shut, hands it over, and lets me go through. He has put a fly in my ointment.

Coming out of China in the early years of the thirteenth century, the Mongols came down like the wolf on the fold. They took Russia for their own from the Urals to the Dnieper. They ruined Kiev, the Mother City of Russia, and they burned the holy city of Vladimir. The metropolitans of the Russian Church, seeing how it was with Kiev, pinned their hopes to Moscow, and they blessed the undertakings of the secular arm. The grand duke in Moscow gobbled up his neighbors. This was unification. Step by step, the metropolitan pronounced anathema on the princes who opposed it. *Bosh-na-bosh.* In the glorifying of Moscow, the Mongols also played a part, and they stamped the city with their image and likeness.

Cruelty, often laconic, participates in this image. The great knout is its emblem, and who can remember when this wasn't true for Russia? You hang up your victim with his feet off the floor and flog him with the knout. If he is recalcitrant, you flog him until he is dead. "Regret is the fruit of pity," said Genghis Khan, the first of the conquerors, and his Muscovite subjects took this to heart.

The grand dukes who ruled in Moscow were hand in glove for a long time with the Mongol khans, and this was how they built their dominion. Being patient, also shrewd, they let the lion wait on the fox. They called themselves Long Arm or Money Bag or Big Eyes, and their statecraft mixed cunning with violence. They practiced blinding, poisoning, drowning, starving, mass deportations, and so they made their way.

But Moscow means pity, as in the great Russian fictions. I think of this when I stand before the house on Kalinin Prospekt where Tolstoy in *War and Peace* lodged his hero Pierre Bezukhov. Pierre, who has a temper, is sometimes a ferocious hero, also the type of the man who takes pity. Andrew Rublev, their great painter and the ward and pupil of hard-visaged St. Sergius, declares this pity for all time. Rublev, like Prince Pierre, is equivocal, though. It pleases him to show you the Archangel Michael, a warrior saint, and the dragon slayer St. George. These ferocious heroes are marching as to war. But the miracle-worker St. Nicholas is another favorite subject. His miracles are worked in compassion.

Compassion is a code word evoking the image of women, and women under the law are the equal of men. In Moscow, however, the woman is the low man on the totem pole. Scut work is woman's work, and the doctor who looks down your throat will likely be a woman. This doesn't mean that women are coming up on the totem pole. Doctor's work is scut work, and men have better things to do.

At the U.S. Embassy they have scheduled a reception for the President of Harvard or maybe Southwestern at Memphis, and Kraisky goes with me for the caviar and vodka. Our visitor is telling us how in colleges back home there are about as many women as men. This changes, though, when you get to graduate school. The further up you go on the academic ladder, the more the men outnumber the women. An interesting point, and Kraisky turns it over. "It is the same in our country," he says. "You want to know why?" The personage regards him politely. "Because women are dumb."

Women being prone to compassion, the Mongols shut them away. Russians did this too. In Cathedral Square they built the Terems, a very private place where they kept the tsarina and her ladies. The Mongol idea that ladies are best when not seen and not heard hung on until the time of Peter the Great. But in the sacred art of Moscow, you feel how the woman means more than the male child she holds in her arms, and the most revered of all their icons is the Vladimir Mother of God.

For us Russians, Glinka says, love "always contains a tinge of sadness." We feel "unrestrained joy or we shed bitter tears." The pages of Radishchev are blotted with tears, and the hero and his cronies pull their hair out by fistfuls. Tolstoy's Levin is like this, pitching between elation and despair. Tolstoy is like this. Pashkov the explorer, whose house lies on my way as I walk from the Metropole to the Lenin Library, made life hell for Archpriest Avvakum. That is only half the story, though. One day a monster, said Avvakum, and the next "he sent us no small store of food."

My lecture at Moscow University is called "Shakespeare ili Pravda." Shakespeare or Truth? What can this mean? I hear the colleagues asking. I see them looking at each other with a wild surmise. Like a portmanteau, "pravda" includes different meanings. It means sensory knowledge and a higher form of knowledge. The Decembrist revolutionaries of 1825 called their manifesto "Russkaya Pravda." Here "pravda" means the truth that makes men free. The Decembrists were sticklers for this truth as they defined it. Where serfdom was the rule they wanted to free the serfs, and they wanted a code of justice based on rational behavior. Benevolent young men, they deserved a better fate. But the fate that overtook them was in the cards from the beginning.

Pestel, their leader, was reason's archpriest. Ryleyev wrote his didactic poems in defense of reason. Bestuzhev-Marlinsky records how he has "memorized Shakespeare's speech of Brutus," and I think you can see why he did this. Brutus is the type of the rational man who looks through men and women, appealing to a higher form of knowledge. "We all stand up against the spirit of Caesar," Brutus says in the play, "And in the spirit of men there is no blood." However, blood drenches them all.

Longing for color on a wintry afternoon, I troop off to Volkhonka Street to see the Impressionists in the Pushkin Museum. *Nyet, nyet.* They aren't having any today. A block or two away in the direction of the river—but the river is everywhere in Moscow, mollifying the hard city—I find myself in the little street that bears Ryleyev's name. Wanting to make the crooked straight and the rough places smooth, he though you had to kill people first. Killing in the name of "pravda" or truth seemed to Ryleyev a sacrificial rite. Tsar Nicholas also appealed to the truth, and he expressed it in the formula "orthodoxy, autocracy, and nationality." Hard of heart and dull of wit, cold in demeanor and banal in his discourse, feline but devoid of imaginative power, a hater of intellect and necessarily an enemy of art, he looks forward to Stalin the man of steel. In the name of truth he hanged Ryleyev and the others.

In my lecture I tell the colleagues how Shakespeare doesn't clarify but darkens the truth. Rational men suppose that the earth must be round or else it is flat. Shakespeare, who entertains these contradictory propositions, is willing to entertain a third. Like Dostoevsky, he thinks that two times two might someday work out to five. His sums are mysterious, the world he inhabits is unpredictable, and the kind of truth that is open-and-shut doesn't get much of a hearing. "Pravda" goes out the window. Wringing their hands, the custodians of the single truth aren't about to give it up. Having your good at heart, they undertake to close the window.

It is turning colder in Moscow, and in the stuffy lecture room all the windows are closed. Kraisky, noting this, jumps up from his seat and gleefully throws open a window. Subdued laughter from the colleagues is followed by applause. They aren't looking at each other with a wild surmise, and if I had thought to stand them on their ear, second thoughts are in order. The colleagues are polite, only they have little to say. This isn't because they are stupid. Self-assured is what they are. Declining to comment, they leave me on the platform, undressed in my amusing ideas. Is that all? their bland faces are saying. I wonder what has happened to the chip on every shoulder.

The annex to the *Pravda* building was brand new in the sixties and fell down when I was there. Like Truth crushed to earth it went up again, though, and it looks pretty solid today. Buildings don't fall down in Moscow anymore, and the nets have disappeared that used to festoon new construction. Cornices don't come unstuck from the buildings, glass windows don't shatter when there isn't any wind, and pedestrians on the sidewalk no longer get brained. The tiny dingy rooms in the University dormitories are still as tiny and dingy as they always were, but the cracks in the walls are plastered over now, the door frames don't run at a bias, and the students have stopped telling you how they only get hot water once a week at 5:00 a.m. The Soviet Encyclopedia is gone from the toilets, where it hung from a nail like the Sears, Roebuck catalog in rural America. Old-time Bolshevik haters, who warmed up the audience with an anecdote about the toilet paper, need a new anecdote.

There is plenty of toilet paper. There is plenty of traffic. Where the vast boulevards used to be empty except for tumblin' tumbleweed, the Chaikas and Volgas muscle each other out of the way, and already Moscow in the rush hour gives a fair imitation of San Antonio, Texas. (New York and its traffic jams to end them all is for the future, like the withering away of the state.)

I confer with my friend Canby about these drastic changes. Canby does the archives at the American Embassy. "What does it mean, to do the archives?" I ask him. "It involves a lot of shredding," he says. Canby runs to fat and looks like a jolly fat man up to the eyes. The job is *comme ci, comme ça*, he says, and as for this posting it beats Kabul by a nose. Canby is an optimist. "Sooner or later," he says hopefully, "we'll blow the whistle on one of their chauffeurs in Long Island, and they'll retaliate by sending one of us home. Maybe me." He has a policy with Lloyd's of London, $50 a year for $5,000 in relocation expenses. PNG insurance, he calls this. *Persona non grata.* He looks forward to the knock on the door.

Canby says that when the Nazis invaded Russia, there were fewer than a million motor vehicles in this country that is a continent all by itself. Forty years later, if you want to cross from Red

Square to Manege Square where the Red Army shows off its hardware on Revolution Day, you have to go underground. To Russians, this means progress. Who is going to contradict them? Not Americans, those prototypical Russians, who invented the cult of progress when Leningrad was still St. Petersburg.

In early October before the killing frosts, I see a ragged old man cutting the grass on Prospekt Mira, near the Cosmos Hotel. He isn't driving a power mower but swinging a scythe, and he might have stepped out of history before they freed the serfs. Looking at him, you feel how nothing has changed. Behind this man, however, is the monument to Sputnik, curving gracefully skywards.

At Moscow University, the gigantic structure in the Lenin Hills where the action is, the important business, says Rector Petrovsky, is science. In these neo-Gothic towers that challenge the heavens you meet the real humanists, going back to the beginnings of the modern age. They make utility their touchstone of value. I walk through the laboratories, and I summon enthusiasm for the geological museum, the autoclaves, the Bunsen burners, the gleaming computers. This mysterious gadgetry suggests that they know what they're doing. Next to the computer you see the abacus, and this is what they use for doing sums.

Getting on the New York subway, you take your life in your hands. I do my best to keep out of the subway. The Moscow subway is a Palace of Culture, marbled walls, chandeliers, heroic statues, a wonder of efficiency, and five kopecks will get you from Planernaya on the upper river all the way to Zhdanovskaya in the south. The statues have it in mind that you should be doing something, and the opulent style might pass for good taste in Houston or Dallas. But you get to Zhdanovskaya in one piece and with your wallet intact.

"He found his people wearing birch-bark sandals. He left them shod in leather. He found them living in thatched huts. He left them great cities of apartments." The beneficent man who did this is Stalin. I have preserved his obituary notice, clipped from the lefty paper I used to subscribe to. The date is 1953, and Stalin didn't live long enough to get everything done. The shoes they pass over the counter at GUM look like the cardboard boxes they came in. "Style is the man" is one saying they aren't partial to. Shoe sizes are negotiable. Maybe size ten is what they have today. When you can't get what you want for the asking, you are willing to take what they give you.

The housing they give you is a cell in an antheap on the way to Sheremetyevo. In Italy also, these self-contained *rioni* are going up everywhere, dwelling places for the future. The future doesn't look good. There is a difference, though. In the micro-cities on the edges of Moscow, personality is muffled. "Friendship Park" is a micro-city where no living pulse beats, and you might as well stay on the metro when it stops at "Friendship Park." Instant aging, Canby thinks, is a consequence of this, or maybe a cause. Where everybody else wants to turn back the clock, Muscovites have found the secret of speeding it up. In a year, the new buildings wrinkle and turn gray. But they keep out the rain and snow, and you have a room of your own if you live there.

At Moscow University downtown, the journalism students have put together a documentary film. This is like a term paper, and I am invited to attend a private showing. The subject is Paris. Someone should tell these students that the Party in Paris has gone middle-class and the hard line is in limbo. No doubt someone will tell them. As the movie begins we hear ardent music, the "Marseillaise" mingling with the "Internationale." Ardent young men and women are selling *L'Humanité*, the Communist paper. The camera pans to the offices of *L'Humanité*. We see the house where Lenin lived, also a monument to the Communards of 1871. A voice-over tells us about the Communards. The voice is lugubrious but inflected with hope. These early revolutionaries didn't make it in their own time. The future beckons, however, and in the East the sky is red. The camera's eye moves to the Lido, dancing girls in the buff except for a few feathers. Outside the theater a hapless *clochard* is drinking up the steam that comes from a grate in the sidewalk.

"He found them weak from disease and living in filth," my yellowing obituary notice continues. "When he died, disease was only a memory. He found the women oppressed, wearing horsehair veils. Many were still prostitutes. When he died," etc. I stroll out of Red Square and turn into Razin Street, wanting to inspect the old churches. The Znamensky Monastery has been liberated, though, and the tiny church of the Conception of St. Anne is only an apricot-colored façade. On my right hand, dominating the Moskvoretskaya Embankment, stands the Rossiya Hotel, bright as a new coin in the wintry sunshine. I make a dejected setoff between this huge pile of glass and stone and the churches which used to be churches that flank it.

But I have been here before and I know what the hotel replaces. Here in the filthy slums of the Zaryadiye, the prostitutes lived, and the *khuligany* beat up on their victims. Disease bred disease. Today in Moscow, prostitution is out, unless for the fun of it or as the KGB suggests, and the new Puritans and their face masks are putting disease to flight. Cleanliness is more than godliness. No graffiti in the subways, no obscenity, no scatology. You think twice in Moscow before you knock out your pipe or drop a match on the sidewalk. This inspires satisfaction and a proprietarial point of view.

Outside the Beriozka shop across the street from the Novo-Devichy Convent, I see young German tourists hammering the tops off their bottles of beer. They are dressed in jeans and sneakers, and like American boys and girls they have an air of free and easy. I like them for this. But I become aware that they are throwing their bottle tops every which way on the ground. I want to expostulate. They are littering my city.

Like the medieval anchorite with the skull on his desk I have a thing for last things, and when I lived in London I used to go up to Highgate Cemetery and visit with Father Marx. In Moscow when I feel these promptings, I go to the cemetery at Novo-Devichy. Granitic and marmoreal, it helps to order my priorities. Waxy flowers decorate the graves. Grief-stricken angels are out, but busts of the dead are plentiful, also photographs, alarming in their wire-rimmed glasses and stiff collars and cravats. This might be Lisbon on the other side of Europe, superstitious and Latin. In Novo-Devichy, the dead are still quick.

The Christian cross is visible, but mostly they dispense with this. Gogol is buried here near Prokofiev and Scriabin, also their famous ill-starred poet Mayakovsky, and Peter Kropotkin, the Anarchist Prince. He wept bitter tears when his father lashed the serfs. They told him his tears were idle, and said how, when he grew up, he would do the same thing. They were wrong about this, and Kropotkin thought that serfs were people.

In a tiny corner lot lies Stalin's wife, Nadezhda Alliluyeva. A plain white statue marks the site. Tragedy followed this woman to her grave. She died by her own hand, or maybe Stalin shot her. "He found his people deep in race hate. He left them marrying across national and religious lines, as did he himself." That is what Stalin did, and some of his best friends were Jews.

The Constitution is color-blind, and the Third World, taking notice, is all over the lot. Africans in native dress or beautifully tailored Western dress are a striking presence on Moscow streets and in the shops and the subway. Look cross-eyed at one of them and you will find yourself in big trouble with the omnipresent militia. Lumumba University caters to these black men and women. But they have stuck it out on Donskoy Proyezd on the other side of Gorky Park. "Truth to tell," Canby says, "Russians don't like to mix cream with their coffee." Black men, he says, have learned not to promenade with white girls in Gorky Park. The *khuligany* have taught them this. He opens his desk drawer and shows me a greeting card that has come in the mail for New Year's. A crude gallows is etched on the face of the card. Probably, Canby thinks, this comes from a disgruntled cleaning person who works for the embassy. "But we get things like this all the time," he says. "We" doesn't mean embassy. Canby is black.

I make it a point to stop by his office when I visit the embassy to catch up on the *Herald Tribune*. It isn't much of an office and not much of an embassy, no reading room in Swedish modern, no library to browse in, no glossy handouts extolling the Land of the Free. I sit on the edge of an undertaker's chair in a warren of a room with gunmetal bookshelves. They hold copies of *Time* and *Newsweek* and the Sunday *New York Times* and the *Trib*. Thanksgiving and the football season have come and gone, but the big news on the sports page is the Dartmouth-Princeton game. A young woman typist in a jean shirt and striped knit pullover tells me to put out my pipe. They wouldn't let her through the door on Madison Avenue. Across the hall, three American girls and their Russian instructor are getting on famously. My name is Olga. I am happy to meet you. OH-chen pree-YAHT-nah. Repeat after me, please.

Embassies tell you something, and they ought to think twice about what they are saying. In London, Saarinen's moated grange dominates Grosvenor Square and is saying "Verboten" to the neighborhood. The American Embassy on the Via Veneto looks like a set for Il Duce. This rinky-dink place looks like nothing at all. Where grandeur is the rule, that seems appropriate.

I am a patriot and salute the Grand Old Flag, but my patriotic flame burns higher the further I get from home. Sometimes I stop my ears so I won't hear America singing. Getting away from home is partly a fiction, and what I thought to leave behind me meets me on my way. "We flee from Russia," said Herzen, "but Russia is everywhere," a land of mountains and plains and rivers, also an idea. Writing his memoirs a long way from home, Herzen the exile tried to put the idea in focus. I am like Herzen, always packing my bags, and the place where I come from sharpens in focus the more it recedes. It has its dark underside and its good residual thing.

The huge isolated map of the U.S.S.R. in the offices of Aeroflot looks like a distended version of the U.S.A. The resemblance, my idea, isn't letter perfect, and "Florida" is too small where "Long Island" is too big. "Lower California" is north of where it should be. But I feel how I might be confronting a mirror image.

They are playing dance music in the style of the forties over dinner at the Cosmos Hotel, sedate pelvic movements, shifting neon lights, and everything is coming up roses. The men in the band wear gold lamé jackets, and the long dresses of the women glitter with sequins. Though the bubble-making machine is broken, the champagne girls on the bandstand have that wholesome look about them. It suggests the girl next door. Cheesecake is out, and none of these girls are showing much knee. "You're just wunnerful," the man with the baton might be saying.

Solzhenitsyn, an Old Believer got up in modern dress, bears revolted witness to the way they live now in Socialist Land. But he doesn't like it much either in the Land of the Free. "Out there" in America it is all rusted hub caps, fast foods, the hard sell and the soft core, a land of functional illiterates who want your money or your life. Solzhenitsyn stops his ears so he won't hear America singing.

On Fleet Street in London I used to go to El Vino's for a glass of sherry in the late afternoons, and a very superior English journalist I knew there declined to see the difference between Socialist Land and the Land of the Free. "Of course you have the freedom to be banal," he liked to tell me. "Old boy." My patriotic blood boils and I could tear my hair like Radishchev. But I am looking for answers. "When found, make a note of," says a dogged character in Dickens.

Big black Volgas weave imperiously through the traffic around the Kremlin. Their rear windows are closed with curtains to protect the VIPs, and there is one law for the carriage trade and another for the hoi polloi. Looking after the men in their Volgas, cops and soldiers are everywhere, like a banana republic or Greece under the dictatorship. This jackbooted swagger would bring down the house where I come from. It is hard to bully the hoi polloi when they are laughing at you, and if you push them around they push back.

At seven thirty at night, I have finished my dinner. They have rolled up the sidewalks, and Moscow goes to bed early. No nice espresso bars, no sidewalk cafés, no hanky-panky either, and the *dezhurnaya* on the floor has eyes like a house dick. I am back in Berlin where the Wall surrounds the city, an up-to-date city, and if you like German food an okay place to be. Only there aren't any doors.

Clarence Canby is a rock fan, fan as in fanatic. To his father's annoyance, he sits in with a pop group called Plastic People. They jam once a week in a hole in the wall in an alley off Frunze Street. Dostoevsky used to live around the corner. For the time being, however, Plastic People is in abeyance, charged with "Disturbance of the peace." They would have locked up Canby Junior with the others except for his privileged status as an embassy brat. A chip off the old block he isn't, and he would sell what he has and give it to the poor if they would give him the new tape by Frank Zappa. There is not a chance that they will do this. They reserve the darkest inch their shelf allows to rock music. Where this orchestrated chaos makes my head ache, it sends them into the streets with their billy clubs and rubber hoses. Like the trumpets of Jericho or the *Dies Irae,* the sound of rock is saying no to the wormy chestnuts that were good enough for our fathers.

Off the lobby in the Metropole, the new color TV invites my inspection. Bosom Buddies à la Russe. He Is My Brother. Some Call Them Freaks. Mom and Dad and Buster, bovine to their fingertips, are jumping through hoops at the Four-H, it looks like. I have seen them before, the time I smashed up my car and had to spend half a week in East Liverpool, Ohio. But not everybody swings, and this gemütlichkeit they go in for has its limits. The TV screen, a little world of its own, defines the limits. Up on top in the greater world, the crowd in the Kremlin has stern words for violence, also for cheesecake. In their entertainments, they keep the wind between them and this malodorous stuff. There are no guns on the tube, not even bows and arrows.

In the Labyrinth Bar at the Hotel Intourist, I hear a Third Worlder say how freedom of the press is a bourgeois illusion. He is wearing a white turban and a wrinkleproof suit and he inserts his Dunhill cigaret in an elegant meerschaum holder. The important thing, he is saying, is to protect the people from lies. I think of William Jennings Bryan, a badly flawed hero, and how with all his flaws he came closest to defining the good residual thing. "The people," Bryan said, "have the right to make their own mistakes."

When I finish with my antiquarian research on the Dartmouth-Princeton game etc., I go out to lunch with Canby. I do this once a week. Sometimes we are adventurous and journey afield. We go to the Uzbekistan on Neglinnaya Street, where the decor is Central Asian, or we go to the Ararat just up the street. The Ararat is Armenian. The Praga in the Arbat is more or less Czech. There are German restaurants and Georgian restaurants, and they have hung Chinese lanterns in the Pekin on the Ring Road. At the Pekin we order Druzhba Salad. "Druzhba" means Friendship. They aren't friendly any more with the folks in Pekin but Druzhba Salad is still on the menu. Pieces of squid are mixed in with the lettuce and noodles. This sounds decadent. The Moscow Food Trust is vigilant, though. It prepares all the menus, and restaurants in Moscow are separate but equal.

At the National on Gorky Street, the waiter starts us off with sturgeon salad and cold potatoes. He is an old hand and we leave the ordering to him. After a long hiatus, the next course comes to the table, sturgeon boiled in tomato sauce. Why change horses in midstream? Lenin used to live upstairs in a room above the dining room, Canby tells me. Being preoccupied with the World Over Yonder, he called himself a materialist. This enduring confusion is a legacy of his to the present. Munching on a dessert roll topped with crudded milk, I think of the great gorging days of Gogol's Chichikov. All that pastry and stuffed shoulder of mutton he put away with Sobakevich, and where has it gone?

With lunch we take tea. When you open the packet, the string and tab come loose from the tea bag. The bill, when it finally arrives, is all wrong. It is totaled by machine, and how can it be wrong? Our waiter, a man no better than he should be, might have fiddled the bill if he thought he could do this, rich Americans being fair game. His frustration is apparent, though. This machine, he says defensively, was imported from France.

Gogol's Chichikov, says Prince Mirsky in his history of Russian literature, is the incarnation of *poshlost*, an untranslatable word he proceeds to translate. "Self-satisfied inferiority, moral and spiritual." Under this aspect, Gogol saw the reality of his own time. You can say he bore witness, but he wasn't long on ideas and unlike Lenin he doesn't ask you What Is to Be Done. "I must present life as it is," Gogol said, "and not write essays about it."

Chichikov is a rascal, also a bumbler, who acquires title to dead serfs at bargain basement prices. He uses this as his collateral when he wants to buy live serfs. The foolish gentry on whom he imposes are rascals, too. They are glad to take a fool's money for their title to dead souls. The government is rascally and levies a tax on this title. Getting round the government is child's play, however. A thousand years ago when the people of Kiev converted en masse to the new Christian religion, there was joy in Heaven for all the souls that were saved. But the Devil groaned: "Woe is me! They are driving me out of here!" They didn't drive him out. This crooked community, disgraced and saved by its ineptitude, isn't shamed by it, though, and is not about to mend its ways. Gogol said how he intended a happy ending for *Dead Souls*, where Chichikov & Co. were going to mend their ways. This happy ending eluded him.

"What a sad country Russia is!" Pushkin said when he read his friend's novel, and he said how behind the laughter you feel the unseen tears. The tears don't deny the laughter, and the other way round is true. "Long live comedy!" Gogol said, intending by this a mingling of laughter and tears. His clerical hero in "The Overcoat" works his fingers to the bone, and all he gets is a metal disk in his buttonhole and a stitch in his side. We laugh at the foolish hero, but his folly makes us sad.

Reading this catholic and slippery writer, I turn away sheepish but secretly pleased, having looked at myself in the mirror. He makes me take the sense of the old chestnut that says how we aren't any better than we should be. This is depressing but exhilarating, too. Moral and spiritual inferiority describes us, and we live on easy terms with the description. Anyway, we understand how no remedy offers. Gogol understood this, being blessed and cursed, and when the balance tilted in favor of depression he quit living.

Twice now, on my visits to the reading room of the Lenin Library, I have encountered Molotov, an ancient of days. Though he is over ninety, the jutting jaw still declares him. In the crowded room, he has a table to himself. This isn't from deference. Molotov is a survivor, like the hammerhead shark, and in the Lenin Library they give him plenty of leeway. Periodicals are scattered over the table, and he turns the pages idly. Looking up from his reading, he finds my eyes on his face. But his eyes are unseeing, and Molotov is looking straight through me. This man, born Scriabin, rejected his name. Scriabin evoked the composer and his music, a world of form where activity is self-delighting and has no purpose but itself. Molotov, by contrast, signifies the Hammer.

I pity my bumbling waiter at the National Hotel, and I pity the rest of us, poor feckless men. Gogol is our chronicler, and what he knows about us denies perfectibility and jeopardizes the future where they are pulling themselves up by their bootstraps. The promoters of uplift, seeing this as a problem, have seen their way to resolving it. They have clarified the doubtful image of the weird tormented man and replaced it with an energetic Gogol. If this skeptical writer couldn't finish his novel on an upward curve, they undertake to finish it for him.

Stalin, passing Gogol's statue on the boulevard which bears his name, didn't care for it. He said this statue looked morbid. Gogol is a capacious writer, familiar with men of all classes and kinds, and already he has Stalin to the life. "Men like you, my pseudo-patriots, stand in dread of the eye which is able to discern." The year before Stalin died, they took away the offending statue and put another in its place. Uninspiriting Gogol went up again elsewhere, in a corner where the great man wouldn't see him. Intourist guides leave this corner alone.

No. 7A Suvorov has a recessed courtyard. On the benches in the courtyard, two old women with string bags and a young militiaman are fighting off a postprandial snooze. The heavy traffic at the corner, where Suvorov meets Kalinin, sounds remotely here, beside this house where Gogol wrote his *Inspector General.* The man on the pedestal is asking, "Who, if not an author, is to speak aloud the truth?" He is reproving the custodians of the single truth, and his expression is somber but you wouldn't call it lugubrious. Stalin is lugubrious. Also Stalin was evil, etc. But the dark and secretive man in the courtyard, who used his talent for mimicry as a weapon against the darkness, says that Stalin was more and less than evil. How commonplace to ask for a good-natured Gogol.

Walking away from the house on Suvorov, I cross Kalinin Prospekt and head for Volkhonka Street and the Pushkin Museum. Hope springs eternal, and maybe today they will let me have a peek at Gauguin and van Gogh. My best route takes me south along Gogol Boulevard. Not for the first time I pass Stalin's

Gogol, looking over the traffic that eddies at his feet. Heroic but composed, he might be directing traffic. *Poshlost* isn't in it for him. Like Marx on his pedestal he is full of good cheer, and like Dzerzhinsky full of purpose. Smiling, this Gogol says that all's well in Socialist Land.

TEA AND BLINI AT THE TRETYAKOV

My cousin Irma has come to Moscow for a visit with her husband, Al Grunewald, in tow. Irma has a shopping list and means to get through it: Beriozka dolls, a fur hat, an antique samovar if she can find one, those lacquered boxes with handpainted scenes of old Russia. Al wears a long face and says he'd rather be in Moscow than pushing up daisies. He knows better than to argue with his wife.

Irma is small-boned, high-breasted, manicured but not obtrusively. Small black curls are shaped close to her head. Her skin is dark and speaks of winter holidays in warm places where you need a lot of money. There are touches of healthy color underneath the dark skin. Irma is forty and looks a lot younger. Al looks a lot older. His face is seamed and liver-spotted, his hair thin on top but luxuriant around the ears. He has a belly he doesn't try to hide. "After forty," he says, "a man has the right to let down his belly." Al owns and runs a furniture factory in Grand Rapids,

Michigan. He wears Harry Truman shirts, high-top shoes, and suspenders. In the pocket of his shirt he carries a clutch of Write Bros. pens. The name of the business is printed on each. Al is Four-H, BPOE, and his politics are vintage McKinley. His vendetta with the Russkies is deeply personal, and he'd rather be called a rat by a Red than a Red by a rat. Like the Russkies, however, he looks for the bottom line. Things that work get his earnest attention. He likes to stand in the subway and time the digital clocks at the entrance of the tunnels and watch as they switch back to zero. They do this whenever a new train pulls in, and he reckons that an average cycle takes no more than three minutes. In Moscow, the trains run on time. "Why shouldn't they run on time?" Al wants to know. Nonetheless, this makes an impression.

Irma goes to church but Al has got religion. Hepplewhite or Chippendale, straight lines or crooked, it makes a difference to him. So does the grain of the wood. He is partial to walnut where the grain runs close together, and turns up his nose at yellow pine. A scale model of the old sailing vessel called "The Falls of Clyde" sits in his office at home. On the deck are tiny capstans, and he has carved a Scottish lass on the bowsprit. This affection for detail that has no point but itself isn't just the same as seeing to it that the trains run on time.

Tour guides in Moscow are eager to impress you but have a mind of their own. They will show you the old churches, if that is what you want to see. What they really want to show you is the new shopping center across the street from the Dom Knigi, the tractor factory, the glassworks, the House of the Collective where four hundred workers' families live, or the monument to the battle and labor exploits of the people during the Great Patriotic War. This is in Yaroslavl, a way out of town. Al would fare better with a guide from Intourist. I am family, however, and do the familial thing.

At the State History Museum, we look at the pointed helmets. At the Geological Museum, we see a lot of rocks. The National Economic Achievements Exhibition is a must. The Central House of Aviation on Red Army Street shows us the world's first airplane. Kitty Hawk isn't mentioned, and Al begins to get hot under the collar. His collar pinches at the Polytechnic Museum. They tell us how this first radio receiver is the work of one Popov. Al wants to remonstrate. "Who do they think they're kidding?" He doesn't know the language, though, a blessing in disguise.

I can't be with them every day, and that is a mixed blessing. The Cosmos Hotel being out in the boonies, you have to take the metro if you want to go shopping or look at the sights. Signs in the metro are conspicuous and neatly lettered but they are lettered in Cyrillic. Al for once is more crushed than indignant. Reading Cyrillic is like looking in the mirror, where inversion is the rule. You recognize N and R, but they have printed them backwards. Even worse, these old friends are not what they seem. P is R, C is S, and B turns into V. Sometimes, however, they don't want you to pronounce it, and evidently B stands for beguiling.

Russian is peculiar, a language like painting where Chagall is the painter. He is turning the world upside down. Men are bigger than the houses they live in, and the houses undulate like licorice or the ropy tobacco preferred by Father Marx. The Cyrillic alphabet is like that: haycocks, a cloven apple, the klobuki hats resembling stovepipes they still wear at Zagorsk. I have dreamed in Cyrillic, visualizing the alphabet, and an ancient Citroën, the symbol for D, is coming at me head on. Against this obdurate language you can crack your head. That is the glory of Russian. "Our great Russian word, free and pure," Akhmatova called it in one of her war poems. "Free" means fettered with a hundred shades and meanings, and "pure" defines the lucky mixture that is history's gift to a living tongue.

In the meantime, Al has a problem. I know how he copes with what he calls the language barrier, having seen him in action before. This was on their trip to Rome when I was studying at the

American Academy there, and Al and Irma were installed in a new hotel near the foot of the Via Cavour. Out in public with Al I did my best to fade into the scenery, a blond Italian from the Veneto, just happening by. "This man is a friend of yours?" *Non parlo inglese.*

When in Rome, if you are Al you don't do as the Romans do. You climb on the bus through the doors marked for egress. You flash a wad of what he calls the Monopoly money they use in that country, and let the conductor extract what is due him. You catechize him in English, raising your voice an octave and enunciating with the clarity reserved for deaf mutes or the mentally retarded. "Where do we get off to see Michael Angelo's Moses?" Sometimes in Italy, this gets results. The Gianicolo where I was living isn't a far cry from English Janiculum, and an Italian if he cares to will understand your drift when you want to know the way to St. Peter's. In Moscow you cannot bank on these rough approximations.

Toilets are toilets, give or take a few letters, and this is all to the good. But what seems an invitation to knock on the door denotes the kiosk where you buy the morning paper. On the Moscow subway, hieroglyphics confront you as your train eases into the station. "Ve-De-En-Kha." That is how they call the station where Al and Irma began their daily tussle with the language barrier. The Cyrillic characters that purport to tell you this look like concrete poetry, however. In this temple at Karnak, the priests serving the temple keep tight on what they know.

"Only one thing to do," said Irma to Al, and being herself she mastered the alphabet. This took two days, and I got a note at the Metropole to call her. Would I meet them in Red Square to help out with the shopping? "KRAHS-noy PLOHSH-shah-dee?" Irma said doubtfully. "Spoken like a native," I told her.

Three hundred years ago when they gave the square its name, *krasnaya* meant both red and beautiful. Today this ampler meaning reduces to one meaning, and Red Square is the color of perturbation. At one corner Lenin's tomb, a pyramid of red granite, anchors the huge oblong, at another the dull red brick of the Lenin Museum. This nineteenth-century mill town remembers Lawrence or Lowell, but the factory workers and their families have all gone out of town.

Sometimes they straggle back, and there is always a queue before the tomb of the Founder. On Fridays, a day for weddings, photographers set up their beach umbrellas and offer three "scenes" for forty-five rubles. In the Place of the Skull or by the statue of Minin and Pozharsky, young couples in their best regalia strike awkward attitudes and look straight into the camera. For the anniversary of the Revolution the powers that be appreciate a big turnout, and they can shoehorn two million people into the square. When people agglutinate on this scale, however, it isn't easy to discriminate between them.

Most days, the great square seems empty. Partly that is a function of size. Six or seven football fields laid end to end blot up a lot of people. Muscovites are in a hurry to click off the yards. They are emerging from cover, or they feel how the immensity dwarfs them. In winter, this place is frigid, and largely silent at all times except when stridor is the order of the day. Benches are verboten, also cafés, and there isn't any loitering unless to watch the changing of the guard, every hour on the hour before the Lenin Mausoleum. You are here to pay homage and move on.

Rome when I studied there wasn't all study, and I used to go for cheap vacations to the Yugoslav coast. In the ocean around Dubrovnik, you can swim well into the fall. The Placa in Dubrovnik is a long way from Red Square, not only as the crow flies. They are drinking beer in the Placa at tables on the sidewalk around the baroque cathedral, and boys are playing soccer and using the cathedral wall as their backstop. The narrow streets twist and turn as you go up from the square. Bedsheets and underclothes are drying on clothes lines between the old buildings. Atop the Roland Column, a medieval soldier holds his buckler and sword. For the medieval city, his right forearm provided the measure of length. They call this measure the Dubrovnik cubit, not a yard or a foot but the length of a forearm. Legend says how Roland, Charlemagne's nephew, gave his column and a constitution to Dubrovnik. The local legend that tells about him is attractive, unlikely, and important.

Not far from the Kremlin, the rickety old building in Novaya Square houses the Museum of the History and Reconstruction of Moscow. This is one of the high spots in the earnest man's itinerary, and I hit it with Al and Irma on the afternooon of the day we did the Polytechnic Museum. Old maps with Latin place names and old paintings by the bucketful peel away the centuries, showing you Red Square in the days of Boris Godunov. Market stalls fragment the great open space, breaking it down, a human space alive with people who aren't in a hurry. No wooden-faced militiaman is moving them on. He would have had his hands full. Tom, Dick, and Harry are a law to themselves, and their contempt for law and order turned this city upside down in the old days. Boris Godunov could tell you.

About Boris Godunov, Al has little to say. But he votes against the past for the orderly present where the trains run on time and they have drained the Pontine marshes, etc. I prefer the disorderly past to the present and wish they had called off the Revolution. Hobson's choice. Al's vendetta with the Russkies won't let him give credit where credit is due. I give them more credit than he does. Bad food, worse manners, barbed wire, the debasing of the word, and I lay it all at their door. Each of us is wrong.

Paris is to Moscow as peaches to pears, but they have their points in common. In the huge square before the Panthéon in Paris, they will let you be august. They won't let you be intimate, however. No eccentricity or clutter tells of where you came from. A provincial abbey church named for St. Genevieve used to stand in the square. Unlike the old church, the Panthéon is catholic, and its comprehensive truth blots up a whole calendar of saints. Catholic doesn't mean inclusive, though. Pretending to include everything, the Panthéon comes up empty-handed. It opened for business in the year of the French Revolution, not a banner year for nice distinctions. The Panthéon, having no taste for nice distinctions, shows you an unbroken space. No environing chapels invite the eye to pause, no gargoyles on the roof mix whimsy and terror. Fragonard and Watteau have their whimsical eye, not appropriate for church, and no seraphic courtiers look down from the ceiling. This ecumenical church is dedicated to all the gods. Ecumenical works out to anonymous.

When the Revolution in France sent the king to the guillotine, the Empress Catherine in Russia took to her bed. Historians like to tell you how she got up a changed woman, no more liberal panaceas for her. The French Revolution is her legacy, however, or you could put it the other way round. Like the men of the Directorate, she lived much in the mind, a parvenu, self-engendered, without lares or penates. The eye she turned on the past was indifferent. Red Square and its clutter, coming down from the past, were like a red flag. All they had to do was wave it, and she created the modern city with a vacuum at the heart.

From the center of the city, wide thoroughfares move outward. They are straight as a die, and the enlightened despot can sight along them. An inner ring of boulevards cinches the inner city, and an outer ring locks the city in place. The Bell Tower of Ivan the Terrible, the tallest building in old Moscow, marks the center of the circle within a circle. In the Kremlin, the enlightened despot looks over the scene. The empty space is a theater where the despot harangues the people and marshals the troops.

Space is what you make of it, and the dialectic notwithstanding, the future is still up for grabs. Prague is a baroque theater where the past and present struggle for the future. The powers that be have allowed the old city of Charles IV to run down, preferring to put their money on the new subway system. They are glad to let this city run down, not wanting the past to speak to the present. Prague today is empty space filled with echoes and depression.

Warsaw is like the South Side of Chicago, Studs Lonigan country, and you wouldn't want to sentimentalize the Poles. They have their piety, however. In Castle Square and Old Market Square after the rising of 1944 there wasn't a stone on a stone, only empty space. Poles have built it up again in the image and likeness of the past. The Sigismund Column is back where it used to be, and the cobblestones are back in place in the scallop-shape of Castle Square. The cafés have reopened in Old Market Square. Boys on skateboards crisscross the square, wimpled nuns go in and out of the rebuilt cathedral. The stenciling is rococo on the houses in the Old Quarter, gilt tracery around the windows, gilt scrolls above the doors. In Warsaw they remember where they came from. This attention to the past says that Warsaw has a future.

Russians want to remember, but there is fear in a handful of dust. St. Isaac's Cathedral in Leningrad still stands on the Neva but they have stored it with instruments of medieval torture, and St. Isaac's is an atheists' museum. Across from Novo-Devichy, the Andronikov Monastery with its Archangel Church leans into the river, a mining town in the Old West. The lodes were depleted a long time ago. You can take a photo of the Archangel Church, the oldest house of public worship in Moscow. Andrew Rublev worshiped here at the end of his life. They aren't about to tear it down, but this church is still virulent. Not even a gauze face mask will get you past the door.

In the Great Patriotic War Stalin invoked the image of Holy Mother Russia. He appealed to the shades of Minin and Pozharsky who fought the Polish invaders three hundred years ago. Al resonates to this and has a sneaking admiration for Stalin, who smoked a pipe. He was Uncle Joe, not an intellectual like Lenin and Trotsky. Americans also appeal to the past, and have something in common with these Russians who aren't pious but only pietistic. In Suzdal north of Moscow, the reconstructed wooden houses show you Russia as it used to be in pioneer days. When I go to Suzdal I am back in Greenfield Village outside Detroit, a monument to the past. Henry Ford whose work this was destroyed the past when he made his automobile.

Catherine the Great called her new city on the Black Sea Sevaste-polis, an august city that remembers Augustus Caesar and the First Rome. She was putting down roots out of old mythologies, and the roots were made of papier-mâché. It is true she took lovers, and this argues flesh and blood. But Catherine has had a better press than she deserves. Mostly she looked through flesh and blood. She liked to read Locke and Bentham and the French *philosophes*, and she gathered from her reading that man is a blank page. Paper, said Stalin, will put up with anything you can write on it.

With Catherine the Great and Peter the Great, you wouldn't care to play a hand of piquet. But these disagreeable personalities are unmistakably themselves. The new autocrat is incorporated, like the First National Bank. He has no personality, and indigenous things get on his nerves. The poetry of Little Russia being indigenous, he won't let them teach it. He won't let them speak Ukrainian. He takes order with everything Polish. The Armenians in the Caucasus have their own thing, and they aren't so far away but what he can see them. It isn't so much that he is anti-Semitic. But Jews are peculiar, so he institutes the pogrom. Religions are peculiar and have their niggling distinctions. "He who does not hold two fingers in making the sign of the cross—be he damned." A little later, however, they are holding up three fingers. Their finicking temper tries the autocrat's patience, so he closes the church or sets up as Pantocrator in a universal church. His ideal city is denuded, not stripped to the buff but titivated with fig leaves and geegaws. Symmetry is his passion or maybe his fixation. The Lubyanka is symmetrical, like Bentham's ideal prison.

Symmetry binds where asymmetry loosens, so down with the onion domes of Moscow. Napoleon, when he got to Moscow, didn't know what to make of the onion domes. He knew he didn't like them, and he stabled his horses in St. Basil's Cathedral. This man of the Enlightenment wanted to tear down the cathedral. Al wouldn't go that far but is not about to contribute to the Fund for Restoring St. Basil's. "Coney Island," he says succinctly, and there is something to be said for this opinion.

As you emerge from the metro and enter Red Square, the crazy quilt that is St. Basil's meets you like a blow to the head. It just misses being vulgar: crazy-colored stripes, poles before a barber shop, inverted ice cream cones, ovoid cupolas. Each of the nine cupolas, differing from the others, stakes out its own claim to attention. The eye, looking for order, doesn't find it and comes to a stand. This is unsettling, and Al turns his back on St. Basil the Blessed.

I tell him he has to look longer. St. Basil's says how, if there is order in us it is the order of change, not the order of mathematics where the sums never vary, but the disconcerting order of the living man himself. Ivan the Terrible, who built this church four hundred years ago, blinded the architect when the building was finished, that is what they say, and St. Basil's is one of a kind. Tsar Ivan devoted his mornings to prayer. In the afternoons, he came to St. Basil's through the Gate of the Savior. He watched them torture his victims in the Place of the Skull, a round white stone platform like a giant well cover or a theater-in-the-round. The appointed victims in this theater were knouted to death or scalded or they drank boiling lead. "I too believe in God," Stalin said once. His bust beside the Kremlin Wall looks across Red Square to this resort of his favorite tsar.

A great disorder is an order, St. Basil's, for instance. Its impulse is centrifugal, and the only unity it acknowledges is the unity of what comes next. Already when they were building it the Pope in Rome was knocking down old St. Peter's and clearing out

St. Peter's Square. St. Basil's, being a house of many mansions, assimilates contradictions without obscuring the point. There isn't a point.

If you are going to come to terms with the old churches of Moscow, you must look for analogies in nature. The hemisphere dome is the head that crowns the body. In the Orthodox churches of ancient cities like Constantinople, the head sits on the shoulders, and Sancta Sophia is like a man without a neck. Churches in Moscow have their tropism, though, and tend upward towards the light. Russian church architects, squeezing the hemisphere with powerful fingers, forced it into a bulb that narrows at the top. The ancient helmets of Russian soldiers in the Armory and the State Museum in Revolution Square are like this, shaped into onions, and the blows which might be mortal slide away. Or the domes are burning candles that aspire to heaven. Bad poetry, but that is what they look like.

On our left hand as we walk back towards Revolution Square, the Spasskaya Tower carries on its mute dialog with the cathedral. The gate in the tower opens on forbidden ground. Before the Revolution, when you entered the Kremlin through the Savior's Gate you had to uncover in front of the icon of the Savior that used to hang over the entrance. Bells are chiming the hour, beginning right on the dot. You can set your Exakta wristwatch by the bells in the Spasskaya Tower.

Goose-stepping soldiers are coming out of the gate from their quarters in the Kremlin. They form a single body with the arms and legs swinging in unison, a textbook illustration of the drill-master's art, and are silent except for the slap of their boots. Evidently the soldiers are coming straight for us. They don't look to right or left, and don't break formation until they ground arms before the portals of the Lenin Mausoleum. The guard is changing, and I feel the small hairs begin to stir on the back of my neck.

GUM, the State Universal Store, faces Red Square and has a block to itself between Kuibyshev and 25th October. The plate glass windows, full of goods, look out on the Kremlin Wall and the Lenin Mausoleum in the foreground. Where the Mausoleum presses earthward, GUM is buoyant and blithe. Unlike the Mausoleum, it has no uplifting message to communicate. GUM is sending out signals, however. Let the dead bury their dead.

Kazan Cathedral used to stand beside it, not challenging the heavens but aspiring to heaven. After the Revolution, the icon-smashers had their way with the cathedral. They called themselves the League of the Militant Godless. Had they known what was good for them, they would have swept the board clean. GUM is vestigial and reproaches the militant present, its old-fashioned elegance having no point but itself. That is how it was with the old-time religion, where the end in view was not salvation, whatever they tell you in church. Sanctity was the end in view, and sufficient in itself.

Graceful arches carry the glass-roofed arcade, and daylight, refracted, softens the electric light. Inside, the walls rise two stories high. The eye follows them upward, looking for the light, and finds the little bridges that span the huge bazaar. In the harmony of soft color, pale blue, pink, and green are the dominant colors. The fretwork on the coffered walls is rococo.

From a balcony on the second story, I look down on the crowd. This isn't a synoptic view, as when you look down from the Ferris wheel in Gorky Park, and it isn't a mob scene assembled for one of Eisenstein's spectaculars. People are vociferating, there is plenty of clutter and shove. But this crowd is from the neighborhood, "Fish Lane" and environs. The faces in the crowd are vivid, and I follow the fortunes of Tom, Dick, and Harry pushing from one alcove to another. Dozens of alcoves are selling different things. Tom, Dick, and Harry are clamoring to buy, and the sellers are anxious to please them.

I am waiting on Al and Irma, and this amiable fiction is a product of time on my hands. Like the meanest store front in

Moscow, GUM is owned by the state, and the clerks who serve the state are insolent and bored. You can't fault them for this, they having nothing to lose. Conceivably, though, they have something to gain. When his vendetta with the Russkies is going full steam, Al equates gain and loss with dollars and cents, and he trumpets the virtues of the free enterprise system. In his heart, he knows better. It isn't profit that kicks him into gear in the mornings. Al is a hard man underneath the soft exterior, and pride is the master motive for him.

No dice on the samovar, he tells me. Otherwise this excursion is a success. Laden with our bundles, we push through the doors that lead to the street and turn right at my direction on 25th October. There are things I want them to see.

Color sends out signals. Green is cool but viscous green is sinister. Yellow is romantic, the color of far-winding horns. Cities have their characteristic color. Burnt sienna is the color for Italian hill towns, blinding white for Greek villages on the Aegean, and for Cairo, earth browns and egg whites. The color of old Moscow is pastel, lavender, pistachio, apricot, dusty chocolate. In the narrow streets around GUM and running down to the river, the eighteenth century is still alive, and the frivolity of the Yellow Nineties in the years before frivolity went out of style. This Moscow of the mind's eye is a fading seaside resort, Brighton by the sea where the Prince Regent in his frivolous Pavilion counted none but sunny hours.

The antediluvian city hints at a carnal life, and who knows what goings-on it used to accommodate. Not putting man on a pedestal, Muscovites didn't ask you to be mindful of him. Their decorators and architects, going in for jeux d'esprit, made whimsical curlicues in plaster of paris. Lacking function, they ought to be vulgar. Form follows function. That was the first commandment, handed down by the Bauhaus or International style. We were all moral fiber when I was growing up.

For the first time in years, I think of the early Victorian lamp my great-aunt Hilda gave me once upon a time. Shaped like a globe, it was decorated in low relief. I wanted to tap off the vine leaves and acanthus with a hammer and chisel, preferring the unaccommodated thing. Away with bric-a-brac, etc. No house room if it doesn't function to hold up the house. Like Rector Petrovsky and his colleagues in the Lenin Hills, I didn't have much to say for the lilies of the field.

But function, like "pravda," is a portmanteau word. This is what I keep discovering as I wear down, and I have stuffed the portmanteau with any number of eccentric definitions. Great-aunt Hilda, a shrewd and civilized old lady who lived on the income from government bonds, crossed over the river a long time ago, and when my marriage broke up her wedding present went the way of a lot of other superfluous things.

Above Lenin Prospekt as you turn your back on Gorky Park, Yury Gagarin stands on his pedestal, an aluminum shaft celebrating the flight of *Vostok*. This celebration diminishes where it ought to ennoble. Anyway, it diminishes me. It isn't Gagarin, a heightened version of myself, who spurns the delimiting earth with his foot. I am looking up at Superman, self-confident and poised for his leap into space. His eyes don't blink nervously but gaze into the sun. His palms don't sweat with fear. The man on the pedestal is ignorant of fear, and I know I can't follow him where he is going.

On the walls of the Faculty of Journalism in Moscow University downtown, a heroic portrait of Fidel Castro assesses me skeptically. I can tell that I don't measure up. There are no warts on this Castro. I pick through the posters in the House of Books on Kalinin Prospekt, and like a bad penny Andropov keeps turning up. He is bright as a penny, though, not getting any older. Pictures of starlets go for eight kopecks. A good likeness of Andropov will set you back sixty rubles.

It is when the rhetoric heats up, all that hectic insistence on man's sufficiency and grandeur, that his shortcomings are most naked. I remember a war movie during the War, Van Johnson and June Allyson having a heart-to-heart at the USO tea dance. He has been through hell in the islands. Knowing this, she ventures how he can't wait to get home. The lady is wrong, though. "The shortest road home leads through Tokyo, ma'am." That is what the hero says, and the sailors in the audience laughed until they cried.

"To tell people the truth doesn't mean to tell the bad, to poke into shortcomings." That is the rhetorician, and Solzhenitsyn in *The Cancer Ward* is asking us to take his mark. The rhetorician is a paperhanger whose job is to paper over the cracks. In Dzerzhinsky Park on the way to Al and Irma's, you can't see the park for the paper. The Worker and the Collective Farm Girl guard the entrance, setting me a standard I can never hope to fulfill. They are all kinetic energy, no harelip, mole, or scar. This stainless-steel ensemble is looking straight through me.

Flapping in the wind, red and yellow banners proclaim "Peace to the World" *Miru—Mir*! When I hear this heartless equivocation, I want to reach for my gun. On billboards in the park, the soldiers and Stakhanovites have picked the grime from their fingernails and got rid of original sin. Taking hands with each other, they are grinning infectiously, and would like to take hands with me too. I would like them to keep their hands to themselves. They are the people, but they aren't my people, and anyway, says Tolstoy's hero, "That word 'people' is so vague."

In Mainz after the War, I had a chance to examine the incunabula in the Gutenberg collection. This placid city on the Rhine is like Cincinnati or Louisville, not a site for Armageddon. I wondered how it must have looked under Hitler. At a guess, not much different, except for the posters. Shining and optimistic, they never leave you alone. *Ad astra,* mein Herr. All that exhorting defeats itself, though, and cynicism is the product of hoopla. The rhetorician, who is out to deceive you, isn't deceived himself.

Old Moscow, understanding how man's reach exceeds his

grasp, makes room for shortcomings, also gratuities. It does better than this. It stamps them with approval. The approval is ambiguous, prompted partly by fatigue, and cynicism has a corner in it too. Not everyone is willing to confer this approval. "What is to be done?" tiresome old Chernyshevsky wants to know, and Lenin echoes this question. In Tolstoy's novel, Oblonsky, having quarreled with his wife, raises the question again. "But what is to be done?" Tolstoy tells us how he found no answer.

There are windows within the windows on 25th October Street, like the little doors on Advent calendars you pop open one day at a time. They serve for ventilation, but a little ventilation does nicely. The merchants who used to live here liked to look out the windows. Also, having their priorities, they liked to keep the great outdoors in its place. Alfresco living is for poor naked man, and winter in Moscow is no friend to society.

The old and debonair buildings are built to human scale, and don't let on if they think of imposing. You see a lot of sky above the roofs of the buildings. They don't ask you to look on their works and despair, like Karnak in the time of the Pharaohs. The city as it used to be turns an indifferent eye on posterity and its approval, one reason it still survives in the present.

Moscow in the present has its virtues, however. Living here, you find out who you are. I am like that small poet in the older time who loved littleness almost in all things, "a little convenient estate, a little cheerful house, a little company, and a very little feast." Aeroflot, on the other hand, is "the World's Biggest Airline." This accurate description makes me think of Flux, Utah, where I gassed up my car once in the World's Biggest Gas Station. Serving more countries than any other carrier, Aeroflot flies routes that, all told, are twenty-five times longer than the equator. You could lay a lot of equators end to end, if you wanted to do this, and they wouldn't have a patch on Aeroflot.

Russia is a country "where nearly everything, from plains to human feet, is, rather, on the gigantic scale." Gogol says this, and

I believe him. Russians are like grand opera. In 1825 one of the Decembrists said to his regiment how "without freedom there can be no happiness." The soldiers of the regiment were willing to drink to that. They drank two hundred pails of vodka in five-gallon pails. This works out to a gallon per man.

In Cathedral Square, at the foot of the bell tower named for Ivan the Terrible, I have put my finger on the world's biggest bell. The Tsar of Bells measures sixty feet in circumference and weighs two hundred tons. Around the Tsar Cannon I certify the great cannonballs, each a yard in diameter. My guide says regretfully that the Tsar Cannon has never been fired, and the Tsar of Bells has never been rung. I tell him to consider the lilies of the field.

The monumental look of Moscow nags at Irma. This isn't the Central African Empire, and what are they trying to prove? For the Red Army there is nothing to prove, and like Aeroflot it serves a lot of countries. The generals who run this army have their dropping-in place on the corner of Frunze Street, named for the soldiers' general Stalin shortened by a head. Around the Ministry of Defense they are strutting like Chanticleer, short, barrel-chested, and they know where their next meal is coming from. Nicholas I, a brutal man, when he wanted to palliate his brutalities appealed to the general well-being, "le bien-être général en Russie." This was said to mean: "It is well to be a general in Russia."

Ostentation in Frunze's time counted as a shameful relic, like the ribbons and sashes they flaunted at the court of the tsar. Today on Frunze Street they are hosting a costermongers' convention. The delegates to the convention are anxious to hook your eye. Where a discreet rosette used to hide in the buttonhole, a sunburst of color covers the chest. Even the civilian clerks have this bedizened look about them. They are telling you who won the Great Patriotic War, or perhaps they are telling themselves.

The Ministry of Defense makes a huge quadrilateral, supported by white pillars. Filled with rubble, like pillars before the house of a man with pretensions, they aren't whimsical but minatory, another word for defensive. For the tops of the pillars, Corinthian is preferred. The more scrollwork they can manage, the better.

"Why not rest on their laurels?" Irma is exasperated and misses the point. They were building Chartres Cathedral when you hear the first mention of Moscow. The first Russian university opened in Moscow a few years before they opened the University of Tennessee. Monteverdi was dead a long time and Mozart was still alive when they performed their first Russian opera. Where GUM now stands, Ivan Fyodorov printed the first Russian book. We pass his statue on the corner of 25th October. Ivan the Terrible paid for the printing press, and the next year he let the mob destroy it. This happened in Shakespeare's lifetime. The first printed book in Montenegro appeared a hundred years before. In England they had a literature in three different tongues when Yury Dolguruky was putting up his log cabins on a rise above the Moscow River, and the great days of the London theater were ancient history when they opened the first theater in Moscow.

Like the First Rome, this city thinks it has something to prove. Following the analogy, I liken America to decadent Athens. Analogies are tricky, though. There is nothing decadent about Al Grunewald, and when I am tempted to contrast this with that, Flux, Utah, brings me up short.

Across the street on our left as we head for the metro in Dzerzhinsky Square, a rampant lion and a unicorn confront one another. Theirs isn't a real confrontation, and the modest façade on which they are posturing looks a little diffident when you put it against the mock-Gothic skyscrapers, Stalin's seven deadly sins. Quartering the sky, these buildings say how man is the master of his fate. Like sand castles at the water's edge, they are gray where the water has caught them and dripping with gray globules of sand. This look of running down doesn't signify erosion, Stalin Gothic being built to last. Those vesicles and blains on the face of the buildings are there to catch the eye. Al says to Irma, "Like that wedding cake we saw in Rome." Gingerbread describes the monument they put up to King Victor Emmanuel in Rome, and Romans, understanding this, have turned it into a laughter. The pointed tower in the Lenin Hills, with its illuminated Red Star like a parody of the Christmas Star, isn't a theme for laughter. It hangs over this city like the stuff of vertiginous dreams, and its quarrel with death is a quarrel with life. Stalin the uneasy parvenu walks up and down in Moscow, and what he made declares the horror of a vacuum.

Far to the west in Smolenskaya Square, the skyscraper Stalin built to house the Foreign Ministry dominates the humbler buildings around it. Molotov had his offices there. He was Old Stone Bottom, whose homilies radiated assurance. The assurance doesn't rub off, and the arrogance which might astonish doesn't take fire.

Nobody sleeps late in Moscow. At first light the trip-hammers are going, and the radio in the hotel room starts up an hour later. Old Moscow smelled to high heaven but you could hear a pin drop in the center of town. Modern Moscow is spick-and-span, no garbage in the streets, and the clamor comes at you in waves. Loudspeakers edify you on the streets and railroad trains. If you take a train from the terminals around Komsomolskaya Square, you hear the glad tidings from eight in the morning to eleven at night.

The radio in the hotel room has a mind of its own. It wants you to be up and doing, and I imagine it proposing that we gather for calisthenics on the roof of the hotel. But the radio is willful and goes dead without warning. You can deal with its vagaries by main force, a satisfaction to Al. Even so, he complains how he can't get a decent night's sleep. They don't tuck in the blanket when they make up the bed, and from the foot of the bed his big feet keep protruding.

They can't tuck in the blanket, "as any fool can see." Al has eyes in his head but refuses to see, and doesn't take kindly to

Irma's suggestion. The bed sheet is two-layered. It makes a sack or shroud, and they stuff the blanket through a circular hole. Gingerly does it, no tossing and turning, and you don't want to rumple the bedclothes. This arrangement doesn't play to Al's strength.

On Sunday morning in Moscow, the hammers are quiet. Irma isn't for sleeping in, though. Even in Moscow Sundays are for church, most of all in Moscow, she says. I am summoned to act as their usher.

Moscow of sixteen hundred belfries, they used to call it, and Muscovites called their city Jerusalem. They said how they were living in the New Israel, and they had a vision of this city standing outside human time. The Third Rome was also a heavenly city, and the role of Moscow was to challenge the secular world, making ready the dominion of Christ.

Coming up Razin Street on a late October day, I have caught a glimpse of the heavenly city, candor beyond imagining. Gold leaf shivers on the domes of the Assumption Cathedral and the clustered domes of the Terems. Eleven of them, matched like bells, make a silent harmony each under each. The Tsars of Muscovy were crowned in the Assumption Cathedral, and later the Tsars of all the Russias. They were Vicars of Christ on earth.

Sun glints on the facets of the Granovitaya Palace and the nine domes of the Annunciation Cathedral, where Rublev made his icons for the greater glory of God. Over all, the white stone tower remembers the crimes of Ivan the Terrible. But good hope is working in me, and bright sunshine plays tricks. The monument to tyranny is an exhalation like prayer and the decorative towers in the Kremlin Wall are like the ramparts of heaven, where the five gates in the wall are the portals of heaven and give entrance to the City of God.

Time has had its way with the belfries of Moscow, and when you open the drawer in the end table by the bed you don't find a Gideons Bible. No icons hang on the wall. Fifty years ago, "Destroy the Icons" days came round in the calendar like movable feasts, and they got rid of a lot of icons in Moscow. But the worship of graven images answers a need for Russians. Where the Pantocrator used to look down from the domes of the churches, they have devised a new theophany. Old Tver is now Kalinin after a hero of the new dispensation. In the agitprop on Nogina, a framed photograph of Lenin stands on a velvet-covered table. Burning candles illuminate the Pantocrator's face. Only the costume is different. This tangible image gives you something you can hold on to.

In Tver the Shock Brigade catechized the workers: "Will you prove your atheism by handing over your icons?" They made a big fire, and when the icons were reduced to ash they marched in a body to the center of town and signed up for the Atheists Union. On the Unter den Linden, they were burning the books when Moscow abolished the ringing of church bells. The local soviet said they did this to satisfy the demands of the people. Anyway, no church bells ring for service on Sunday mornings, and only a small fraction of Muscovites still go to church.

This is a problem they are doing their best to resolve. They haven't resolved it yet, and you can find working churches if you know where to look. The Baptists have their meeting hall, the Jews have their synagogue, and there is a Roman Catholic church behind the Lubyanka Prison. The Third World counts in Moscow, and there is even a mosque near Kommuna Square. Moscow has a long memory, however, and the Lutherans, who stirred up trouble in this city, have been sunk without trace. For Irma this is disappointing, and we settle for an Orthodox service.

Novo-Devichy Convent in a bend of the river above the Sports Palace keeps to itself behind its crenellated wall. The metro doesn't stop there, and outside the Cosmos where the taxis are waiting, we tell our laconic driver what we have in mind for Sunday morning. Cab drivers around the world will rain on your parade if you let them, and this one is no exception. The little man in the cloth cap minds his p's and q's, but we see him gain in stature as he climbs behind the wheel. His lips curl, the eyes narrow. He is Basil Rathbone in *A Tale of Two Cities*, sneering from his carriage window at the peasants in the street. Or he is a knight on horseback, and when he comes to a crosswalk he puts his lance in the socket and charges.

It was this way in London just after the War when money was scarce and consumer goods were scarcer. The automobile stood for privilege then, and for persons of privilege the Edgeware Road was like the Grand Prix. In the affluent society, they aren't so keen on asserting their manhood. Today in London the right to a Morris Minor has become an inalienable right, and you can enter a crosswalk without putting your life on the line. A mini Moskvich in every garage is my one best hope for the future.

From the Cosmos Hotel, all pomp and circumstance, we drop down Prospekt Mira, turning right on the Ring Road, and enter a new dimension in time. The New Maiden Convent is a step back in time, not frozen, but verging on decay. Outside the walls the clock is still ticking, and this weedy, dejected place gets older by the hour. The eccentric splendor of the five golden domes underlines the general look of not caring. In Orthodox churches there must never be less than five domes. You can put up more domes if you want to, but they haven't cared to do this. The domes are Oriental turbans remembering the Mongol past, and the battle towers in the wall remind you that this used to be a fortress. The towers stand tall, throwing down a gauntlet to the new Sports Palace below the main gate and the Lenin Stadium in the distance.

Some historians read history as the conflict of mighty opposites, Christ against Caesar, Dmitry Donskoy against Khan Mamay and his Mongols of the Golden Horde. Tacitus, in his annals of imperial Rome, says how, from pondering matter-of-fact, most of us learn to distinguish right and wrong. History makes sense or it teaches a lesson. Hunting for the figure in the carpet, I think of the graven image at Herculaneum, the earliest Christian cross to survive from Roman times. In 79 A.D. the gods put on their instruments to punish an impious world, and that is why the cross survives. No one knows who cut this image in the upper story of a little house overwhelmed by the volcano, perhaps a Christian convert who lived in Judaea and received the Word from Christ himself. If you are hopeful, you will feel how this modest cross means more than all that rigamarole of the Caesars. Real history begins with Christ, said Pasternak in *Dr. Zhivago.*

Damp wind from the river scuffs the leaves along the ground and picks up the candy wrappers and fragments of old newsprint. Patches of mud show where the overgrown grass is worn thin. The trees have lost their leaves, their black boles drip with wetness, and there are ghosts from an earlier time among the trees. Peter the Great came to Novo-Devichy to deal with his rebellious soldiers of the palace guard. He hanged three hundred of these Streltsy outside the window of the cell where he kept his troublemaking sister Sophia. She wanted the throne for herself, and he cut off the hand of her principal supporter and nailed it to the door of her cell. Sophia is buried in Novo-Devichy.

The Laurentian Chronicle instructs me how Gleb, a summary man, once ruled in Novgorod, the oldest of Russian cities, where a priest of the old religion was stirring up the people. He looked into the seeds of time and said what would happen tomorrow and what would happen before evening. Gleb the prince took an ax, hiding it beneath his cloak, and went forth to deal with the problem. "Do you know what is to happen to you today?" the prince inquires. "I shall perform great miracles," the troublemaker says. "But Gleb, pulling out the ax, cleaved him so that he fell dead, and the people dispersed."

Rough-and-ready goes back a long way in Russia, and the corollary is ancient history that says how "the people dispersed." The Church of the Archangel in Cathedral Square shows you history with its moral. Tsars and princes and grand dukes lie together in death, and only a few of them went off from natural causes. The knife, poison, and the rope took most of them off, and

Ivan the Terrible is here with his murdered Tsarevich. Tacitus, who thinks we ought to read history as a moral fable, has another reading in spite of himself. Summing up the crimes of Nero, Tacitus says, "this monotony of incident, this slavish passivity, this torrent of wasted bloodshed wearies, depresses, and paralyzes the mind."

Russia is a citadel like this convent, or it is like that necropolis the early Christians made in Kiev. From the friable rock of Kiev they hewed out the Lavra Caves, and built a monastery underground on the banks of the Dnieper. In dark galleries underground they starved themselves to death, and had themselves half buried before they died. The world outside was a temporal place of skulls.

When Grand Prince Vladimir declared for Christianity, his subjects in Kiev followed the leader. He was "the new Constantine of mighty Rome who baptized himself and his subjects," and he led them down to the Dnieper where they all took the waters together. Municipal Stadium in Cleveland, Ohio, stands on the shores of Lake Erie, and between the World Series and the beginning of the football season they had a convention of Jehovah's Witnesses there. This was in the fifties. They went into the lake in their thousands and tens of thousands, praising the Lord, and it must have been like that in Kiev. It is still like that in Kiev, where Lenin is the second Vladimir. The people of Lenin don't go to church. They go to the polls where they vote a single slate, but they aren't long on politics either.

I have been to Zagorsk and its Trinity Monastery, wanting to photograph the wall paintings they have there. Sergius Radonezhsky is on the wall of the cathedral, built over his grave five hundred years ago. He was the spiritual leader of Russian Orthodoxy, and today the Patriarch of All the Russias is still Father Superior of the monastery at Zagorsk. The new patriarch and the autocrat hark back in their alliance to the days of Dmitry Donskoy. Grim St. Sergius who rallied the people in the war against the Khans is like Father Sergius of Moscow. This modern patriarch wrote "The Truth about Religion in Russia," saying how "Soviet order means the rule of the people."

In Russia, said Custine, what they call the public order is "a dismal tranquillity, a frightening peace, for it is like the peace of the tomb." This French aristocrat, coming to Russia in 1839, did for the Slavs what Tocqueville did for the Americans. A witty, perceptive, and vastly opinionated writer, he said how Russians took naturally to the peace of the tomb. In Novo-Devichy, though, they are mining dark galleries, like the Lavra Caves or the Church of the Catacombs where early Christians prepared a challenge for the future.

The Church of the Transfiguration of Christ is closed, says the sign, "till 17:30." It tells us this in four languages and leaves no room for doubt. But how can the church be closed, and why until 17:30? A whiskery old woman is climbing the steps, and we follow her hopefully. She is the *upravdom*, a concierge who sits in judgment like Madame Defarge or St. Peter at the Gates. She is wearing round-toed shoes, a lumpy coat, and two or three sweaters that come down beneath the hem. A head scarf like a bandage is tied under her chin. At the top of the steps she unlocks the door. Looking over her shoulder, I glimpse a shining iconostasis. In the gloomy interior, it gathers the light. I want to see more. *"Nyet,"* however, and she closes the door in my face.

But the Smolensk Cathedral is open for business. Grand Duke Vasily built this church for the Mother of God when he annexed Smolensk to Russia. This was in 1522. Blind beggars, some without arms, squat before the church doors. They sniff for sound as they hear us approach, and show us the whites of their eyes.

The Smolensk Cathedral is a national treasure in Socialist Land. Eighty kopecks apiece, says the man in the kiosk, and clutching our tickets we enter the cathedral. The service is progressing and the congregation is on its feet. They do without pews in these old Russian churches, and you must stand through the Orthodox service.

An illustrated altarpiece closes off the sanctuary from the body of the church. Between the Virgin and the Baptist stands a faintly epicene Christ imagined as by Burne-Jones. The baptistery fount is hidden behind a gold screen. Crimson cords with gold tasseling bring you to a halt, and much of this church is off limits. Quadrilateral pillars carry the high ceiling, and frescoes adorn the face of the pillars. The coloring is too vivid, there is too much clarity of line, and evidently the restorer has been here before us. Nothing is left to the imagination, and every inch of the surface is encrusted with paint.

More is less, they say, but old churches in Moscow don't share this point of view. The Church of the Annunciation in Cathedral Square is a vase filled to the brim and overflowing, and a painted carpet of stylized flowers covers the walls of St. Basil's. Moscow, a city of empty spaces, cringes before its emptiness. The wind blows through Red Square and Manege Square, a vast prison yard. The dissenter Kopelev in his memoirs called the yard of his prison Donkey's Manege.

Around the Golden Ring of Moscow they have their Romanesque churches, and St. Demetrius in Vladimir is centuries older than the Smolensk Cathedral and almost as old as the Romanesque churches of France. You wouldn't know this to look at it, though. Except for Christ on the tympanum, the great church at Vézelay is simple and severe. St. Demetrius isn't simple, and its limestone walls are pestered with shapes. The Greek thing, Pliny says, is to conceal nothing. The Greek Orthodox thing says that bare bones are unseemly, and I have felt this fierce aversion to nakedness before. In the Orthodox churches of Serbia and Montenegro, they see to it that their frescoes cover the walls. Elijah on the walls is looking away from this place of skulls to the World Over Yonder. On the other side of Europe, the Alhambra in southern Spain, veiled like an Eastern bride, suggests how Islam is like the Greek Orthodox thing. On the walls of the Alhambra, geometric forms displace the physical world.

Sentimental icons crowd the walls of the Smolensk Cathedral. This religious art of the seventeenth century isn't much worse in Russia than anywhere else. Like the art of the movies, where reality depends on what you are wearing, it formulates a dress code and gives a specious solidity to the shadows on the walls. The painters who made the icons didn't look hard at the men and women they were painting, understanding how truth is simple.

The priest at the altar turns his back on the people and bows low before a jewel-encrusted icon, flanked by burning candles. The Smolensk Mother of God holds her wonder-working Son, and only the face and hands are visible to say that this is a physical presence. But physical doesn't mean real. The Real Presence is powdered with onyx and pearl, a glittering surface almost three-dimensional. The adoring posture of the priest and his flock tells you that the god himself is enclosed beneath the surface.

Emblazoned in gold thread on a banner by the altar, the motto reads: *In hoc signo vinces.* "In this sign you shall conquer." The Roman emperor took heart when he saw the Cross in the heavens at the Milvian Bridge. Maxentius and his pagans scattered like straw, and Constantine annexed the Rome of the Caesars to Christ.

A young man from Intourist is standing behind us, Christ among the Sanhedrin. He wants to clarify the meaning of the three-tiered iconostasis. Having it all by heart, he doesn't need a ferrule, and his schoolmaster's voice rides right over the priest. A well-set-up man with a black curly beard, the priest is singing the service in Latin. Maybe fifty people, mostly old women, are making the responses. In Novgorod and Kiev, when I went there in the sixties, the churches were empty except for these women, and it seemed to me then that the Orthodox Church would die of starvation when they died. The stock of old women keeps getting replenished, however.

These women wear black, like the Three Marys looking for

the grave of Jesus. Some of them are on their knees and touching their foreheads to the pavement. Outside the Trinity Church in Zagorsk, water bubbles from a shrine like the fabulous rock when Moses made the water flow. The women of Zagorsk bring their bottles to this shrine and siphon off the holy water. No holy water bubbles up in Novo-Devichy, but on the lectern before the priest a large folio lies open and the women are coming forward to kiss the open page.

In a corner by themselves, three Soviet sailors have their eyes on the priest. They aren't joining in the service, not knowing the responses, but they haven't come here to scoff. These sailors are all eyes, and I think of my friends who call themselves atheists as a matter of course and how a lot of them seem to breed religious children.

The voice of the priest lifts and grows stronger. He is sure of his artistry, aware of his priestly role. I feel the music in my head and bowels. I am standing in the choir loft in my red and white surplice, and the choir director is raising his hands. "I'd rather have Jesus than silver or gold, I'd rather have Jesus than everything that this old world affords today." I turn and glare at the guide from Intourist.

The congregation is a harp swept by gusts of emotion, and the strong fingers of the priest are playing on the strings. The people respond when this virtuoso bids them. He is appealing to a higher truth beyond our temporal place of skulls. I want to join hands with the priest and his flock and sing along with them. But I have been here before, not just as a child on Sunday mornings in the choir loft. At a rally in the Polo Grounds for Henry A. Wallace, I stood at Armageddon to do battle for the Lord. I wasn't old enough to vote but they let me hand out leaflets and sing the old songs. They found new words for us to sing, and this political crusade was like a revival meeting. "Hallelujah, I'm a-travelin' down Freedom's main line." At the end of the rally they had us link arms, and we sang "Solidarity Forever."

When I sailed into Patmos it was Greek Easter Sunday, the

stroke of midnight, and the town went berserk. Rockets and firecrackers lit up the sky, bells clanged, and except for the *1812 Overture* in the Albert Hall I have never heard anything like it. "Pray for me," said the black-bearded monk as we coasted up to the quayside. He made the sign of the cross with three fingers. But we had shared the same table on our way down to the Dodecanese, and I wasn't going to pray for him. All dandruff and arrogance, red lips and long hair, he made a sucking noise when he spooned up his egg lemon soup. He hadn't much to say to women, and my wife at the table was the cross he had to bear. Later that week, she and I climbed up to the monastery where St. John the Divine had his visions. But the Orthodox monks were inflexible, and she waited outside the gate while I went through the monastery alone.

The beggars are gone and the wind from the river is blowing harder and promises rain. As we hurry out the gates of Novo-Devichy, I look back for a last look at the cathedral. The five golden domes are surmounted by the Russian cross, and the crescent is under the cross. It bisects the lower vertical, like a new moon or the crescent of Islam. "In this sign you shall conquer." The hammer and sickle remembers the old Russian cross.

They are doing Shostakovich's Fifth at the conservatory on Herzen Street, and the student performers give it their affectionate best. But I like music for a small room. Against this music that wants to burst out of the room and take over the sidewalk, I put up my hands. It begins with the largo of the masses working underground, where the accelerando corresponds to the subway system. The allegro in its turn symbolizes gigantic factory machinery and its victory over nature. This is what the program says.

I grew up on program music, *Romeo and Juliet* and the tone poems of Strauss, and the luscious sound of these composers is easier to listen to than the "Symphony of Socialism." But I don't know that they are really all that different. When you soft-pedal the meaning, the page fills with a hundred meanings and they spill over into the margin. If you put your money on the meaning, you find yourself out of pocket. "Play the record again." That is what Sibelius said when they asked him about the meaning of his Fourth Symphony.

Outside the conservatory, the railing makes a mosaic of musical notes. It remembers the music of Tchaikowsky, the opening bars of the *1812 Overture*, the signature of the Black Swan. He stands beside the railing, Olympian and a little bemused. The lady they commissioned to do the statue, wanting to suggest his roots in folk art, proposed an ensemble where a shepherd boy with open arms was welcoming Tchaikowsky. The artist gives a tongue to the popular wisdom. Knowing their Tchaikowsky, though, they thought twice about the shepherd boy, and the composer has the pedestal to himself.

His name is lettered in Cyrillic, but I don't trust the sculptor to tell me who this is. I look at the notes in the railing. Put a helmet on Tchaikowsky and a horse between his legs and he might be Yury Long Arm in Sovyetskaya Square. Or give him a musket and a little less forehead and he could take his place with the others in the monument to the Turkish War on the corner of Bogdan Khmelnitsky. This Polaroid art is the product of iconophobia. The man on the pedestal has two eyes and ears, a chiseled nose, a head of hair. If there is more to him, they prefer that he keep it under his hat. The violet color of late Monet, the hollowing out of the faces in the sculpture of Donatello, the way the strings confront each other in Beethoven's Great Fugue, all this is off the point. Don't trust the artist, trust the tale. That is what they are saying, but the tale is already written. They have it on file in the office.

For once, Al is with me all the way. "Socialist Realism!" More sins on their head, but Al has got it backwards. This nondescript art isn't Socialist and it isn't realistic. Under the sculptor's chisel, truth to life has leaked away. Socialism is a cry of pain, like the sense of reality, and the man they call Tchaikowsky has never suffered unless from a toothache.

Already in their older art, like the icon paintings of the seventeenth century, Russians understand how only weak men suffer and strong men are impervious to pain. They have hard words for the reclining pose of the Virgin in Nativity icons, where the Mother of God is like the merest woman attended by a midwife and otherwise alone with her pain. "There was no pain, no weakness in birth, only joy." That is what they thought three hundred years ago, and they wanted the Mother of God to sit up straight and look into the camera. Artists who painted "according to their own understanding" gave them trouble a hundred years before this. They said in the Kremlin how "sacred tradition" tells the artist what to paint. Between the Artist and the Commissar, Prokofiev and Stalin, Ovid and Augustus Caesar, the quarrel won't be settled tomorrow.

Like President Eisenhower when he painted, the artist in the older time followed the dots on the canvas. They said how this was following "an inviolable law and tradition of the Orthodox Church." To the holy fathers "belongs the composition, to the painter only the execution." The holy fathers aren't Russian, though, and this reminiscence of an Ecumenical Council in Christian Byzantium dates from 787 A.D. The Russkies make a good target and Al would be lost without them, but the diminished view of the artist and his business isn't peculiar to them.

In New York not less than Moscow, they don't want to confuse you. Their monumental art goes in for typecasting. You can't tell the players without looking at the program. From the program, you gather a simplified psychology. Father Duffy is compassionate, General Sherman soldiers on, and William Cullen Bryant, being a poet, has his head in the clouds. Al like these others is a bundle of contradictions, prickly and accommodating, fatheaded, shrewd as shrewd. When they put up his statue in Grand Rapids, however, they will make him down-to-earth and leave it at that. Otherwise his own mother wouldn't know him.

The artist in a free society helps create a better future, Al tells me. He gets my vote for the next vacant seat on the presidium but thinks I'm kidding when I say this. I recite for his approval an ironical version of the artist and his business. The artist's duty is to rise. "His dwelling place should be the skies, His theme and inspiration, beauty." Pushkin, I tell them. "Not bad," Al says grudgingly. He isn't persuaded, however.

For their last full day in Moscow, I take them to the Tretyakov Gallery. The brothers Tretyakov, Pavel and Sergei, began this collection of Russian art a hundred years ago. In the old mansion that smells of beeswax, six thousand paintings hang on the walls. Every year a million people come to look at the paintings. There are always a lot of children who are glad to be let out of school.

It is pelting down rain, the temperature is falling, and by late afternoon the rain will turn to snow. For the taxis on the street, competition is fierce, and someone else is always getting in before us. This isn't a day to love your neighbor. Irma wrinkles her nose at the exhalations of salami in the metro, body odors, brilliantine. The metro stop at Novokuznetskaya isn't just around the corner from where we want to go. My rubber boots have sprung a leak, water squelches in my shoes. I can wriggle my toes but can't feel them, and the blood has left the tips of my fingers.

When Marco Polo came back from his travels in the East, they told him how the cold in Russia was hardly to be borne. He listened and gave Russia a wide berth. I think of Napoleon getting his cold comeuppance on the roads that go east, and the Marquis de Custine who felt how Moscow wouldn't repay him for the trouble he had taken to come here. "Let us give up Moscow," said this sensible man, "and order the postilion to turn around and leave in all haste for Paris."

The Church of All Sorrows, obscure in the rain, looks like itself and we hurry to put it behind us. Under the portico, half sheltered from the rain, a drunk is sleeping it off. Russians, said Marco Polo, have great drinking bouts. In the taverns, men and women pass the entire day. When Prince Vladimir in Kiev decided to abandon the faith of his fathers, he thought at first of going over to Islam. But they don't drink in Islam "and it is the Russians' joy to drink," said Prince Vladimir. "We cannot do without it."

There isn't a grog shop in sight, and I herd Al and Irma into the *stolovaya* on Lavrushinsky Lane. An Amazonian female is swabbing the floor tiles. She is the Genius of the Place, shapeless, stolid, and generic, and the dogsbody work is her business. In the metro she carries a birchen broom and a dustpan, and when it is raining she ladles up the slop and hauls it away. She cleans the public toilets and the cages in the zoo. She takes your coat in the cloakroom. On every hotel floor in Moscow, she sits enthroned behind a desk and looks you over as you enter and leave. You will catch her smiling at you, as Khruschchev used to say, when shrimps whistle.

I call for a bowl of kasha and she brings it to the table. The cabbage soup is thickened with flour, a lump of meat swimming on the surface of the broth. Never mind the kasha, and I push it away. The babushka takes note. "In this cafeteria, food is provided by the Institute of Scientific Research and Design." Under the eyebrows she looks at me warily. Then a grin splits her face and she shows me a row of steel teeth. "If you go to bed with dogs, you wake up with fleas."

Through the streaking rain the façade of the gallery, gilt, red, and cream, combines an Orthodox church and a pagoda. St. George in bas-relief is killing the dragon. In the center of the courtyard stands a nineteenth-century gent. The inscription on the pedestal says that this is S. M. Tretyakov. The olive-clad policeman won't let us in, though. His eyes flick to the glazed poster on a sandwich board beside the doors. They have scheduled a lecture on the work of A. Ivanov, the nineteenth-century painter who thought that art was uplift. Without a ticket, you can't go in. "Lifting men up and away from worry and grief to the finest moments of life," said Ivanov. This was the business of art. I can do without this painter and his divine afflatus, but Irma is sniffling, Al looks at me reproachfully, and I would give what I have for a ticket.

At my elbow, the young Oscar Wilde is holding out a fan of tickets. A plastic flower droops in his buttonhole, the nap of his velveteen suit is dejected, and the points of his wide lapels are curling in the rain like wet cardboard. He is one of those aberrant souls they call *stilyagi* in Moscow, a jaunty caryatid who has got tired of supporting the weight of the future. He isn't dejected, though, and might be singing in the rain. This style-boy is saying how six rubles apiece will persuade him to give up his tickets. I hand over the money, ten rubles for the three of us. This transaction is petty but like the gift of grace. Where we were invisible, we are visible now, and the cop on the sidewalk understands that we belong.

The Tretyakov brothers had their eye on the present, and the paintings they assembled say how the past is prologue. Here is Repin's haunted version of Ivan the Terrible, the murdered Tsarevich dead in his arms. Vrubel's nightmarish Satan still walks up and down in the earth. *The Massacre of the Streltsy*, the chef d'oeuvre of Surikov, is like a lurid photograph in this morning's paper. Was it hatred or compassion that inspired this artist? The play of light on texture was the inspiration, Surikov said. He remembered the reflection of a burning candle seen accidentally against a white shirt.

Massive paintings crowd the rooms at the head of the stairs. Norman Rockwell is the painter. Soldiers and sailors are striking fraternal poses or going into battle. Tank traps poke up in the streets of wartime Moscow. A bride and her groom walk into the future, where new construction is rising. Work for the night is coming, and I think it would play in Grand Rapids. A golden boy sits astride a fiery red horse. I pick up a catalog from the resident babushka, and read how Petrov-Vodkin's *Bathing of the Red Horse* "symbolizes a breakthrough into the beautiful future." I want more from this painter about the horse and his rider, and I remember Satie on the "Afternoon of a Faun" saying to Debussy how much he liked that little bit at half past two. A lot of talk at half past two and not enough music, Satie is saying. Where the end is more important than the means to the end, they leave the gallery in droves, or would do this if it ever stopped raining.

Two connected rooms on the bottom floor are reserved for religious paintings, icons and frescoes. The Virgin in her sleep like death is getting ready to take flight for heaven. St. Michael presents the warrior, and St. Nicholas the type of the eleemosynary man. The Jesse Tree shows you the lineage of Jesus. His progenitors in the dark backward of time are remembered in the voluted scrolling of the family tree.

Al and Irma aim to please but don't like the icons, and it isn't hard to sympathize with them. From the two-dimensional planes perspective is absent, and the folds of the Virgin's dress lie flat on the surface. This rectilinear art has no humanizing curves. Religious painters in Russia haven't heard how the Word was made flesh. They breathe the air of the sanctuary, hieratic and forbidding, and their paintings aim to keep the viewer out.

But Andrew Rublev, the master of convention, raised his back above the element he lived in. This painter of the early Renaissance cared more for the Word than he cared for men and women. The Word as he presents it is always incarnate, however. His *Old Testament Trinity* is inscribed within a circle. It makes a harmony of colors and circular strokes, deep red and golden ochre, light blue that deepens to blue-gray and green. The shape of the single chalice in the center of the icon is repeated in the shapes of the angels that surround it. Rublev in his icon in depicting the virtues of self-sacrifice, the chalice being a symbol of sacrificial death. The catalog tells me this and lets it go at that.

A grandmotherly woman in a flowered print dress is recalling for the audience Lenin's golden words. We tiptoe through the doors and make ourselves inconspicuous in the back of the room. The narrow table, covered by green baize, holds a silver samovar, just what Irma has been looking for, a sauce boat, a jam pot, and bone china plates piled with blini. Hundreds of sketches fill the walls of the room, each a study for Ivanov's *Appearance of Christ to the People*. For twenty-five years Ivanov labored this painting, finishing in 1848, the Year of Revolutions. This was auspicious. He dreamed of the better future that is always receding before us, like the Third Rome where history ends. Wanting to proclaim the "golden age of all humanity" when the followers of John the Baptist acknowledged the Messiah, he identified this age with his own generation. Russians, he said, were "the last of the peoples of the planet." The destiny of Russia was to prepare the triumph of "one kingdom and one pastor."

Like an enormous icon in a secular church, the canvas of Ivanov hangs behind the speaker. She holds a ferrule in her hand and passes it from left to right, pointing the moral and clarifying the tale. Christ stands alone in the upper right-hand corner, a reluctant Messiah, wraithlike, almost a homunculus. If He has words for the people, you know they will fall on deaf ears. Lost souls in the foreground, seminaked grotesques imported by this artist from the Sistine Chapel, dominate the canvas and turn away from the Messiah. The prophet who comes before Him is more impressive by far. This wasn't what Ivanov intended, and his hortatory painting is like the mountain that labored and brought forth a mouse. But it makes an honest failure. Don't trust the artist, trust the tale, where the tale itself records a failure and the voice of John the Baptist still cries in the wilderness. "Ivanov died still knocking." That is how Herzen remembered this artist who spent his life looking for a new religious type. However, "the door was not opened to him."

Just enough light remains to look out the window. It frames the green domes and tent roof spire of the Resurrection Church.

Snow, falling on the domes, makes crazy patterns on the glass of the window. The patterns are formal but empty of meaning. Having divulged Ivanov's meaning, our speaker has launched into her peroration. She quotes Musorgsky on the aim of the artist. "Life, no matter where it finds expression; truth, no matter how bitter it be; fearlessness and words of sincerity to the people . . . that is my bent." Sooner or later, Al will add these words to his quiver.

A burst of applause winds up the lecture. Man, who can't live by bread alone, can't live without it, and the three of us head for the table. The scalding hot tea is served in chased pewter stakans, the blini in sour cream with a dollop of jam. Fortified to greet the world again, we leave the old gallery by the polished mahogany staircase. Tretyakov in the forecourt wears a blanket of snow. I think of the drunk in the porch of All Sorrows and wonder if the falling snow has caught him.

THE SWAN ON THE NEGLINNAYA

A PREFABRICATED CITY on the surface of the moon, that is Friendship Park out Chimky-Chovrino way in the northwest corner of Moscow. The cosmonauts who put this lunar city in place have neglected to bring with them the green belts and banks of flowers that are featured in the architect's mock-up. Here today, gone tomorrow, so why take thought for today, that is what the new buildings are saying. Elsewhere on the planet, even in fraternal lands, these same expedient buildings blossom with boxes of flowers. In Yugoslavia, for instance, the moonscape is a palette of color. Balcony by balcony, the colors are different, depending on the eye of the resident artist. This difference identifies the people who live there.

A pulse beats in Friendship Park, though, belonging to Bogdanov. He was straddling two chairs front and center in the lecture hall the first time I saw him, and where the others were pacific he had obvious designs on my person. Like Tolstoy's hero

Pierre, he came across as "too large and unsuited to the place." The magnified eyes would have pinned me to the wall had I let them. What Bogdanov calls his blinky glasses transform this nice man to a colonel of the KGB, a mad lepidopterist, a dentist.

Unlike his colleagues, Bogdanov had something to say about my lecture. He said he didn't like it. This was a week later, when we bumped into each other on the steps of the Lenin Library. Being polite was good manners but buttered no parsnips. A club was what I wanted, not a stiletto, and the thing was to whack them over the snout. Bogdanov teaches English at Moscow University and a course in journalism when they need him. This academic detests his fellow academics, and intellectuals in general get the back of his hand. Intellectuals in particular are a different story. When we walk down Marx Prospekt, he tips his hat to the statue of Michael Lomonosov who founded this reliquary institution where he teaches. Lomonosov was a poet and weighed his words, also a man of action. Bogdanov, approvingly, says he didn't take the word for the deed.

"Useless knowledge" sends my friend into orbit. He puts sincerity over knowledge and prefers "the path of experience" to books. "Beware of the merely learned man," he tells me, "an idler who kills time with study." Evidently this is a quotation, and I wait for the source. "Bernard Shaw, the English playwright." Bogdanov has an itch for literary allusions. The dean of the faculty in the journalism school is a bookful blockhead ignorantly read with loads of learned lumber in his head. "Alexander Pope." For this learned man who turns all colors in the house of learning, a gulf opens between the "elite" and the "workers." He would rather be with the workers "even drinking sour wine." They are light years more intelligent, if you can believe him. On his lips, the word "elite" is like a bad smell.

"The emancipation of the workers must be the task of the workers." That is the great imperative in the catechism according to Bogdanov. His dissenting colleagues are priests of Baal who worship false gods, Kraisky, for example, "a glorified cop." He could solve all by himself the fertilizer shortage in the Soviet Union.

Bogdanov, a son of the working class, makes you feel that his lineage is nobler than the blood of Riurik, the ancient king of Russia. "Kind hearts are more than coronets." He grew up in Babuskin when it wasn't a suburb but mostly open fields, and his father the cabinetmaker had his own shop out in back of the house. They took away the house when Bogdanov was a boy and collectivized the carpenter's workshop. However, they let it stand empty. "It wasn't losing the shop that killed the old man," says Bogdanov. "But if they had to take it, why didn't they put it to use?"

After the War, a huge apartment house went up on the spot where Bogdanov used to live. It sits on the right off the Yaroslavl Road just before you come to the Ring Road that circles the city. A brightly tessellated shelter marks the place where you wait for the bus. This pilgrimage is gloomy, but Bogdanov insists. Block letters stand tall on the roof of the apartment house. GLORY TO THE COMMUNIST PARTY. The word for "Glory" is "Slava," and he makes it a scorn and a byword. *"Slava! Slava! Slava!"* Even when he is woebegone, he can't help being comic.

When I go back to America, I mustn't expect to get letters from Bogdanov. His correspondence is carried on by postcard, "to save them the trouble of re-gumming the envelopes." He has been in hot water with the powers that be, but his derring-do in the battle for Tula and the military medals he won't wear set him clear. He makes no bones about his feeling for the powers that be: "comrades," and he spits out the word. This coffee klatch of reformers betrayed the Revolution. "But outside of anarchy," says Bogdanov, "there is no such thing as revolution." When he talks like that, I study my shoes. There is nothing to fear from the comrades, however. "Bourgeois," he tells me, "sleep undisturbed."

Despite the fire and brimstone, the mad lepidopterist wouldn't hurt a fly. Living in the midst of evil, he holds fast to his belief in natural goodness and says how all tyrannies are fastened on us from the outside. One evening a week he works as a nurse's aid at the Red Cross and Red Crescent on Kuznetsky Most. They don't pay him for this. A compulsive vegetarian, he hasn't been able to eat meat since the War unless it is cooked to a crisp.

The *upravdom* in the glass cage beside the lift worries about Bogdanov and how his rough-and-tumble might unsettle the neighbors. *Nekulturny* is their word for the uncultured man, whose lack of proper culture is a spreading stain. There goes the neighborhood. The *upravdom* does his best to keep Bogdanov under wraps. When I knock on the cage and ask for this friend's apartment, he lets me feel that he'd rather not say.

Old terrors from childhood come back to haunt you in Socialist Land. Mostly they are unfounded, as when you look under the bed for the bogeyman. The KGB is a bogeyman, and in every two-bit factotum I detect its intimidating presence. A big bald dome, rubbery lips, and exophthalmic eyes, the *upravdom* swims slowly to the surface of the cage and flattens his face against the glass.

The lift is out of order, and in the darkened stairwells they have taken the bulbs from their sockets. Clutching my bottle of Armenian brandy, I trudge up the six flights of stairs. "*Nichevo,*" Bogdanov says, not to worry. Besides, the mind is its own place. Under this rubric, he and Marina have converted their instant slum to a temple in Arcady where the Professor of English dwells with Beauty and Truth. Carpets from Uzbekistan brighten the floor in the tiny bedroom and the living room. The linoleum on the kitchen floor is antiqued and resembles parquet. A Socialist version of the Murphy bed stands against the wall between the windows in the living room. This is for the nephew who stays over once a week on the weekends.

On a white enameled cabinet beside the kitchen table, the bust that says Shakespeare looks like a self-satisfied butcher.

Books and papers make a pile on any plane surface that invites them. There are sets of Shakespeare and Milton in English and Russian, selected poems by William Morris and his *News from Nowhere*. Dreiser and Dos Passos lean against assorted novels by Upton Sinclair. A heavily scored copy of Mark Twain's *Connecticut Yankee* lies open on the coffee table, beside it *The Grapes of Wrath* marked down to five kopecks, the cost of a fare on the metro.

Where there aren't books there are pictures. Marina on the wall is hugging a rag doll half as big as she is. Bogdanov looks much younger in his Red Army dress. Father Christmas is wearing glasses and a bushy white beard. He is Peter Kropotkin, the Anarchist Prince. A thumbtack fastens the white anemones to the wooden frame. "The soul of a beautiful white Christ." Oscar Wilde said that, Bogdanov tells me. He says that the withered flowers come from Kropotkin's grave.

A kindly astigmatic man, his photograph says. For Kropotkin, the path of history led upwards. The enemy was out there, blocking the path. Like most men of his century, Kropotkin had no inkling of the enemy within. He fled the house of privilege, wanting the workers to make up the vanguard where they wanted to go to the grogshop. The apocalyptic man looked down the path for the return of the good prince Dmitry. Like Marx he saw how history was ending, and he saw the pot of gold at the end of the rainbow. Like Lomonosov, he put his faith in science. They gave him a medal for his early work in geography. He broke off this work, however, and was willing to take the word for the deed. Towards the end of his life, Kropotkin burst out: "I would like to finish my *own* work."

At Columbia University when I was teaching there, they made a hero of Kropotkin and waved the black anarchist flag. Also they blew whistles and banged the lids of garbage cans outside my classroom door. "No more laws! No more judges!" They quoted this secular saint with approval when he said how "Any authority can only be harmful." That was America in the sixties, ancient history today, and the beautiful white Christ isn't widely remembered.

Above the headboard in the bedroom hangs a copy on wood of the Vladimir Mother of God. The Church like the State is bad news to Bogdanov, and he disclaims any part in this relic of "outworn superstition." Loving his wife, however, he accommodates her woman's weakness. They painted the icon in Constantinople nine hundred years ago, and the men of the Second Rome handed it on to their successors. Pious Russians will tell you that St. Luke the Evangelist was the painter. This emblem of authority, like the ark or the palladium, appeals to a higher order transcending the self. The order is personal, unlike the Dialectic. An old man with a beard sits on top of the heavens, and God's eye is looking down on the sparrow.

In the Third Rome they gave credit to the icon when Ivan the Terrible overcame the Mongols at Kazan. They called the sacred talisman Our Lady of Tenderness. From their old religious readings, Russians learned how the Virgin went down into hell and won a respite for the poor damned souls every year from Maundy Thursday to Whitsunday. The sad haunted face has little in common with the hard happy faces you see on the posters in the Dom Knigi. The eyes are slanting but not avid, and the pursed lips say how trust in earthly things is vain. Acquainted with grief, this woman is fallible. The tiny Christ in her arms is holding on for dear life.

How Bogdanov and his wife live together on easy terms in this module of theirs is a comment on the natural goodness of man. "But everyone should have it so good," says Bogdanov. Marina shrouds her eyes when he says this. She remembers Nagatino south of the river and how, when there weren't enough beds to go round, they turned her parents' house into a commune. The local soviet gave the three of them a room in the attic. "A kind of rough justice," says the equable man. Four of them in the attic when Bogdanov moved in, this is how they lived for thirteen years.

Lath and rough-cast covered the aspen logs, like the *izbas* where the peasants live if they don't want to live in the House of the Collective. You still see these old houses on the Warsaw highway as you go south out of town. They are painted in pastel and glorified with painted stenciling around the door and under the eaves. Hand-carving adorns the eaves. This gingerbread house had a vegetable garden where they grew their own cabbage and okra. In the spring the clumps of peonies made a palette of color against the fence that surrounded the yard. No vegetables are growing in Chimky-Chovrino, no peonies either, but Friendship Park, says Bogdanov, is like the Promised Land. This isn't the first time that things have worked out for the best. Marina was forty when they got the apartment, too late to have a child. "Disappointing for Bogdanov," she tells me.

When they made Bogdanov, they passed an electric current through his Medusa's head of black hair. His hands are like shovels, he has feet to match, and has never been sick a day in his life. Icy showers are his fetish. He likes to spend Sunday mornings at the Sandunovsky Baths where they parboil you first before you go into the water. My first cold of the winter is a personal affront, and he wants to know if I have any vodka. "Take a snort of vodka when you get home." That is what I expect him to say. However he says, "Rub some vodka on your ankles."

Bogdanov has an all-purpose specific. He is one of the Seals, that is what they call themselves, and they swim all winter long in the pond underneath the Ostankino TV Tower. Of the seventy men, a handful, I observe, are elitists. Most of the Seals are horny-handed, however. They break a hole in the ice and go down a ladder into the water. It takes them thirty seconds to swim a lap. Some stay in the water for almost a minute. "I do this twice a week," Bogdanov informs me, "and that is why I have never been ill." At the Intourist on Gorky Street they have a large poster of the Ostankino TV Tower, the tallest building in Moscow. Tsar

Ivan's bell tower is small potatoes in comparison. An inscription on the poster inquires rhetorically: "Who would not wish to visit the Ostankino TV Tower, 540 meters high?"

Even in November Gorky Park has its patrons, Bogdanov among them. On this pewter-colored day, I hurry along in his wake. The leaves that still hang on the trees have gone yellow. Large birds like rooks are cawing in the trees, gunmetal blue and dove-colored gray, and in Moscow even the rooks are larger than life. The enormous portrait of Lenin is made of living flowers, tuberous begonias, marigolds, and red salvia. The flowers are cast down and bedraggled, however, and the frost has raised hell with the portrait. In cafés on the midway, men and women are drinking beer and fizzy kvass. I settle for an ice cream like an Eskimo pie.

The open-air theater has closed for the winter and the kiosks have boarded up their half doors. But in the shooting gallery, teenage boys and their dates are potting away with air rifles. They aren't taking dead aim, this is only a lark, and the wooden ducks on the rifle range will make it through another day. Kids are pedaling in the pedal cars and riding the Tilt-a-Whirl. The whirling cars, little rocket ships, identify themselves as *"Vostok."* They don't look like rocket ships, they look like toy cars, but the children, pretending not to know this, have entered into a conspiracy with the grannies who have them in charge.

A lot of grannies and old codgers but not many young adults are spending the afternoon in Gorky Park. The absent parents are working, facing into the wind. The old folks are beyond this, and the initiating of the children is for another day. Sufficient to the day. This brief respite belongs to the very young and the old. They are doing their best to support one another. Symbiosis in the Park, Socialism à la champagne. No runny noses, no tantrums that don't get a hearing, and no grannies and codgers who aren't given a new lease on life. The little Eskimo children are bundled up to the eyes, some wearing furs. I wonder what this has to cost. "An arm and a leg," says Bogdanov. When it comes to children, they don't count the cost. Moscow loves its children.

In the Dom Knigi, I have bought a storybook for Al and Irma's *malenki malchik* back home in Grand Rapids. The story is in Russian but there are pictures on every page, and the face in the pictures is familiar. This life of V. I. Lenin is entitled "Lenin Loved Little Children."

A sign in the metro tells you that children have first claim on the seats. Green space is their playground, and nobody badgers them to keep off the grass. Log cabins, little windmills, and wooden figures of animals flatten the grass here and there in Gorky Park. Smoky the Bear isn't saying how we have to be careful. A wooden bear provides the fulcrum on which the seesaw is resting. Two children are going up and down on the seesaw, and haven't a care in the world.

Lenin and his thirty-five-foot portrait seem out of place in Gorky Park. His resolute profile faces into the wind. He is the master of his fate, and like the fierce enchanter in Shelley's poem to the wind he is driving dead leaves towards the future. The man with a mission couldn't listen to music. It affected his nerves and made him want to say amiable things. "Stupidities," he called them, and he stifled this impulse. "Today is not the time," he said.

On the eastern edges of the park over towards Lenin Prospekt, new construction is going on. The planners have decreed a bigger park for the future when a toy railroad will run from the Krymsky Bridge to Gagarin Square. This waits on the future, and in the meantime the present looks good. The joggers on the footpath aren't climbing the highest mountain. They don't leave us in their dust, and the ubiquitous old women with their picks and shovels and raggedy shawls aren't digging for treasure. At the rate they are going, they won't make it to China today.

Two or three skaters have the rink to themselves. They want

to do something fancy but the ice is still too patchy. The rowboats in the river beside the Pushkinskaya Quay are submerged to the gunwales. A young woman with her sketch pad is estimating the scene, torpid but not gloomy, fall going down to winter. This rhythm commends itself to her artist's eye. The shouldering brown water rides through the park as it has been doing from time out of mind. There are ducks on the river, moorhens like sooty balls, and all they want to do is paddle. The statue of a diver is poised to take the plunge, not a leap into space. Beside the path, a masterless bitch wanders into the bushes. Two aimless young men are strolling arm in arm. They would like to be delinquents and are studying to get the hang of this. Why aren't they in school or punching a time clock? In Russia, says Bogdanov, the corpse has proved stronger than the surgeon.

On the midway, the Ferris wheel continues to turn. The gondola we sit in only sways a little, not wanting to scare us. When we come to the top, it pauses and lets us look down on the city. In this palimpsest of a city, the new sits on top of the old. Cranes are everywhere in Moscow, a city on the move. There isn't much traffic on the river, however, and the tourist boats won't start running again until spring. On the prow of the police launch, the red flag snaps in the wind. A string of ancient boxcars crawls across the old railroad bridge. Behind them, the locomotive is making haste slowly.

The domes and spires of the Kremlin are fairy towers in the distance. Turn the other way, and you see the high towers in the Lenin Hills that used to be the Sparrow Hills. Trees are marching on the land, conifers on the high ground, oak, elm, and ash where the soil is deep enough, birch trees that aren't choosy where they put down their roots. This silvery host says that we are looking at Moscow. Skinny branches sweep the ground, remembering the weight of winter before the winter comes. The leaves on the birch trees are orange-yellow, the hectic color of sickness.

Looking down on old Moscow from the Sparrow Hills, Alexander Herzen and his boyhood friend Nick vowed to sacrifice their lives to the struggle they had chosen. "Write then," said Herzen's friend, "how in this place the story of our lives began to unfold." This is what Herzen did, and his story is exhilarating but the ending makes you sad. When he died in 1870, he knew already that Communism is "the socialism of revenge."

Herzen glimpsed the Pisgah-sight, but like Moses he didn't live to enter the Promised Land. Kropotkin lived longer. His forty years of exile in defense of the future ended in 1917. Don't go to Russia, they told him, but he disputed this counsel. "The greatest day of my life," said Kropotkin. A hundred thousand people followed the coffin when he died four years later, and the soldiers who marched with the people came unarmed. The banners they carried bore the inscription "Where there is authority there is no freedom." The band played Tchaikowsky and Chopin's Funeral March, but they didn't play the Internationale. "The howling of hungry dogs," Kropotkin called it. The Cheka let the anarchists go to the funeral, and when it was over they went back to prison and stayed there.

In Moscow a street and a square are named for Kropotkin, and a street is named for Herzen in the center of town. Kropotkin looks uneasy in their pantheon, though. His socialism was a cry of pain. He said he couldn't take pleasure in life "when all around was oppressive poverty and the painful struggle for a moldy piece of bread." I have gone back with Bogdanov to visit Kropotkin's grave in the cemetery on the river across from the Sparrow Hills. The grave is unquiet, like the grave of Parnell in the cemetery at Glasnevin. "My dead king!" Joyce called this Irish hero. He died a failure, like Kropotkin, who might as well pull up the coverlet around him. Kropotkin said before he died how economic materialism, made in Germany, the forging house of Hegel and Marx, had corroded the high ideals of the past. This was the ulcer that killed the Revolution. So the problem was only another social problem, and Kropotkin had an answer to suit.

In the middle distance, the rooks are black specks against the sky, and the pedestrians on the midway are stick figures in an animated cartoon. From this distance, they all look the same and not much bigger than ants. Russians are prone to the long view. This makes them a little laconic. When the train of history goes around a curve, some men must fall off, Lenin says. "Don't take things so personal," Kraisky used to tell me. "If you split wood, the chips fly." He has his cop's job to do and keeps his head down, so misses the Pisgah-sight. Lenin is more interesting and has an eagle eye. He appeals to history and the greater good. The poet Mandelstam wasn't a victim to tyranny exactly, as when they shot García Lorca. He was sacrificed, says his widow, to "the inverted 'humanism' of the times."

A Congress on Soviet-Afghanistan Friendship, like a meeting of the Lodge, is playing at the Hotel Ukraine. The brothers wear their pins, and the president of the S&A Friendship Society is extending the hand of friendship to the brothers in Kabul. His words of welcome are earnest but sent into the void like a letter without an address, portmanteau words, Liberty, Equality, and the Brotherhood of Man. They have lowered a bell jar over the hall and created a vacuum at the Hotel Ukraine.

Bogdanov, when he argues, creates a vacuum around himself, not just the same. This honest man is like a filament, and the hotness of his passion, igniting the air, sucks the oxygen away. Sometimes talking with Bogdanov, I find it hard to breathe. God, Man, and the State aren't empty words on his lips but inscriptions on battle flags. When he goes into battle, he holds these flags aloft. He is always on battle stations, having something to fight for. Lacking humor, he has no gossip or chitchat. My talk is only inanities against the intensity of his talk. He is the Russian intellectual, a grand hero of our time. He wears his heart on his sleeve, not caring who sees it. Maybe in the end, this will do him in. But Russians like my friend saved Europe once before. This was when they stopped the Mongols. Madame Mandelstam says that Russia, "by taking the brunt on herself," has saved Europe again, "this time from rationalism and all the will to evil that goes with it."

The poster in the window at No. 3 Serov Proyezd tells me that "Communism is the historical perspective of mankind." My Intourist guide says that this street is named for a hero of Soviet aviation. Bogdanov says, however, that they named it for Ivan Serov, the head of the terrorist branch they call Smersh. A short, balding man, he went mostly unnoticed at the UN when Khruschchev stole the limelight there, banging his shoe on the desk to the scandal of the delegates. I wonder what Serov must have made of this outlandish display.

Mayakovsky had his study at No. 3 Serov Proyezd and looked out from this window until he killed himself in 1930. A poet with a social conscience, he wanted to march with the others. He demanded as his right "an inch of ground in the ranks of the poorest workers and peasants." But Mayakovsky didn't see eye to eye with the powers that be, lacking the proper perspective.

The view from the Ferris wheel has been the favored view in my time. Militant people, finding it to their liking, share a knack for putting things in perspective. The Nazis made short work of Tom, Dick, and Harry, and I remember Himmler saying how what happened to a Russian or a Czech didn't interest him in the slightest. The last train from Berlin pulled out before my time, and what I know about the Nazis is mostly what I read in the papers. But I don't need the papers to tell me what it feels like in Moscow, and I don't want to miss the last train.

Coming out of Moscow is like that scene in *Macbeth* where the king has been murdered and outside the castle they are knocking on the doors. Inside the castle you have been in hell, but until the knocking wakes you up you don't know this. Light thickens and the wind drops, when you go east from Paris to Prague. Like Custine, you want to turn the horses' heads and go back where you came from. If you go west from Moscow to Prague, you feel the wind freshen, however. The city under siege hasn't fallen yet, and in Prague they still know you by your given name and patronymic.

People in Belgrade don't pump your hand or call you comrade. Being Slavs, they aren't always agreeable, only like themselves. There are pretty girls and homely girls who won't give you the time of day. Some of them will. The shop clerks will help you if they haven't got the virus that is going around and haven't been up half the night. Motorists look both ways when they come to the intersection, but some who are *nekulturny* park their little cars on the sidewalk. An impudent jaywalker doesn't scatter when I lean on my horn. I'd like to see him try this in Moscow. In Moscow what happens to a Russian or a Czech doesn't interest them in the slightest. Friends of mine insist that red shirts and brown shirts are different, and I agree that they wear different clothes.

In this prison yard for donkeys I am a donkey, also a private eye, and I want to return to the scene of the crime. All the clues point to Marx, who has that hangdog look. But Marx is only a stand-in and his guilty forebears go back a long way. These men of good hope are canvassing problems. They want to rationalize everything under the sun, and they can tell you how all problems are social. Sometimes your own time is illuminated for you in a vivid phrase. When you hear it, all the pieces drop in place. "My *personal* I has been killed forever." Bakunin said this the first time he read Hegel. Marx didn't like this Russian anarchist and he didn't like anarchists, etc. But Marx also got rid of his personal I. Blood was thinner than water, and he didn't like his brothers and sisters. Living in London half his life, he might as well have been living on the moon. Odd about Marx, who put the physical world above everything else.

At Sheremetyevo when you enter the Arrivals Lounge, the first thing that strikes you is the overpowering smell of shit. I wince for the Customs man at his winnowing labor beside the public toilets. But he lives in a vacuum where men and women are pure as pure, not an impure amalgam. You can't blame the body for taking its revenge. This stoical man in his olive drab and red epaulettes was a slovenly muzhik not so long ago. He held the plough and sowed seed and brought the harvest in, not an easy life, but that isn't the rap against it. In Socialist Land they want us all to be like Jove who had his birth in the clouds. No earthly mother suckled him.

Once in a while but not often, they give you a hard time at Sheremetyevo. Mostly, they let you sail through. They turn an indifferent eye on my bottle of bourbon and all those tins of tobacco I have clearly brought in over the limit. If I want to ruin my liver and lungs, that is up to me. But they X-ray my bags for papers and books, and look hard, riffling pages, at my copy of *Barchester Towers*. They don't know about Trollope but they know about the word, not the hot gospel but the mollifying word. If you take it personally, the jig is up with them.

Backward places are best in cities on the move. In Moscow, I spend a lot of time at the zoo. Zoos around the world are a passion of mine, and it doesn't put me off if they don't rate a star in the guidebook. In Santiago de Compostela they have a black swan with a flaming red neb, and the tropical birds steal the show in Honolulu. There aren't a lot of carnivores or pythons and such. Muscovites don't go in for this either. The amber-colored dogs look like house dogs to me. In the little aquarium, the fish are mostly no-colored, but one startling black carp has a chiffony tail as long as he is. Outside the aquarium, seals are coming up from under. The walrus on the other side of the paling is irascible, not loving a wall. Swimming up to the paling, he mugs for the camera.

This place needs work. The circular pound is piled any which way with old fence boards and old wire fencing. Piles of dirt and dead branches wait for someone to cart them away. Evidently the old zoo on Bolshaya Gruzinskaya isn't high up on their list of priorities. It looks unkempt and running to seed, like the U.S.

Embassy just around the corner. To their orderly paradigm, this disorderly place adds a footnote. As yet, the future hasn't found it.

Disorder is lese majesty in Socialist Land, but their passion for order has its esthetic side. A poet friend of mine, when I praise a new poem he has written, agrees complacently that there is nothing left over. They are like this poet in Moscow. Gratuities depress them, and they want to clean out the icebox. Nothing is left over, everything has its place. I recognize this finicky impulse in myself. On the underside of composition, the Artist meets the Commissar. Damned if all those lively things-in-themselves will escape their appointed shackles.

In the time of Catherine the Great, Russians made a lot of Jeremy Bentham. He meant his Panopticon for her new city on the Black Sea. In this ideal prison, a central observer looked into all of the cells. Bentham wanted "a method of becoming master of everything which might happen to a certain number of men." If you found the method, you could see what the men were up to and spy out their connections and every circumstance of their lives. The warden's eye is on the sparrow in the Panopticon, where nothing and no one can escape the desired effect.

A version of the Panopticon, Yeliseyevsky's on a Saturday afternoon looks like the climax to Glinka's *Life for the Tsar*. It pullulates with Russians, and above the body odors rises the tang of caviar. The rococo fittings have lost some of their shine, and since the Revolution Yeliseyevsky's has had a new name: Food Shop No. 1 of the Moscow Food Trust. But as Bogdanov will tell me, a rose by any other name would smell as sweet, and this is where I go for the good things of life.

Everybody knows his place in Food Shop No. 1. On their own initiative, these Russians have formed up in lines. The first line ends at the red and gold counter. You tell them what you want and they tell you what it costs. Three rubles twenty for a bottle of vodka. But they are selling fresh caviar for ninety kopecks an ounce, a bargain at the price. I join the second line for the *kassa,* hand over my money, and pick up my receipt. They send me back to the line where I came from. Madness in reason, this isn't a bargain but a heist. Caviar I can do without and am almost ready to give up my vodka.

Kopelev in his prison memoirs, reflecting on this problem of order and disorder, decides that formal deportment is good. "The precisely prescribed, standard gestures and words, although they express subordination and obedience, nevertheless allow one to maintain one's human dignity." In Moscow, formal deportment doesn't get high marks. There is a lot of prescribing, however. I have friends who want to lump the two together, a good Protestant impulse. It slices through much cant and says how clothes and what have you don't make the man. But petrified behavior in a boiled shirt isn't just the same as the consciousness of form, and living in Moscow makes me want to distinguish between them.

When the Red Army took Bucharest in 1944, the comrades, says Bogdanov, were appalled at what they found there, nightclubs and bodegas, frivolous places. Even in wartime these Rumanians had a good time. In *Pravda* the comrades made bitter fun of the "well-dressed people sitting in the cafés," and they warned the Russian Ivan not to be deceived by "these outward signs of so-called civilization." Bogdanov says that the comrades are killjoys and he lays this finger-wagging to "the deadly Puritan strain." He harps on religion and how its hangups are still with us. "Thou hast conquered, O pale Galilean," etc. But this doesn't do justice to the comrades. They understand in their bones how "outward signs" make the difference. If you want to break a man down, the first important step is to get rid of his well-tied boutonniere. Who knows or cares what the spirit is doing? It is the letter that saves or kills.

Waiting in freezing rain to view the mummy in Red Square, I suck on my pipe, holding it upside down, until they let me know that this is *nekulturny*. The orderly line of Russians stretches to infinity like the algebraic curve. Silence, reverential, is broken only by the hiss of rain on the cobbles. Fraternal delegations carry wreaths and wear long faces. The militiaman jumps them to the head of the line, and Russians in the line don't complain. Inside the mausoleum, a soldier stands at attention every three yards. Pinkish lights in the semidarkness pick out the waxy features of the man in the coffin. Vladimir Ilyich is an icon, and only the face and hands are visible. The peace of the tomb settles on us like a blanket. Wouldn't you know that these Italians are going to spoil it.

Schoolteachers from Bologna, they are doing their best to keep the volume down. But they can't help what they look like, smart in their furs and stylish leather boots with the leather flaps folded over at the top. *Che contrasto!* this is a scandal. The spiky heels are an absurdity, but as they tell the girls in Texas, beauty knows no pain. The subtle makeup on their faces is like a work of art. Even in the rain every hair is in place. Also they smell good. They are cheerful, unself-conscious, and their black irreverent eyes tell you what is going on in their heads. "Looks plastic to me."

The formal figure Lenin makes is vivid with meaning, however. It enacts the triumph of death over life. They make this triumph incarnate in their old churches where they keep the saint's body under glass. You can't win, evidently, when you start a revolution. The usury of dead institutions mounts up from the past, and the present is still footing the bill.

Like Lomonosov, Bentham was a teacher, but not cut from the same cloth. He proclaimed this triumph of death in life when he founded the University of London. He told them in his will to produce his dead body at meetings of their board of trustees. For a long time they did this, and in a cupboard in Bloomsbury you can still see the mummified corpse of the founder. Mussolini also had his plans for the future. *Non omnis moriar,* and he wanted to be buried in the Augusteum on the Tiber. But his irreverent subjects set their lively form against his petrified form. He wanted to make them Germans but they wouldn't measure up.

In 1922 Russians tried to get rid of the Orthodox Church. They created a "Living Church" to replace it. Saying one thing but meaning another, they said there wasn't room for "soulless formalism" in the Living Church. Soulless formalism is the nightmare from which they have yet to awaken. What they got rid of is form. The Japanese on their islands, a lot of people in a little room, are formal out of necessity, the mother of decorum. The drillmaster thing where everything is ordered isn't formal but fetishistic, and resembles the peace of the tomb.

If you are going to Moscow you will want to buy a map before you go. Maps are hard to come by and what they show you is selective, also faintly wrong. At Intourist, they button up or give you the wrong information. Generating information isn't their strong suit, also it isn't their pleasure. But this Rube Goldberg contraption that passes for a modern state is letting you in on its secret. "Trust no one." That is what it says in their phylactery. Close the windows when you leave, lock the door, and chain up the Bible.

Some things they do better than anyone else, and when it comes to cross-referencing they have written the book. The computer has been a big help to them here. Begotten by a technocrat on the old tsarist censor, this prodigious offspring leaves nothing to chance. "Thanks to the censorship," said Herzen in his memoirs, "we are not accustomed to anything being made public." Tsar Nicholas saw to that, and his State Department of Police with its bullies and spies and agents provocateurs didn't need Dzerzhinsky and the Cheka to tell them.

But where the job of the censor is to bury the present, the computer's job is to dig up the past. It has a capacious memory, and nothing and no one is too picayune for its unwinking eye. Someday they will ask the computer about me, and it will tell them that back in Moscow my friend's name is Bogdanov. If by this time he is out of harm's way, there is always his wife or his nephew.

To beat the computer, you must speak with forked tongue like a white man. False noses and wigs, a nom de plume and dark glasses are the writer's stock in trade. True confessions are out. Like the clerks at Intourist, you don't put your cards on the table. Aesopian language is the language of survivors, not saying one thing and meaning another but saying one thing in terms of another. The form his poetry makes, Voznesensky says, is "a wrathful parabola." But that is how all writers write, if they understand their business.

By and by the computer will do it all for them. As it is now, when you enter your hotel you have to show a card to the doorman. You hand over this card to the *dezhurnaya* on the floor, and that is how you get the key to your room. If you want the card back, you must give up your key. Contingencies don't faze them, even acts of God. A notice in the corridor tells you what to do in case of disaster. "Dear Guests," and they want you to keep out of the elevator and walk down the stairs to the lobby.

Outside the Cosmos, I wonder impatiently where Al and Irma have got to. They are red in the face when they finally show up. Al explains how the elevator had other things on its mind and they walked down the stairs to the lobby. This is not a good idea, there being no access to the lobby from the stairs, and the exit door in the basement is locked. For good measure, the handle has been unscrewed. Backtracking up the stairs to wait for the elevator, Al wants me to know that he won't take the stairs again.

Courtesy of the folks at Intourist, I have a pair of tickets to the Bolshoi Ballet. Bolshoi means big, as in big productions and big crowds clamoring for tickets. They could fill their Sports Palace, still leaving a crowd of people on the outside looking in, but they know better than to do this. Ballet is the ultimate fiction, remote from sweat and strain, and says that everything the body does is easy. This look of being easy doesn't go with being natural. Petipa, the greatest of their ballet masters, tells of a *première danseuse* in St. Petersburg and how they made her "professor of the class of perfection."

Bogdanov has come down with a bad case of the sniffles. I know I ought to commiserate but this evidence of his mortality doesn't come wholly amiss. I suggest a little vodka on the ankles. To hear Bogdanov tell it, he isn't long for the world. Like Boris Godunov making his last adieus, he sends Marina and me out the door. She is all dolled up in a new cloth coat faced at the cuffs and collar with marten, it looks like. A little fur hat is perched on her head. Gold earrings match the wedding ring on her right hand. A head shorter than her husband, Marina is taller than most. She has thin angular shoulders like a sad Picasso clown, and her blond hair is streaked with gray and combed into a bun. Pinched at the mouth and sad around the eyes, she knows how to smile when Bogdanov comes into the room. Tonight she is all smiles. *Swan Lake* is her favorite.

"Confectioner's art!" Bogdanov says fiercely. This famous balletomane tells us how *Swan Lake* is a copout. Petipa in his staging wants us to turn our backs on reality. "An enchanted swan queen, I ask you!" Out there in Moscow the real world is doing its disorderly thing. Teacups rattle in their saucers, door handles turn, and men and women are dressed in the costume of today. If important business is getting done out there, I need the regisseur to tell me about it. His art of fairy tale does this. Messy life clutters the truth, and he keeps the footlights between the crowd and his confection.

Preferring the real world, the crowd squirms at the sharp definition of the footlights. Petipa tells how once one of the players jumped across the footlights to the applause of the crowd and began a revolution in the streets. "Not even changing his costume." That is the real world, appealing from order to chaos. You can read about it in the papers. In the ballet, the last thing you want is reality breaking in.

The artificial form requires its setting, and summertime in Moscow is the time for ballet. The lights go up in the elegant old theater at the head of Sverdlov Square, where the great portico remembers the improbable world of Alexander III and the rearing horses on their columns are harnessed to the chariot of Apollo. The horses and their rider are full of ardor but no sweat, and the art of the sculptor communicates repose. This is wintertime, however, and the Bolshoi Theater is dark. Leaving the metro at Marx Prospekt, we head for the Palace of Congresses just inside the western wall of the Kremlin.

A thoroughfare, the white Trinity Bridge makes a trap. Like a giant portcullis, the iron grating slammed shut on Napoleon when he won the battle for Moscow and entered the Kremlin by the Trinity Bridge. On the western end of the bridge, the Kutafya Tower is a squat stone warder that keeps Marx Prospekt under surveillance. Closing off the other end, the Trinity Tower stands gigantic in the dusk. To the south, the red neon star that tops the inverted cone of the Borovitskaya Gate grows brighter as the daylight fades. In the sunken gardens beneath the bridge, lime trees define the walkways, and light from the floodlights throws the shadows of the trees on the grass. By the artificial light, men are digging trenches. The Neglinnaya River made a moat around the Kremlin until the tsar put the river in conduits underground. He created these gardens that still bear his name as a respite from the thundering city. Alexander I, the conqueror of Napoleon, did this in 1820.

Marina says that the underground waters supply the Sandunovsky Baths. The pickax brigade, a scruffy detail fom the occupying army of Khan Tokhtamysh, is repairing the conduits. The men wear shapkas on their heads. Across the top, the white lacing looks like dirty white laces from gym shoes. These maintenance men in the Alexander Garden are only doing what comes naturally, and their slow-motion movie is slipshod and amorphous. Some are going through the motions, the trick being to do this without breaking a sweat. No baths tonight at the Sandunovsky Baths.

The crowd on the bridge is letting me know that clothes don't make the man. The women have stitched together old potato sacks, and the ragged men are getting ready to storm the Winter Palace. Their ballerinas are beautiful, though, Semizorova, for instance, our Odette and Odile. I remember Toumanova, near the end of her career. Outside the old Stoll Theatre in London, I waited to see her. A body that sang, it never hinted at effort when she danced her whipping turns in the coda of the Black Swan. Ballet tradition calls for thirty-two turns, no more or less. This tradition is what you inherit. Style is how you cope with your inheritance, and personal to you. Yeats says in a poem of his how even daughters of the swan have something in common with every common paddler. Maybe you could put this the other way round. Between the theater and these theatergoers, there is nothing in common, however, and real life is over there across the footlights.

The Palace of Congresses has that new-car smell about it. In the baronial lobby, the emblems of their fifteen republics are vivid scutcheons on the walls. The stage looks big enough to accommodate the *Hindenburg*. You get a good view from every seat in the house. They don't discriminate between the peons and the carriage trade, and I wish the rest of the world would take notice. Once, for a performance of *Billy Budd* at Covent Garden, I sat up top with the peons. When they hanged the hero from the yardarm, you could see a bit of shoe underneath the proscenium arch.

All the same, I prefer the old theaters, like the old Met in midtown Manhattan. A nightmare backstage, that is what they say, but full of grace notes up front, swags of gilded flowers, winking chandeliers, and red plush on the seats. The bronzed termini pretended to hold up the ceiling. Austere Russians used to complain about the carved scrolling in their old churches, all those unicorns, monkeys, and impudent devils. What did they have to do with religion?

Concluding Act II, the traditional French dance in three-quarter time gives everyone a breather. This dance is meditated, the look of spontaneity most of all. Music and motion heed one another. Marina, taking note, speaks her contempt for Bogdanov's indifferent colleagues and students. Mostly they are mediocrities in the journalism school, where the good drives out the best and the bad drives out the good. They never heard yet how the career belongs to the talents. Putting in their time, they are only killing time. If you task them with this, they reproach you with being elitist. That is their word for Bogdanov, says Marina.

This egalitarian friend of mine has only himself to blame. In everything he does he shows himself an elitist, and his distinction between the elite and the workers is real but not a class distinction. The egalitarian man, calling himself an atheist, bristles at painted icons on the wall. It seems to me that in a time when nobody much goes to church anymore, the only religious people are the men and women who give themselves to the struggle they have chosen. They aren't climbing the ladder, unless to fight with the angel, and they don't measure themselves against Tom, Dick, and Harry but against the demands of their craft. Casey Stengel, a grizzled hero of our time, used to say that the world divided up between professionals and ribbon clerks. There are a lot of ribbon clerks in Socialist Land and the Land of the Free, and if Gresham's Law holds, the future belongs to them.

Swan Lake flopped badly the first time around. This is hard to believe, and Tchaikowsky blamed his music. Petipa saw how the fault was in the staging, and said how the choreographer must make the dances conform to the music. This prophet died without honor but vindication came later, and at the ballet in Moscow they are burning candles to Petipa. They don't deviate much from his Peasant Pas de Trois. The divertissements for the ballroom scene still follow the design he worked out in the nineties, a grand design for this ballet to end them all. I am with Marina in giving first place to *Swan Lake*.

But where Petipa turned the world of ballet upside down, his successors have left it where he left it. A hundred years or so later the lava has cooled, and his revolution in staging wears a mortified look, like Herculaneum after the volcano came down. If their younger choreographers have a quarrel with this frozen city, it doesn't get an airing at the Bolshoi Ballet. The old revolutionary has become the establishment. In the wings the whole of modern dance is still waiting.

Out there in Moscow, *Sovyetskaya Kultura* is saying *Nyet* to the rising tide of protest. They have taken up the cudgels in behalf of tradition, as when you take arms against a sea of troubles. Socialist dancers will vindicate themselves by holding fast to realism, "the only general and firm base of art."

No one is more real than Semizorova, a woman alive in her body. She makes the White Swan incarnate. Dancing the Black Swan, she gives you another version of herself. Swan and Princess and Woman, Odette and Odile, they look in different directions but the same heart beats within them. Arms ripple and flutter, and the slightest tremor of shoulder communicates a world of loss. The proud flesh, conscious of itself, isn't ingenuous, and the sexuality doesn't hide itself but cries for attention. This is every paddler's heritage, but not amorphous and not simply generic. The emanation of personality, scents and unguents on the air in the Palace of Congresses, is peculiar to one woman alone. Split leaps, hardly credible, dramatize the doomed passion. They are real, being formal.

In the frosty night air outside the lobby, floodlights define for us the undulating battlements of the Kremlin Wall. Down there in darkness at the base of the wall, the river used to flow. Swans lived on the Neglinnaya in the older time, an invitation to fantasy. Are they redeeming or reproving? "God bless my second fatherland," said Petipa the Frenchman. His love for Russia, he said, was something he had learned.

Across Marx Prospekt, they have turned out the lights in the enormous room where the Presidium receives the people. Lights are going out in the Armory below us. But there is action in the Kremlin Palace, and in the Alexander Garden the pickax brigade is still doing its desultory thing.

My three-day holiday in Leningrad has come to an end, and I am flying the friendly skies of Aeroflot back to Moscow. Five minutes out of Leningrad they tell us that we won't be landing at Sheremetyevo. "Dear passengers," but they don't tell us why and they put us down in Tula, bringing us into the city by bus. Canby at the embassy has his intelligent ear to the ground and I get the bad news a day later. An Aeroflot jet taking off for Dakar and Freetown, and a petrol tanker on the runway where it had no business being. You can number the survivors on one hand. The runway, Canby says, is still closed. This news not being fit to print, I won't read all about it in *Pravda.*

I take back to Moscow a head stuffed with pictures and poems, "Art and Poetry in Russia 1900–1930." All these paintings and manuscripts they are showing at the Hermitage haven't seen the light of day since Stalin put them in the attic. This was fifty years ago. Now here they are coming out of the attic, Tatlin and Kandinsky, Mandelstam and Chagall, trumpets of a prophecy. Maybe they will blow the house down.

Or maybe not. The world outside the front door is partly what you say it is, and first of all you have to see it. The tree that falls in the forest where nobody sees it is a nontree in Socialist Land. In their early Bolshevik journals, Trotsky pokes up his head. This is a problem but the curators at the Hermitage know how to cope. I leaf through a copy of the magazine *New Life*, and they have pasted a correction slip over the name of the left-wing opportunist.

Poems by Mayakovsky are on display at the Hermitage. He is summoning the proud to lift up their heads. "We will wash every city in the world with the surging waters of a second Flood." If Mayakovsky had his night thoughts, this doesn't appear. In the catalog the suicide of the poet goes unmentioned. It wasn't their fault exactly that Mayakovsky killed himself, but even so they wish you wouldn't bring it up. I ask about Repin's canvas of the murdered Tsarevich, and they say how this death was accidental.

Malevich said he wanted to destroy "the tyranny of easel painting." They keep this to themselves, but show you without comment his "white on white" series of 1918. Day one at the Hermitage, the cat is out of the bag, and the crowd wants to know what this painter thought he was doing. In the night Malevich disappears from the wall, and on the wall in the morning there are Revolutionary posters by Denisov.

In Russia, they shoot people for making up poetry. This anxiety of theirs has its endearing side. Poetry to them isn't only moon-June. But I wonder if they aren't being alarmist. Getting on with poetry involves more than hefting a book in your hand, and real seeing involves more than eye contact. For eye, ear, and touch, the rule is the same. Trumpets sound in Trotsky's *History of the Revolution* but Russians don't hear them, and in Socialist Land the three monkeys have made a new troika. Hear no evil, see no evil, speak no evil. If they dropped the state censor tomorrow, not a whole lot of people would notice.

Bogdanov, believing in the power of art, would give what he has to tag along on this cultural safari. He tells me, quoting aptly, how art strikes the shackles from the mind and makes us free. Catharsis is his word, and he talks about the precious lifeblood of a master spirit. Like the blood of the lamb, it washes you clean. Before I set out, we spend an hour together at the Druzhba Book Store across Gorky Street from Yeliseyevsky's. Bogdanov has been singing the praises of Chagall, a great painter. Unconvinced, I turn a deaf ear. Maybe they have a picture book and it will help to convince me.

Nothing doing, however, but not because they don't care for Chagall. The fact is, says the clerk, they can't keep him in stock. Their biggest black market is in books, Bogdanov tells me, art books most of all, and in Moscow they would rather read than eat. When I am back home where they would rather eat than read, I will find the book we are looking for. Maybe the scales will drop from my eyes. But I won't send a copy to Bogdanov. If I sent him a copy, the censor would purloin it. The censor has taste. This doesn't interfere with the job he is doing.

Riding the metro, most of them are reading, even when they are hanging on with one hand to the strap. They prefer books to the daily paper, an index of taste. Many prefer poetry to prose. They read patriotic poets like Simonov and Surkov, but highbrow poets don't scare them, Akhmatova, for instance. She is handing on the Russian word to their children and grandchildren and saying how the word will save the children from bondage forever. Bogdanov's life of Milton had a first printing of one hundred thousand copies, and in six weeks every one of them was gone. *Slava* to these readers in Socialist Land. Only diet books and sex books sell like this where I come from. But I know from morose experience that you can read Milton like a Hallmark greeting card. "Sporting with Amaryllis in the shade."

Beebee is the nephew who comes to visit on the weekends. He is Boris Bogdanov, and his uncle has wangled a place for him at the journalism school. This sober young man smokes a pipe and hasn't earned it, but speaks better English than some students of mine. He likes reading Galsworthy, bad Mark Twain, Salinger, Maugham, and the novels of George Eliot. *Daniel Deronda* is his favorite. They have given him a ticket to the room in the Lenin Library where foreign periodicals are locked away and the hoi polloi can't get at them. Once a week he goes over there and spends the afternoon looking through the *New York Times,* the *International Herald Tribune,* and the *Washington Post.* It helps him to keep up his English, says Beebee.

"Real materials in real space." That was Tatlin's credo. He worked in glass and steel, intractable materials forged in the fire, meaning their power to assail you like a sea of flame. Mostly what he meant went untranslated, or they trimmed his fire and let it illuminate their new egg-crate school of design. He spent thirty years working on his giant glider that looked like a bug. This glider never flew. In Petrograd the authorities consulted their fingernails when he wanted them to build his monument to the Third International. However, the model survives.

The three revolving tiers are shaped like a cylinder, a pyramid, and a cube. An enormous spiral coils around them. This was the symbol, said Tatlin, of a new dynamic spirit, the Communist spirit. He wanted it to challenge the bourgeois horizontal, symbolizing the spirit of greed. Directly behind his three-dimensional model, the exhibitors have hung an immense photograph of Lenin, like the heroic statue devised by the bureaucrats in Washington, D.C., to stand before the monument to the war in Vietnam. If they have their way they will blot out the monument, and you won't think about Tatlin and his new dynamic spirit.

Like Ivanov or Kropotkin, Tatlin is a failure whose voice cries in the wilderness. Looking at these relics of the Constructivist style I think of all the good men who fought and lost the battle, and how the thing that they fought for comes about in spite of their defeat. "When it comes," said William Morris, another prophet without honor, "it turns out not to be what they meant." But Tatlin cared for the work he was doing, while he was doing it, and by and large for its own sake.

The little airport south of Moscow is just big enough to take the big jet, and we circle Tula, sweeping lower, until they give us permission to land. Down there young Bogdanov shed blood for Holy Russia in the Patriotic War, and incidentally won the medals that have helped to save his skin. To the north and west, Kutuzov in 1812 bled the Grand Army at Borodino. Napoleon, then Hitler, and in the long past the Mongols and Dmitry Donskoy. In the bloody land, the rivers are one river engorging another. They hold the land like the coiling serpent that figures eternity, the Moskva and the Oka, the Nara, the Protva, the Vozha where Russians caught the Mongols napping. This was in 1378.

Seen from above, the Krasnaya Pakhra is a lumpy girdle on the land, and doesn't look red or beautiful. Once it looked red. In the waning summer six hundred years ago, Prince Dmitry called his vassals to help him. "They flew together like eagles from all the northern land." The old chronicle poem has them saying, "Let us cross the river Don and compose a wonder for other lands, a tale for old men to tell and young men to remember." This is what they did, and the armies came together at Kulikovo Pole, the Field of Snipes. As we start our descent, I can see the open plain where the Nepryadva flows into the Don.

Tolstoy in *War and Peace* has a chapter on how great men are "history's slaves." He pokes fun at Napoleon who thought he was moving the pawns on the board when he was only another chessman himself. This doesn't mean for Tolstoy that history is bunk. History is necessity. In 1812, men in their millions "had to go from west to east to slay their fellows, just as some centuries previously hordes of men had come from the east to the west, slaying their fellows." Tolstoy is remembering the Mongols. Reading Vernadsky and his history of the Mongols, all that blood-letting, I leave off bruised and sore. If history isn't bunk, what is it then? Marx thought that history was progress or might be, and he thought that things got better when you exasperated the conflict of classes.

Like most of his people, Dmitry Ivanovich, the Grand Prince of Moscow, couldn't read or write, but he "had the holy books in his heart." St. Sergius and the monks let him feel how life on earth was the war of good and evil. His role in this conflict was clear. First he ruled in Moscow and then in Suzdal-Vladimir, the City of God. In Suzdal the purple domes were inlaid with gold stars and the wooden belfries gleamed like standards as the aspen wood darkened with age. This Russian hero, inbred with love of God and love of the land, fought like a Tartar on the Field of Snipes. In my imagination he wears the golden helmet on the high drum of St. Demetrius, the old church in Vladimir.

The Golden Gates of Vladimir have seen a lot of history, and the diorama in that city brings it vividly to life. The Mongols stormed the Golden Gates, and they opened in triumph for Alexander Nevsky. This was after the famous victory in the Battle on the Ice. Most people wouldn't care about it one way or another if it weren't for Prokofiev and his music. The Peoples' Militia on their way to fight Napoleon marched through the Golden Gates. Up the hill and down again like the Grand Old Duke of York.

In the old religious poem the Mongols are approaching the upper reaches of the Don, and Dmitry is in church with his princess and his boyars and his glorious generals. Just before they sing the hymn to the Mother of God that opens with the words "It is meet, in truth, to bless thee," the hero leans against a pillar and sees in a vision the plain of Kulikovo, strewn with corpses. The Christian dead glimmer like candles and the Mongols are black as pitch. Over the plain walks the Mother of God and the Apostles and angels. They are chanting the requiem for the dead. "And where is Prince Dmitry?" He is not in his place but his place is appointed, and "he shall lead the throngs of martyrs," says the Mother of God, "and his princess shall be in my train."

The vision fades and the hero weeps, supposing that the hour of his death is at hand. But he summons the troops and honors his rendezvous with Khan Mamay. Two years after the Russian victory, a more resolute khan sat down before the city of Moscow. He sacked and burned the city, and the work of redeeming Moscow from the Mongols was all to do again. Meanwhile, half the army never came back from Snipes' Field.

Bogdanov's war was like this. Fighting for Russia, he helped to ratify the triumph of Stalin. Other times, other villains, and you could say the same for Kutuzov. When everything was battened down again, Custine came to Russia and asked himself what man had done to God that sixty million of the human race should be condemned to live there. Avvakum the Old Believer has an answer to this. He says that Satan has obtained from God "our bright shining Russia, that he might purple it with martyrs' blood."

In the wall behind Lenin's tomb, martyrs and scoundrels are buried impartially. Dmitry Donskoy tore down the wooden wall and rebuilt it in stone. Inert and forbidding, this jagged range of mountains rises higher and lower as the ground rises and falls. A fortress in the Badlands, the wall is slashed with sentry boxes and loopholes for guns, and pierced at the top with crenels and machicolations. Look out below for boiling oil. Stark white like a sepulcher, red like the sighs that run in blood down palace walls, the Kremlin Wall does this to you. The nineteen towers are peaks thrusting at heaven or giants in the earth. They will gobble you up if you linger.

Stalin is buried just outside the wall, and John Reed is buried inside it. Everybody knows his *Ten Days That Shook the World*, and they have made a movie about him. Only a few old men remember Big Bill Haywood and the IWW, but he is buried in the Kremlin Wall too. John Reed was a friend of his from the other side of the tracks. They fought the Revolution to get rid of the likes of him. Maybe he knew this. Bill Haywood is the working class and said how the Revolution was the victory of his class, "all feathered out!"

This angry man hated the power of money. But he didn't talk glibly about "the money power," a different kettle of fish. A socialist of the heart, not of the head, his socialism was a cry of pain. His life story shows the good and bad of this. Running from America where they wanted to lock him up again, this time for good, he came on deck as they were passing the Statue of Liberty, "the old hag with her uplifted torch." He said, bidding her goodbye, "I am now going to the land of freedom." Like Kropotkin he thought that anarchy was freedom, and he dreamed of a "Kids' Town" that might be a model for grown-ups. No boy there would think of being a policeman. Soldiers wouldn't be needed there. No fighting with others, no prisons, no banks, "and none of them said anything about churches." The Revolution, said Bill Haywood, was "what we have been dreaming about" all our lives. Had he lived a little longer, the Lubyanka would have gobbled him up.

Until ideas possessed him and he ran down hill like the Gadarene swine, this American hero wrote a good prose and his autobiography makes an American classic. Recall is absolute in Bill Haywood's Book. What he remembers is people, all the good men and women who fought and lost the battle. Gene Debs and Tom Mooney. Altgeld of Illinois, the Eagle Forgotten, a poet called him. The Haymarket Martyrs. Emma Goldman. The Molly Maguires. Like Herzen and Nick, they gave their lives to the struggle they had chosen. Some of these American heroes were blind and missed the shape of the future. It is hard to read the future, and Bill Haywood didn't have a crystal ball. However, like Shakespeare's character he drew a good bow and he shot a good shoot.

Russian land is soaked through with the blood of martyrs, and rascals will tell you that they died to make men free. Mostly what they fought for turned out not to be what they meant. The wisdom of hindsight says that they were fools to give their lives to the struggle, but that is only the wisdom of hindsight.

Gogol, concluding the first part of *Dead Souls*, tried to read the future. He saw his native land in a vision, a speeding troika that no one could overtake. The road smokes beneath the wheels and the bridges thunder as the troika rolls across them. Along the road, the spectators are struck with the portent and ask themselves if this is a thunderbolt from heaven. "Russia of mine . . . What does that awe-inspiring progress of yours foretell?" Waiting for an answer, Gogol says how "no answer comes."

As I tiptoe away from Socialist Land, I have my own vision of the future, a double vision, this being permitted to writers but not to men of action. As the War was winding down, Stalin dusted off the Russian Orthodox Church and took the old patriarchate into his establishment. In 1945 the new Patriarch Alexis ascended his throne. This was cause for rejoicing, and they threw a big party in Moscow. Dignitaries came from all around the world, and one of them remembered the messianic traditions of the Orthodox Church. He said how Moscow even yet might become the Third Rome.

The vision fades, like the dream of Prince Dmitry in the Assumption Cathedral. Another rises to confront it, Mayakovsky writing poetry just before he died. "I know the power of words," he said. "They make the coffins break loose and walk off on their four oaken legs." He left his poem unfinished, though. One way or another, the future will fill it out.

CONSTANTINOPLE

CROSSING GALATA BRIDGE

THE TURK from old times is malignant and turbaned. A figure out of nightmare beaked like a bird of prey, his thick black mustache turns up at the ends. I see him with the mind's eye, committing unmentionable acts on Colonel Lawrence or pursuing Greek peasant girls over the mountain crags. The girls have a lot of décolletage and this inflames their pursuer. They are throwing themselves down from the mountains, however, preferring death with honor to a fate worse than death. The "unspeakable Turk," said Gladstone with a shudder, but this time he is balked of his prey.

The airport is Yeshilkoy, meaning "Green Village," but the green has all gone into concrete. I enter the Arrivals Lounge, having come to the Holy City of Byzantium. Mustachioed desperadoes on the other side of the barrier press their fierce faces against the plate glass. Leathery old men are playing Anthony Quinn, one of his character roles somewhere east of Suez. Most could do with a shave. In the ceiling, the low-wattage bulbs show as dim aureoles of light. Coal dust on the wooden benches and metaled radiator covers feels like granules of sugar. The smell of burning coal, mingling with tobacco smoke, brings back London in the old days. Dickens had a phrase for this. "Inspissated gloom."

A djinn or a dervish materializes out of the smoke. He is offering *simit,* chewy bread shaped like a doughnut and dotted with brown seeds, "the insane root that takes the reason prisoner." I am not about to sample his wares. Shoeshine boys with their kits and slurred importunate voices want to know why I don't want a shine. A gnarled old woman all in black meets my eyes accidentally and looks away in a hurry, drawing the long *charshaf* over her face. Soldiers in combat dress, wielding machine pistols, say that Istanbul is under martial law.

"Tuvalet nerede?"—everybody's first phrase when you cross the language barrier. They show me the way to the toilet. An adolescent boy is standing in the doorway and wants me to cross his palm before I go in. This boy's face is half eroded, he has eyes like muddy water, flaring holes for a nose. He tries to make me understand him but can't articulate speech. However, they have given him something to do. He is the keeper of the toilet.

Over the revolving doors, the man in the portrait wears a black tie and mourning coat, a gold chain across his belly. In the heavy sensual face the washed blue eyes are lowering and melodramatic. This is Mustafa Kemal. Ataturk, he called himself, the father of the Turks, and he said how Turkish people were lepers and pariahs alone with their customs of another age. "Enter resolutely into modern life," he told them. He wouldn't take no for an answer.

A neighborhood bully, partly a comedian, also a hero, Ataturk defines the great man. The people he bullied made him their idol, like Peter the Great. He was the *Gazi,* the Conqueror and Destroyer of Christians. The *gazi* "cleanses the earth from the filth of polytheism," says an old Ottoman poet. In 1921 King

Constantine of Greece, believing in three gods, sent his army into Turkey. He wanted to rule in Constantinople, like Constantine the Great. But Mustafa Kemal destroyed the Greeks at Sakarya. This was how he earned his title. In the War for Independence a *hodja* or holy man invoked a blessing on the Gazi. "*Mashallah*," he said. "God save him from the evil eye." It is going on fifty years since Ataturk died in the grandiose palace that looks over the Bosphorus to Asia. But the eyes of Father Turk are still quick in his head. No evading them either. *Mashallah*! Like the old woman, I feel for my *charshaf*.

Out on the tarmac, the plane revs up, getting ready for departure. But I have come to Istanbul on the track of East Rome. Duty before pleasure, and writing a book is like picking oakum. Also this plane is bound for Bursa and Ankara. Out of the frying pan, into the fire. I settle for a taxi and it takes me into town.

Istanbul is a graveyard where old American cars go to die. The '56 Chevvy is a bull on the rampage. That is what the driver thinks, and he drives with the heel of his hand against the horn. This car has the staggers, only two gears engage, and the tail fins have rusted through and make an obtuse angle with the body. These Stamboullus in the street aren't hurrying to get out of the way. They think that Istanbul belongs to them.

"The peasant," said Father Turk, "is the master of this country." He breathed the unpolluted air of the Anatolian plateau. You couldn't do this in Constantinople. The ancient city on the Golden Horn was "the harlot of the ages," never mind that Turks and Byzantines had made it their capital for sixteen hundred years. It was time for a change, Ataturk considered, and he built a new capital in the open spaces of the East. "Constantinople," he told them, no longer existed. He said that they should call it Istanbul. But things changing remain the same, and this man who despised the past resumed the past without knowing it.

A thousand years ago Byzantines with superb assurance called their city "*he polis*," The City. Muslims lived across the water on the outside looking in. They adopted the Greek usage and spoke of going "to the city," "*eis ten polin.*" Already in the tenth century this was Istanbul.

On the outskirts of town, the cobbled streets are deserted. Garish billboards flank the streets and proclaim a cult of beauty. In Latin countries they want you to think about your liver. "*Fegato! fegato! fegato!*" Here in Istanbul it's what's up front that counts, and these billboards are selling hair oil, depilatories, and face cream. Plumes of yellow gas jet from the refineries. The fitful illumination silhouettes the coal dumps, the earth movers tethered for the night, the boxcars at their sidings. You see them as the light flares, then they go dark. The peeling factories sit back from the road, eczema in their bones. On our left hand is the Coca-Cola bottling plant.

Yeats, a great poet who has a lot to answer for, said that if they would give him a month of antiquity and leave to spend it where he chose, he would spend it in Byzantium a little before Justinian opened Sancta Sophia. This was in December 537. When the emperor came to the finished church, he held out his arms in prayer and said he had beaten King Solomon. In the Holy City, Yeats said, "religious, aesthetic, and practical life were one." All the things that count came together for a moment, caught in luminous mosaic. "Maybe never before or since."

Cold sweeps in from the Sea of Marmara, and on Edirnekapi Caddesi the new apartment buildings hug themselves and turn blank faces to the street. The car heater doesn't work. Outside the Edirne Gate we pass a hillside cemetery. Cypress trees, tall among the gravestones, blot up the last of the light. People make love in the cemeteries that surround Istanbul, and the dead and the living make a fraternity in this city where life holds more terrors than death and every dismal fact is up front. Turbans in stone crown the tombs of the dead men. On the tombs of the women, the rounded stone suggests a scarf or *charshaf*.

Four hundred years ago a French traveler came this way. He

said how all other cities were mortal but Constantinople would endure "as long as there are men on earth." Sometimes old means enduring. Mostly it means emptied out, like a cistern emptied of water. The older the city the less that is left, Ravenna, for instance, where the Byzantine exarchs made their great churches. But the Lombards took the city the way a terrier takes a rat. The Franks came later, then the Guelfs and Ghibellines and everybody knows how they were always fighting, then the armies of the Pope, the Venetians, French, Germans, and Spaniards, and little is left of the ancient city in the marshes. In modern Ravenna they make macaroni, fertilizers, synthetic rubber, and cement. To recreate the city as it used to be, you must work on your imagination.

Take the word "divan," a backless couch with pillows. You set it against the wall, and I have one at home. However, this description is only bare bones. To Ottoman Turks, the divan meant the center of state. The sultan sat on his divan and his ministers of state sat around him. This was like the old French levee, only these meetings meant more than getting dressed and being obsequious. Here in Istanbul I try to recover the ampler sense of the word. At first the sultan presided at meetings of the Imperial Divan. Then his interest began to wane. He spent more time with the girls of the harem, letting his grand vizier run the meetings and do the conferring. This administrative change or gradual letting go says how Turkish power declined. The more virile at home, the less virile abroad. In Istanbul today there is neither sultan nor divan, and the Ottoman Empire is a thing of the past.

The grand vizier had his residence in Topkapi Palace, and you went in to see him through the Bab-i-Humayun or imperial gate. The Sublime Porte, Westerners called this gate. They made it a synonym for the government of Turkey, the way we speak of the Kremlin or the Court of St. James. Over the gate were the heads of offenders. When they had too many heads they displayed the ears and noses alone. High-ranking offenders had their heads displayed above the Ortakapi, the gate that opens on the second courtyard. If you are a tourist, this is where you buy your ticket. To take your camera in, you must buy an extra ticket.

The land walls are upon us and we drive through the Edirne Gate. Turn the car the other way and you come to ancient Adrianople, Hadrian's city on the eastern edge of Europe. Turks have renamed it Edirne. The Roman Emperor Theodosius began the land walls sixteen hundred years ago. They made a rampart from the Golden Horn to the Sea of Marmara. From the bottom of the moat to the top of the towers, the land walls rose a hundred feet. These walls were convex. The seawalls curved inwards, shunning the water. They began just below the little village of Eyup at the head of the Golden Horn, and ran down to the Bosphorus. Rounding Seraglio Point where Topkapi Palace stands, they ran along the Marmara shore for another five miles, rising straight out of the sea. Centipedes and scorpions have taken over the seawalls, and green borage and pink oleander flower in the cracks. The leaves of the borage are hairy. Altogether these walls were fourteen miles long, and for more than a thousand years they stood guard before Constantinople. In the fifth century they saved the city from Attila the Hun. From the tops of the towers, the defenders hurled their missiles and "Greek fire." Of the ninety-six towers, only a handful are left. In the moat outside the wall, kitchen gardens are growing, faded grape hyacinth hangs from the dripping stone, and lean-tos are built into the arches. Squatters live in the lean-tos, my cab driver says.

Just inside the gate, a single minaret pricks the sky like a hypodermic needle. Sinan their great architect built this mosque the year Shakespeare was born. The princess Mihrimah Sultan who commissioned the work found the money, they say, from the sale of jewels that adorned a single slipper. Seven domed bays make a graceful porch in front of the mosque. A second porch used to stand here. Its broken columns still lie on the ground, toppled where the earthquake left them.

Moscow, the Third Rome, is beating in my mind. "The Third Rome stands," said Philotheus the monk. When Moscow lay deep in forests dreaming its dream of hegemony to come, Constantinople embodied the finished fact in precious metal and tessellated stone. "Before the Emperor's seat stood a tree made of bronze gilded over." An Italian bishop who traveled to the city remembered this tree. He said how the branches were filled with birds, "also made of gilded bronze, which uttered different cries each according to its varying species." All summer long, they commended whatever is begotten, born, and dies.

I read in an old writer how the old city was beautified all through "like a robe woven to the very fringe." If we have to have a garment, let it be spotted and torn. "The spider holds the curtain in the Palace of the Caesars." Mehmet the Conqueror said this when he walked through the ruined halls of the Great Palace of Byzantium. Constantine built the palace and Justinian rebuilt it, and now, said the sultan, "the owl hoots its night call on the Towers of Aphrasiab." Gibbon, a heavy ironist among historians, liked these lines and used them to end his story of decline and fall.

The new moon is rising over the city, like a thin sickle of Cheddar cheese. This lurid coloring is a function of the smog that insinuates itself everywhere in modern Istanbul, glamorizing the pocky landscape below. By the light of the new moon, ancient Byzantines detected the invading army of Philip of Macedon, and they invested the moon with numinous power. "In this sign you shall conquer," like the Christian Cross that appeared in the heavens to the Emperor Constantine. Mehmet the Conqueror suppressed the Christian Cross and the two-headed eagle, but the crescent moon of the Byzantines became his own emblem. He enlarged it with his "star." Above the Sixth Hill of the city, a single star trails the crescent moon like a spur, and I am looking at the battle flag of Islam. There are a lot of stars in the sky tonight, and the shape they make is in the eye of the beholder.

Gashes wrinkle the land where the earth-movers have been.

They don't spare the spreading chestnut and don't take the long way around. Featureless boulevards cut through the old quarter, Ataturk Bulvari, Vatan Caddesi. When Ataturk was a young man growing up in Macedonia, he saw the Pisgah-sight, like Moses and Lenin. He organized a Fatherland and Freedom Society, "*Vatan ve Hürriyet.*" But this fatherland he sponsored devoured the land, knowing no provenance.

On our left, the Mosque of the Conqueror looms gigantic, "like a town full of lead-covered domes," someone said. Crowds of men but no women are milling in the courtyard, and from back alleys and cross streets more of these men are erupting. They whizz off in all directions and butt against each other, heated particles in random motion. Istanbul shuts down at night by fiat of the military, and the hour for curfew is approaching. The men on the street appear not to know this, however.

Traffic builds as we come to Fevzi Pasha Caddesi, the center of town, and we bull our way through. The street is slick with mud, and in the broken pavement pools of water have collected. What pavement there is isn't concrete but cheap reddish tile. On the narrow sidewalks of the tributary streets, people can't walk two abreast. Mostly, however, they keep to the sidewalks, not wanting a truck or taxi to crush them.

Turning against the traffic and blocking our way, a truck driver is trying and failing to maneuver his van through the postern of a small needle's eye. Kibitzers on the sidewalk are watching the scene. Appreciative patrons enjoying their dinner, they shout encouragement and offer suggestions. Little boys selling views dart through the crowd like piranhas. One of them raps on the taxicab window. "My name is Ollie," I hear him say. "Ali" is what he is saying, and I shake my head No to his concertina of postcards. A grizzled man wearing a white cap that resembles a yarmulke makes an island in the stream. He is holding up long white strips bunched together at the top, like a giant bunch of white radishes. Foam rubber, says my driver. In winter you stuff it around the windows to keep out the cold.

Men like pack animals are supporting enormous burdens, the panniers strapped to their backs. They carry tinned copper pots and pans, hessian sacks holding who knows what, coils of rope, wooden crates, and cardboard containers laminated with metal bands. Where the bags of millet have broken, white seeds trickle to the sidewalk. They use the seeds for food. Also they ferment them to make the spicy drink called *boza*. The men beneath the burdens are wiry-thin. Having a sixth sense, they thread their way through the crowd without looking. In the city on the Horn there are fewer jobs than people, unlike Moscow where there are fewer people than jobs. No work is too mean for these men who live under the whip.

Where six hundred thousand people lived in Justinian's city, four million people live around the Golden Horn. All of them want a place in the sun. Bigger is better, my cab driver thinks, and if there are problems he doesn't let on. Before the coup of 1980, political killings took the lives of twenty-two people a day, information I don't get from the driver. Politics strikes him dumb, and to hear him these Stamboullus are docile as lambs. Four million Turks but no problems, he says.

On every corner, the armed men are a visible presence. They aren't menacing, only you see them. I spell out the block letters sewn across their tunics. AS. IZ. The Askeri Inzibat or military police hark back to the Muslim Conquest. The last sultan packed his bags and departed in 1922, but the military caste hasn't noticed. Their guns are at the ready, and I want to know what the trouble is. "Between the rights and the lefts," my driver says. "Which is no more."

The street lamps are dim and few and far between, but he doesn't use the high beam. He flicks on the interior lights in the car. They want him to do this. "So they can see what you're doing," he says. A good citizen, he renders to Caesar the things that are Caesar's.

Like a lighted train in a tunnel, the line of traffic approaches the bridge across the Horn. The De Soto just behind us pulls out of line to pass. It barely misses the huge tail fin, a calculated miss. This neatly turned veronica makes us look foolish. The lights are off in the De Soto, and the man at the wheel is sending a message. The peasant, he is saying, is master in this country, and the askeris hold no terrors for him.

In the little *lokantas* or restaurants, dinner is on display behind the lighted glass windows. The layers of strudel pastry are topped with ground walnuts and syrup. This is for dessert. For the main course they are offering green peppers stuffed with rice, broiled leg of lamb, bits of lamb and tomato skewered on spits, bits of swordfish it looks like. They lie on dark green leaves and look good enough to eat. There is plenty to eat, and Turks don't make a cult of deprivation.

In the clothing store windows, there is plenty to buy. However, says my driver, no one has the money. In Moscow they have the money, but there is nothing to buy. Mannequins in Western dress and hairdos stare from the windows at the passing parade. Their unwinking eyes are unabashed and Anglo-Saxon, and their skinny torsos give the lie to the old Ottoman saying: "She is so beautiful that she has to go through the door sideways."

City Hall is at our back. However, the city fathers have gone home to the suburbs. They don't live in Istanbul, where new construction makes an instant slum. The Young Turks who ran this city when the century was younger turned a negligent eye on anything old. They were Talat, Enver, and Jalat, pashas in linen suits, and they spoke for the Committee of Union and Progress. When the Allied armies threatened Constantinople, they knew what to do. They said they were going to blow up the city, antiquities included. Sancta Sophia didn't cost them a night's sleep. "We all like new things," Talat said.

Around the intersection where we cross Shehzhade Bashi, the tumbled ruins of a Christian church invite reflection on the up and down of things. The spires on our right are rockets ready to go. This is the mosque of Bayazit II. Superb on the Third Hill, it looks across the clutter that calls itself a square to the no-nonsense buildings of the University of Istanbul. These forcing houses for the modern world are throwing down a challenge to Islam. My driver wants me to notice. He perhaps is illiterate like most of his people, but these latter-day *hodjas* who don't wear the fez will see to it that his son and daughter can read.

Spanning the boulevard named for Ataturk, the great double arcade of the Roman Emperor Valens is frozen in time. In the mind's eye, however, the aqueduct is marching. It crosses the valley between the Third and Fourth Hills, linking the Muslim mosque with the vanished church of St. Polyeuktos, and the vanished world of the Romans with the modern city of the Turks. The great cistern they called the *nymphaeum maximum* took the waters of the aqueduct and sent them into the city, where they fed the kitchen gardens and performed their ancient task of ablution. Near the site of the cistern, modern engineers have built a waterworks or *taksim*.

Where the massy arches of Valens bisect Ataturk Bulvari, they are sixty feet high. They ran north and west, seeking the waters that rose beyond the Edirne Gate and the Theodosian Wall. Through an opening in the wall the Janissaries in their red tunics poured into the city on May 29, 1453, shouting their battle cry: *Allahuekber*! God is Most Great! From a tower on the wall they hoisted the star and crescent. The red flag of the Infidel is flying from the domed roof of their Municipal Museum as we come down to the water.

Like a sore thumb, the old city sticks out in the water. Seraglio Point is the tip of the thumb. If you stand on the point you are in Europe, but look straight ahead with your back to the city and you are looking at Asia. That is Uskudar on the Asiatic shore, called Chrysopolis in the ancient world, the City of Gold. Below it on the water is the Anatolian suburb of Kadikoy, ancient Chalcedon where all the trouble began. In 451 A.D. the Church met there in council, and decided that the Christian God was both human and divine. This was the rock on which the Church split apart. Some Orthodox Christians were like the Muslims who succeeded them. Preferring an impersonal Logos, they sank the human in the divine.

Muslims think it impious to represent the human form, and the bronze statue of Ataturk, dominating Seraglio Point, was a first of its kind for Turkey when they put it up in 1926. Nobody knew he was coming. A hundred years ago, the old historian Lane-Poole looked back to the days when Turks were simple, honest, and courageous. He thought there was plenty of such stuff in the people still. But where was their leader? "Till Carlyle's great man comes, the hero who can lead a nation back to paths of valor and righteousness, to dream of the regeneration of Turkey is but a bootless speculation." Ataturk was just around the corner.

The man on the pedestal is turning his back on the past. Turks who called themselves civilized had to prove it, he said, "in their outward aspect." This meant shoes and trousers, shirt and tie, jacket and waistcoat—"and of course, to complete these, a cover with a brim on our heads." In backwater Turkey, he showed them a Panama hat. "I want to make this clear," said Ataturk. "This head-covering is called 'hat.' "

Turks wore the fez. When they prayed, their pressed their foreheads to the ground. If you wore a hat with a brim, you couldn't do this. Ataturk dressed like a giaour, not like Byron's romantic giaour but like a "*gavur*," in modern Turkish a Christian or uncircumcised dog. This was deliberate. "If only we could make them Christians!" he said of his people.

Not far from the Gardens of the Seraglio, an equestrian statue on a stone shaft used to overlook the water. It stood in the ancient Forum of the Byzantines near Sancta Sophia and the entrance to the Great Palace. Justinian on the column was dressed in armor, his right hand extended towards the rising sun. The barbarians lived in that quarter, and the emperor, said Procopius the historian, was commanding them "to remain at home and advance no further." He was a man in perpetual motion, wanting to civilize the world, and his people never got to sit still. Procopius, who didn't like him, said he "kept tearing down existing institutions as if he meant to change all things into another form."

The waters make a strait, a sea, and a river. They flow into each other, surrounding the city like a garland, said Procopius. The great ditch of the Bosphorus separates two continents, Europe on the west bank, Asia on the east. Constantinople stands on both continents, and no other city is like this.

The Bosphorus looks like a river but smells like the sea. This tells you where it comes from. For eighteen miles it runs north and mostly east to the Black Sea and Russia, the old enemy of the Turks. At the same time, it runs south. The fresh waters of Russia, flowing south, make a counter current. In winter they carry chunks of ice and are swollen with melting snow. Being fresh, they are more buoyant than the salt water coming up from the Mediterranean, and they ride above it like a foaming collar.

Below Seraglio Point, the garland of waters is called the Sea of Marmara. It flows south around the point and west to the Dardanelles. This was the Hellespont where Leander caught a cramp when he swam across the straits, and Byron, being vainglorious, had to improve on his performance.

The Aegean lies outside the straits, and everybody remarks the improbable blue of the water. Above it, jutting into the water for more than fifty miles, are the ridges of Gallipoli where modern Turkey found its soul. In 1915 Mustafa Kemal held these ridges for Turkey. "I don't order you to attack," he said to his soldiers. "I order you to die." That is what they did, but they drove the British army into the sea.

On the European shore of Constantinople, a third and much smaller body of water cuts the city in two parts. This is the Golden Horn, an arm of the sea probing inland for seven miles. When they looked at the water, Byzantines saw the twisting horn of a stag. Turks were more prosaic, and the Golden Horn to them is only the "Halitch" or canal. States of mind are more important for Constantinople than the lie of the land and water. Stamboul on the south bank of the Horn is "Muslim," and on the other side they are "Christian" and brisk. On the north bank, the lights in the rowdy cafés called *meyhanes* burned through the night, and across the Golden Horn Stamboul lay dead in an Oriental silence. This was before the generals took over. Now the silence is pervasive.

The generals, being prudent, want to save electricity. Also, being puritan, they want everyone in bed. By 8:00 p.m. I have finished my dinner at the Four Seasons, and the waiter bows me out into the street. All the lights have been extinguished. The traffic has vanished, and it was roaring just an hour before. On Istiklal Caddesi, a yellow dog could walk safely down the median line. In the brown light and silence, the old European quarter of Constantinople looks like East Berlin from the roof of the Hilton on the other side of the wall.

Pera dominates the north bank, taking its name from a Greek word meaning "beyond" or "across." On its steep cobbled hills the great Christian powers built their embassies when Constantinople was still the capital of Turkey. Stamboul "over there" was like Sodom and Gomorrah, said the British Commander in Chief in 1915, a "nest of iniquity." Turks were "natives." In the Ottoman city, foreign nationals stood above the law. They had their own law courts, and had their hand on all the levers of power. They advised the army and navy, also the police, and they controlled Turkish trade. They granted loans or didn't, and their pleasure made the difference for Turkey.

The state within a state is an old story for Constantinople. Below Pera is Galata, the old trading quarter on the lip of the Golden Horn. Here the Genoese lived, and they had their privileges too. At the end of Galata Kulesi Sokagi near where the stairs go down, you can still see the ancient Podestat, the Palace of the

Magnificent Community of Pera. From this building, their Genoese governor ruled the state within a state. He spoke Italian, an alien tongue.

In Constantinople, memories of alienation are deeply involved with language. Wanting to challenge these memories, Ataturk set out to purify the language, a serious job that had its comic side. He got rid of Arabic, a language of "incomprehensible signs," and replaced it with the Latin alphabet. Latin characters didn't suggest the alien presence, on the contrary, he said. They were Turkish, and he made fun of Turks who didn't understand them. Once, giving a speech in the Sarayburnu Park where his statue stands, he waved a clutch of papers written in the Latin script and called for a volunteer who knew how to read Turkish. He got his volunteer and proceeded to shame him. "This young man is puzzled," said Ataturk, "because he does not know the true Turkish alphabet."

Coming to terms with the true Turkish alphabet wasn't easy, but he decreed that "the change will happen in three months." He turned the whole country into a schoolroom, and the headmaster was the Gazi himself. "The Turkish people are going to work hard," he said, "until they pass the exam of that school." In Dolmabahche Palace, he set up blackboards in the halls. When dignitaries came to see him, he stood them before the blackboards and taught them how to read. He did the same with his friends and servants. Like a patriotic Frenchman, he said that borrowings from other languages were "linguistic capitulations," and he got rid of them too. He gave himself a new name and invented new names for his colleagues. His prime minister Ismet became Inonu, after the great battles they fought in that place. Also he purified the names of Turkish cities. Angora became Ankara and Smyrna became Izmir. In Istanbul this rite of purification continues, and old Pera is now Beyoglu and Galata is Karakoy. Beyoglu has taken but Karakoy hasn't, and Turks still call it Galata. The Grande Rue de Pera, running out of Taksim Square down to the tunnel underneath the Golden Horn, is known today as Istiklal Caddesi. This means Independence Avenue. But where the name is different, the substance is much the same.

Toiling up Istiklal Caddesi, the jampacked bus bound for Taksim runs out of gas or nerve and grinds to a halt. The bus empties in a hurry. It doesn't roll back down the hill, though there is reason to fear that it will do this. Rain beginning to fall, I summon a taxi. The meter doesn't work and we bargain over the fare. The fare is what you agree on. You are a pigeon unless you agree before the cab pulls away from the curb. It is hard to come to composition with this driver, however. On Istiklal Caddesi, haggling is a way of life. The long twisting thoroughfare, said a resident of the city, "is a narrow as the comprehension of its inhabitants and as long as the tapeworm of their intrigues." Independence Avenue was still the Grande Rue de Pera when he said this.

In other ways, the substance isn't just the same. The automobile didn't figure in the Gazi's design, but it has made a difference, assimilating Istanbul to the rest of the modern world. The T1 bus is my best route home from Taksim to the Pera Palas Hotel. This bus proceeds west and south along Tarlabashi Caddesi, a dreary phalanx of garages, used-car dealers, car rental firms, show windows for new cars, store fronts displaying tires, fan belts, spark plugs, hub caps. You can see your face in the polished chrome surface. From early morning until dark and a little after dark, this street sacred to the automobile stinks with exhaust fumes. Traffic moves downhill in peristaltic motion, squeezing and releasing. The driver shuts off his motor and we wait.

Taksim Square is the center of Pera. On the right side looking down to the Horn, the octagonal buildings look like a *turbe* or tomb. This is the *taksim* that distributes the waters from the reservoirs in Belgrade Forest. Taksim Baba, Turks call it derisively, the tomb of a latter-day saint. In 1521 the young Sultan Suleiman took the Christian city of Belgrade for Islam. He was the Shadow of God on Earth, and like God or Ataturk he gave a name to the forest that lies between the Bosphorus and the Black Sea. Belgrade, he called it. In the valleys of the watershed wild peonies and cyclamen bloom in the spring.

As you walk out of Taksim Square, the Christian churches among the embassies are fish out of water, red brick Italian Gothic for the Franciscan church, pompous Houses-of-Parliament Gothic for the British church that remembers the Crimean War. Ruskin would have felt at home here. In the Swedish Embassy at the bottom of Istiklal Caddesi, the exiled King Charles XII lived for four years near the end of his life. Peter the Great humbled this famous king at the Battle of Poltava in 1709, and the old Russian Embassy is still a ponderous presence just across the street. Nothing suggests its old function. The rooms diplomats used for their business have been cut up to make shops and apartments or storage rooms where the spider builds.

Fire, earthquake, and riot have done a job on Istanbul, and what they left standing the people have carted away. The land walls are still standing, but Mehmet's great cannon has knocked them about, and underneath the seawalls plastic junk that never dies litters the sandy beach. Camel thorn and salt bush poke up through the litter, and this isn't a place to go walking.

On the Fourth Hill the wooden houses of the poor, pieced out with rusting tin and bits of masonry from earlier structures, lean against each other for a little while longer. Among them, looking down on Ataturk Bulvari, is what remains of the church of St. Savior Pantocrator. After the Conquest this church became a mosque, its "Christian" columns replaced with piers. Next door is a pigeon cote. The pigeons who leave their droppings don't distinguish between the church of Christ Almighty and the Molla Zeyrek mosque.

Not far away, the tenth-century church of the Mirelaion is an evil-smelling shell choked with rubbish and splinters of glass. Mirelaion is Oil of Myrrh, and the Byzantine Emperor Romanus

Lecapenus built his palace beside this church. The outlines of the palace walls being flush with the pavement, kids from the neighborhood use the site as a playground. There are slides on the sunken roof of the palace.

In Rome they remember everything, and don't discriminate between heroes and villains. They name their children for Hannibal, even for Attila. Moscow also recalls the past, and on a selective basis they have their plaques and their monumental sculptures. In Istanbul, the dead bury the dead. Likenesses evoking the honored dead are rare, also gratuitous in this city where so many have died. There are exceptions to the rule, like the paintings of nineteenth-century sultans in Dolmabahche Palace, and when you go to Topkapi they will show you a rare portrait of Mehmet II. Ataturk, to nobody's surprise, is an exception. Bristling among the tram lines and billboards in the center of Taksim, another monument remembers the Turkish soldiers who saved the Republic. A few secular portraits survive from the long past. A portrait in mosaic high on a pier in the north gallery of Sancta Sophia shows a Byzantine emperor who ruled in this city a thousand years ago. Medallions flank the portrait, bearing the legend: "Lord help thy servant, the orthodox and faithful Emperor Alexander." After a reign of thirteen months, this alcoholic, mad despot died of apoplexy during a drunken game of polo.

Istanbul by whatever name you know it is a city habituated to violence, and that is the common term in their remembering of things past. Ataturk is the Gazi who fights for Islam, and on the monument in Taksim "the Turk stands up to die." When Mehmet and his Janissaries seized Constantinople, they left four thousand dead. The wheel turned, however. Four centuries later, Sultan Mahmud II penned the Janissaries in their barracks on the site of the old Hippodrome. He fired the barracks, and when they tried to escape the fire he killed them all. "History" in Constantinople is like Fortune's Wheel that moves from apogee to perigee and then turns up again. On the Ides of January 532 the Emperor Justinian trapped the Nika rebels in this same Hippodrome. Thirty thousand died.

Galata on the water is a tangle of alleys and steps going up and down, and you don't see the huge tower until you are almost upon it. The Genoese who built this tower called it the Tower of Christ. Let into the stone walls is the inscription "29 May 1453 Mehmet II Fatih." "Fatih" means the Conqueror. Inside Galata Tower, tourists ride the elevator to the viewing platform. Fire-spotters use the platform, the wooden city of Istanbul being always ready to catch fire. In the café on the upper levels you can buy a glass of *raki,* and if you pour in water it turns a cloudy white.

Sometimes the Golden Horn lives up to its name. This is generally at sunset when the rays of the dying sun appear to ignite the water, and the pollution on the surface shines with a rotten phosphorescence. At all times the air carries coal dust and the smell of sulfur. "Greek fire" seems potential. Only toss a lighted match. Barges bring the soft coal down the Bosphorus from Zonguldak on the Black Sea, dumping it beside the canal. In berths along the canal the old tubs and unpainted scows are decaying, some awash or half heeled over.

The states of mind that are Europe and Asia meet on Galata Bridge. To the left of the bridge as you look at Stamboul, ferry boats are casting off from the *iskele* or landing stage. They connect the city to seaside villages along the Bosphorus, or turn northwards and proceed up to Eyup where the land and sea walls come together and the Golden Horn begins. As you go up water there are factories on one hand, slaughterhouses on the other, and on either hand the slums of Istanbul. The tanneries in the smog are shadowy suggestions just touched with gold. Though you don't see them, you smell them. At Kasim Pasha on the north bank, the naval arsenal is still open for business. In the heyday of Ottoman power the great dry docks accommodated more than a hundred ships. Now half a dozen ships are careened in the dry docks, men scraping barnacles and caulking their hulls. At Haskoy where the ferry stops, Karaite Jews established a colony three hundred years ago. In the hillside cemetery their gravestones lie flat on the ground.

The last port of call is Ayvan Saray or "Great Palace" on the south bank. Here the barges drop their coal and scabrous buildings come down to the water. Mangy curs scavenge for food, Istanbul lacking the wherewithal to support both dogs and people. Around this muddy quay, just inside the land walls, the Byzantines built their Palace of Blachernae. In the palace they kept the girdle of the Mother of God. Once it was the palladium of the "God-defended city," like the statue of Athena that guaranteed the safety of Troy. I have seen this girdle in a little town in Tuscany, and perhaps the Crusaders brought it home in 1204 when they ransacked Constantinople.

The village of Eyup is a place of pilgrimage for pious Muslims, ranking just after Mecca, Medina, and the Dome of the Rock in Jerusalem. The standard-bearer of the Prophet lies buried in the mosque. He was Eyup or Job, and he fell in battle before the city when the Arabs besieged it thirteen hundred years ago. After the Conquest, Mehmet II dug up his body, directed by a helpful councilor who located the place in a dream.

The mosque on the site is the color of honey, and inside the baroque octagon men are praying where they please. The women are shuffled off to a corner, like a quarantine ward where the sickness is catching. In pious isolation they squat on the blue prayer rug, touching their foreheads to the floor.

This place is haunted and auspicious. Adnan Menderes, once prime minister of Turkey, rides to Eyup at night from his prison island of Yassiada. The generals hanged him after their coup of 1960, this being four coups back, two of them abortive. Some Turkish people believe that their hero still lives, like the True

Prince Dmitry who lives for Russian people and will come back to redeem them when time is accomplished. Russians and Turks, who are enemies by custom, both look to last things and have reason. The Third Rome tottered when Ivan the Terrible murdered his son and heir, and they said in Moscow how the reign of Antichrist was imminent when Dmitry, the last son, was murdered too. Or they said that Prince Dmitry hadn't died but was biding his time.

In Istanbul, the martyred demagogue bides his time, like the Last Roman Emperor asleep in an ivory chair in a castle hidden deep below ground. His face is shrouded, though, and his name remains a secret. Above ground, half the people of Istanbul live from hand to mouth in their "night-built" shanties. *Gedjehkondu* is the word for these houses built anyhow between dusk and dawn, and Turks who can manage this hold the land by right of possession. That is what they think until the powers that be disabuse them. Meanwhile they pin their hopes to the Once and Future King, and he rides a white horse on his nightly excursions to Eyup.

The mosque the Conqueror built fell down a long time ago but they have put up another, and the old hollowed-out plane trees still grow in its courtyard, inhabited by storks. Wheeling flights of pigeons darken the sky. In the outer courtyard they come to ground in their thousands, lured by the pilgrims who feed them grain and millet. This way station on the road to Asia is like the great square in Venice, or as it will be in years to come when the waters have risen and the spider holds the curtain in the church of St. Mark's. Graveyards surround the mosque, and the wooden shanties are trimmed with fretwork like the *izbas* where the peasants live outside Moscow. Above the village two small streams flow into the Horn, on the west Alibey Suyu and on the east Kagithane Suyu. These streams are common sewers and once were known as the Sweet Waters of Europe.

The most imposing mosque in Eyup is named for Zal Mahmut Pasha. This Zal was a king-killer, who executed the first-born of the emperor Suleiman. Later he did the same for the brother of Selim the Sot. Selim, being drunk, fell on his head and died. His son Murad, coming to the throne, had his younger brothers strangled. Amurath, the English called him, and they prided themselves on their difference. "This is the English, not the Turkish court," said Shakespeare's hero-king, Henry V. "Not Amurath an Amurath succeeds/But Harry Harry." In France, however, this Harry cut a wide swath. Shakespeare wrote about his wars, and Sinan built the mosque of Zal Mahmut Pasha.

From the *chayhane* or tea shop that overlooks the mosque, you can see down the Horn all the way to Stamboul. New housing tracts and factories hide the meadows between the hills where Stamboullus on holiday used to go for their *déjeuner sur l'herbe*. To a traveler from the West this bird's-eye view looks familiar, except for the minarets. There are more than a thousand of them as you look down, and if Moscow is or was the city of belfries, Istanbul is the city of spires.

But the view from on high, as when you look at Moscow from the Ferris wheel in Gorky Park, is the wrong view for Istanbul. In the terrifying city, everything is too vividly present to the senses. I am worn out by the beggars in the streets, the standing horde in the buses, the *odaji* or room-man who waits with Oriental patience in the bars and *lokantas* and wants to fetch and carry for a fee, the endless chaffering in the markets over things I don't need and don't want. At night, I creep back exhausted to my hotel. Dogs yowl all night long, the cry of the muezzin breaks in on my sleep, and from the balcony outside my room I see that chickens live with people in the apartment house over the way. Now I know why I hear a rooster at dawn in the middle of Istanbul.

This city smells of dissolution. Look closer, however, and you see life peering through the hollow eyes of death. The new life that burgeons here preys on its host. But it gives where it takes, and Istanbul is not a ruin and not a museum where a few vestigial glories are preserved under glass.

From time out of mind, the old city has been ploughed up and ploughed under. This makes Istanbul resemble Ravenna. The resemblance is apparent, dejecting, and partly real. Only partly, though, and Istanbul isn't like Ravenna where you check off the monuments and get back in your car, and it isn't for the long past that you come to this Holy City. Never mind the squalor and the tatterdemalion crowd, Istanbul shows best when you see it close up. This doesn't mean that what you are looking at is real like a movie or a view on a postcard.

Stamboul at first light, seen from the Galata side, is an "unreal city, full of dreams." The air is tangible, impregnated with drops of rain and viscous with black dust, and the pallid sun wrapped in smog looks like the moon. Coming out of the mist above the dark water, the apparition of Yeni Chami, the Queen Mother mosque, is not inert but alive. On the filthy air, it seems to be dancing. The domes and semidomes flow into each other like water, and the porticoed galleries elude the earth and its pull. From the *sherefes* or balconies that wind around the minarets, the muezzins are chanting their weird disharmonious call. They do this five times a day, and you needn't know, unless you want to, that this call to prayer is recorded.

All the great cities are fantastic or partly fabulous, cities of your own devising. Moscow is itself, brassy modern and the city of six hundred belfries, also "Socialist Land," an emblematic city reared by thought and existing only in the mind, and Constantinople is the "God-defended city," also a version of Erie, Pa. When you see it for the first time, you feel at home and your heart sinks. On the water's edge, however, I remember how Yeats saw this city with his mind's eye, "an incredible splendor like that which we see pass under our closed eyelids as we lie between sleep and waking, no representation of a living world but the dream of a somnambulist."

Rising over Yeni Chami, the hills of the city wear their headdress of palaces, mosques, and churches. They create the living skyline, more implausible than Venice seen from out in the lagoon or New York from the Narrows. This skyline is both real and imagined. In Moscow they saw it in the mind's eye, an exhilarating vision, and they wanted to embody it in their Third Rome. Someday, they said in Moscow, "the Russian race shall conquer all the Mohammedans and shall reign in the City of the Seven Hills." Constantinople is the City of the Seven Hills, built in the likeness of the First Rome.

The Byzantines who cultivated this likeness were the new men of their time. When their first emperor Constantine traced the boundaries of the city with his sword, he said he would go on "till He tarries Who goes before." Following Christ, they made a fresh start in Constantinople, and their city was a slate wiped clean.

However, they called themselves Romans. In their own minds they weren't Byzantine, and German scholars, who want us to say "Kaisar" for "Caesar," have created this identity for them. Though they spoke Greek, they called it Romaic. Their empire was Romania, and their capital the Second Rome. There were fourteen *rioni* or regions in old Rome, the same in Constantinople, and Galata, the thirteenth region across the Golden Horn, corresponded to Trastevere across the Tiber. The palace of the Caesars on the Palatine Hill overlooked the Circus Maximus, and in Constantinople the Hippodrome was their circus and they built the royal palace beside it. Five valleys divide the city, running athwartships from the Horn to the Sea of Marmara. Six hills flank these valleys, and though the buildings of the modern city soften their contours, if you look with one eye closed you can still see them all from Galata. The seventh hill stands apart, away to the southwest, the valley of the Lycus separating it from the bony ridge along the Horn.

There were seven hills in old Rome and in the Second Rome, and the fabulous city made a supreme fiction. It stood outside time and appealed to eternity. Muslims knew nothing of the eternal city but they hearkened to this appeal. When Mehmet II conquered Constantinople, he became the Sultan of Rum. His dominion was Rumelia.

On the First Hill, where Byzas the Megarian made his acropolis in 667 B.C., the Conqueror situated the Great Palace of the Osmanli Sultans. The Osmanlis are the Ottomans, and the Palace is Topkapi, meaning Cannon Gate. Once the walls on Seraglio Point shook with the cannon that fired the salute. For the sherbet and iced fruit of the sultan, they brought ice and snow from their Bithynian Mount Olympus. The odalisques in the seraglio ate young turkey, *gallo poulo,* raised on the Gallipoli peninsula. The chief black eunuch had the harem in his keeping. He was the Lord of the Girls. The soldiers who served him and protected the harem girls were Halberdiers-with-Tresses. These soldiers were shamefaced. From their tall hats, false tresses hung down and covered their eyes.

The *saray* or seraglio that gives the point its name is a luscious word for most tourists who come to Istanbul, and it also has its life in the mind. But "*saray*" means a harem only incidentally. In Ottoman usage, it stands for the whole complex of the imperial household. This is Topkapi Sarayi. You are lucky if you come here for the first time at night, when the floodlights pick it out and it shows to your senses like a rocket blazing over the sea.

In the outer gardens of the saray, Haghia Eirene, the Church of the Heavenly Peace, still holds its old place. You can see it from the Horn if you climb Galata Tower, and from that distance who will say that the Greek rite is no longer observed here. Close by on the First Hill is the Blue Mosque named for Sultan Ahmed. Spiky "English grass," green all year long, grows in the courtyard before the kitchens that serve the mosque. Across a pleasant park, planted with tulips and violas and making room for a small soccer field, is Sancta Sophia, the Church of the Heavenly Wisdom. Incredible unless you have seen it, said Procopius, who tells you how he saw it with his mind's eye, a great ship anchored among the neighboring houses.

High above the Horn in the heart of the modern city that was also the heart of Justinian's city stands the Suleimaniye. The vast dome and the four minarets that rise from the corners of the courtyard awake recognition in everyone who comes to Constantinople, the mosque of Suleiman speaking for this city the way St. Peter's speaks for Rome or St. Basil's in Red Square speaks for Moscow. Suleiman is Solomon. But the Turkish Solomon isn't like Justinian, looking over his shoulder, and his Suleimaniye is only first among equals.

Sinan made this mosque for the greatest of the sultans, and in the *turbes* in the gardens he and his patron are buried. Sinan is simply The Builder, *Mimar Bashi Sinan*. "If you want a monument, look around you." Suleiman is the Magnificent who reigned for forty-six years and died when Ivan the Terrible was reigning in Moscow. When the great king was a student they set him to read in Nizam al-Mulk's *Book of Government,* and he read in this book how "Paradise and sovereignty are never united." However, his chronicler wrote of Suleiman: "He subdued the world, established order and justice in his dominions, embellished all the countries which were vanquished with his arms, and was successful in all undertakings." This can hardly be true, but when I look at Stamboul I believe it.

From old times there has been a bridge at Eyup, and if you are coming from Yeshilkoy Airport and want to miss the city you can take the bypass here and head straight for the Bosphorus Bridge. Down stream is the modern crossing named for Ataturk, below this the crossing at Galata where the Golden Horn begins to lose itself in the Bosphorus and the Sea of Marmara. Before Ataturk Bridge existed, two English families lived on opposite shores, like Hero and Leander. One lived in Eminonu around the Stamboul end of Galata Bridge, the other in Galata itself. At night they played cards together, their own variety of whist. But they feared the crossing at Galata where robbers waited to pounce, and they traded engagements, deferring to each other. "Tomorrow," they said, "it's your night to bridge." This is how the card game got its name.

Blackened steel girders rise from steel pontoons. There is always a crowd of men in dingy hand-me-down suits flowing over Galata Bridge. On the quays between it and Ataturk Bridge are the open-air markets. They sell fruit and vegetables, plastic bowls, plastic pocket combs, and throwaway pens and lighters. Sea bass is brought here from the Black Sea. At the water's edge, tiny silver fish are set out for sale on newspapers and trays. Also they sell turbot, swordfish, and red mullet, and if you like caviar you will like the mullet roe even better. The best buy is striped tunny or *lâkerda*, boned and soaked in salt. Flat-bottomed *kayiks* bring it inshore from the fishing boats out in the water.

Lined up along the shore, the *kayiks* wait for business. Some are motor-driven but most are oared, and the men who pull the oars are said to bark like dogs. "Now and then between times," says Purchas the old traveler, "many of them say Bow, bow-wow, bow, bow-wow etc., and then pull some few strokes and tut again." The wide beam of the *kayik* tapers in and turns upwards at stem and stern like the crescent of Islam.

Galata Bridge is ugly and visibly there to the eye. But it has another and impalpable side, and when you walk across the bridge you feel how you are leaving the present for the past or crossing from one world to another. Ataturk, who wanted to reverse this direction, abolished the sultanate when he made his Republic in 1923, and he abolished the caliphate too. This Muslim version of the papacy was only a "tumor of the Middle Ages." Like Peter the Great dispensing with the patriarchate, he cut it away. They woke the last caliph at Dolmabahche Palace in the middle of the night, and by 5:00 a.m. they had him and the women of his seraglio out of Turkey. In this way, said one of them, they blew up the bridges attaching Turkey to the Middle Ages.

The crossing at Galata stands for all these bridges. Muslims who preferred the past and rejected the present disputed this crossing. When Mahmud II, the same westernizing sultan who finished off the Janissaries, rode over Galata Bridge, a dervish seized his bridle and wouldn't let him proceed. He said that the sultan was out to ruin Islam, and perhaps the dervish who took such liberties was mad. He disclaimed this, however. If he spoke the truth, he said, Allah would reward him with a martyr's crown. "Very well," said Sultan Mahmud, "Give the good man his crown," and they hanged the dervish from Galata Bridge.

This was in the 1820s. In the spring of 1909, the editor of a liberal paper was murdered at night as he crossed Galata Bridge. Revulsion was great in Constantinople, and the Young Turks who wanted Turkey to pull itself together understood how this was their chance. They seized the city and deposed the sultan, Abdul Hamid, "the Damned." They sent him into exile with his favorite cat, and in his place they installed a puppet sultan. They too hanged their "reactionary" opponents on Galata Bridge.

These confrontations between the past and present are still vivid in a comic-opera kind of way, but the point they make is merely bookish, as when you read about the westernizing of Turkey or "the rise of the middle class." The crowd on Galata Bridge is "Eastern," and perhaps it looks backward or perhaps it looks nowhere at all. But it isn't "reactionary," and it isn't just like that dispirited crowd imagined by T. S. Eliot flowing over London Bridge. "I had not thought death had undone so many." In the city on the Horn, death is as near as tomorrow. Meanwhile, the crowd on Galata Bridge explodes with vitality. It isn't depressing, it buoys you up, and looking at this standing horde you feel how the East is alive.

WHIRLING DERVISH BY THE HORN

From the other side of the glass doors the lobby of the Pera Palas is all striated marble. The marble is mock-marble, and the old hotel is a dowager who has seen better days but keeps up the appearances. Outside the doors, life is sound and fury and you know what it signifies. Inside, they have the wit to deny this. The inner lobby is an atrium, rising two stories high. In the center, the facets of an ancient chandelier pick up the electric light from the sconces in the wall. Around the chandelier runs a little arcade, like the mezzanine floor in a theater. Antique chairs and settles, some upholstered in fading plush, are backed against the revetments. In the lift is a bench with plumped-up cushions. The gates that open on the lift are done in black and silver filigree, and the vest the operator wears is stiffened with buckram and sewn with gold thread.

The operator is Oguz, pronounced "O-ouze," and hardly into his teens. He has a wistful smile and a speculative look. I think he is speculating what life must be like where I come from. He comes from Uskudar, and every morning at dawn he takes the ferry across the water, then a bus from the *iskele*. He has to change for a second bus at Taksim. Afternoons, he goes to school where he is studying English, and he likes to hone his daily lesson on me. "I am all day long at your service," he says. This is not strictly true but he would like it to be true. When I thank him he answers formally, "Not at all."

To the right of the ornate staircase that winds around the lift, French doors disclose the dining room. Cornucopias spill their riches in the ceiling and on the walls, and most of the time this cavernous place is half empty. Coming down in the morning, I meet the buyers and sellers and the scattering of tourists who can't afford the Etap, let alone the Hilton. We breakfast on black olives, feta cheese, and coarse bread. The strong black tea is diluted with boiling hot water. They go easy on the water, wanting to fortify us for the hard day ahead. A three-piece band plays for dinner, a violin, a bass fiddle, and an accordion. The men in the band wear tuxedos, and at least once a night they play "La Vie en Rose." They do this every night except Wednesdays, when the Rotary Kulubu meets here.

The Pera Palas is a last survivor of the old imperial days of Abdul Hamid II, and travelers who disembarked from the Orient Express used to put up at this hotel. They came into Sirkeji Station on the other side of the Horn. Outside the station, the locomotive that pulled the train is on permanent display. It is like a toy choo-choo with shiny brass fittings, and you wonder how it got the job done. The barn of a bar is called The Orient Express. Under glass on the wall, a framed newspaper clipping tells how many years ago Agatha Christie ran away from England and hid out in the hotel. No one knows why she did this, and that is part of her mystery.

Ataturk in a wing collar confronts you in the lobby, also in the dining room, and you see his portrait worked in crewel as you enter the bar. For a time in the First World War he lived in the hotel, but it is hard to imagine him taking his ease among these Oriental-cum-Italianate splendors. The tired but manful man is trudging up a hill. No name is lettered beneath his portrait to say who this is, only the dates 1881–1938, not much of a life if measured in years. He packed his brief life with drums and cannon. "No, we will not rest," he said, "we will kill each other." This was after they had finished killing Greeks. "When the struggle ends it will be dull; we must find some other excitement."

The restless man lacked convictions, a contemporary said. "He adopted now one thing and now another with the same vehemence and energy, no matter how contradictory they were." So he was opportunistic, like all the great men. "*On s'engage, puis on voit,*" Napoleon said. But Ataturk had his polestar, and this was rational behavior. He made a cult of progress that wasn't linear but deliberate, rejecting the *ulemas* and their backward-looking cult of Islam. The holy men were always talking, and he couldn't see why. They circled around the truth where he was in a hurry and wanted to cut the Gordian knot.

At three in the afternoon it is still too early for cocktails, but in a recessed alcove two bearded men are drinking tea and going at each other in hoarse, conspiratorial voices. They are survivors too, like the Pera Palas Hotel, and their passionate back-and-forth evokes the city of the Byzantines where metaphysics was the breath of life and men argued abstruse questions at the drop of a hat. These two men wear dark suits pinched and corded at the shoulders. One is old and his scruffy beard is gray, the other almost old. Call them Photius and Gennadius, two Byzantine sages come from the fire. Both like to split hairs. Graybeard wants to know if the Holy Spirit proceeds from the Father and also the Son, or from the Father alone through the Son. Greek Catholics and Roman Catholics used to argue this question, and they made it a matter of life and death. Gibbon, when he canvassed the question in his history, decided that Greeks and Romans were absurd. All that to-do about prepositions.

Photius and Gennadius aren't alone in the bar, and to their

annoyance they know this. If looks could kill, they would be the death of Carstairs. Wavy blond hair curls over his ears. He wears a double-vented hacking jacket, velvet trousers, blue suede shoes, and is playing "Here Comes the Sun" on the upright piano. Carstairs lives above me on the fourth floor of the hotel. The steam in the radiators doesn't get up there that often. This means cold baths, and rooms above the third floor are cheaper than other rooms. That is the only difference between them. "There is no hot water," I tell the clerk at the front desk. He is an amiable man with a placatory smile. "Run water four, five minutes," he says. I stick to my guns. "You run water already?" he asks me. I nod and we leave it at that.

Carstairs pays by the week, and this shaves a little more off the room rate. He doesn't know how much longer he will stay here, however. It depends on what is going in the markets and bazaars. A buyer and always hoping, he hopes to get something for nothing. This is what he means by carrying pigs to market. He roams the spice bazaar in back of Yeni Chami, and the vaulted shops and wormy passageways beneath the mosque of Mustafa III. The vine-covered courtyard near the Bayazit mosque is a favorite haunt of his. Secondhand booksellers congregate there, and he picks through the stalls and barrows, looking for pornography. "Turkish delights," he calls this.

Back home in London, Carstairs sells what he buys and scrapes a living on the difference. "You might call it a living," he says, underlining the pronoun. He has a shrewd idea that the Turk, a generic figure, is out to skin him alive. Between him and this figure, a state of war exists. Carstairs gives the devil his due, though. "The Turk is all right," he says, "but you want to remember not to bend over."

The boutiques on Carnaby Street are delighted with Carstairs and glad to take what he can get them. Modish jewelry sells like hotcakes on Carnaby Street, and he keeps an eye peeled for the signs of the zodiac in silver or bronze. His sign is Cancer the Crab.

The crab, being sea-born, is sacred to Venus, he tells me. Carstairs is venereal, also "carapaceous." Like the crab, he has a thick skin.

Leather goods are his specialty, three-quarter-length coats for ladies and gents, also military jackets that cinch at the waist like Eisenhower jackets. This is à la mode. He buys bronze services for coffee, fake faience tiles advertised as from Iznik, Turkish water pipes for hash, and meerschaum pipes carved in the likeness of harem girls and houris. Once at least on each trip out, he picks up a rental car on Tarlabashi Caddesi and drives into Anatolia. In provincial towns like Bursa, embroidered Turkish towels and terrycloth bathrobes go for a song. Carpets and kilims are simply money in the bank and he knows what to look for, but just at this time he doesn't have the cash in pocket. Perhaps I would like to take a flyer?

Outside the hotel we hail a passing *dolmush*, and for thirty-five Turkish lire, about twenty-eight cents, it brings us over Galata Bridge to Stamboul. *Dolmasi* is stuffed, as in stuffed mussels, *midye dolmasi*. These shared taxis don't bely their name. Like the city buses they travel fixed routes. Your fellow travelers may be sitting in your lap but you don't address them and you don't tip the driver. "*Dour*" says Carstairs, an imperative verb, and the driver stops the cab and lets us out in Bayazit Square.

After the '60 coup, Bayazit Square became Hurriyet Meydani, Freedom Square. Skeptics to their fingertips, Turks still call it Bayazit. This shambling place is named for the Conqueror's son, an accommodating man. When the Catholic King Ferdinand and Queen Isabella expelled the Jews from Spain, he welcomed them in Constantinople. Byzantines, like Muslims, had this knack of accommodating. The men of the Fourth Crusade, mistaking it for weakness, called them "wretched little Greeks." Their city was the Oecumene, meaning the world, and in the ecumenical city they accommodated Jews, Armenians, Roman Catholics, and Muslims. Being strong, they found it easy to defer. Justinian their great emperor deferred to "faultless antiquity" when he made his legal code, and Greeks in Constantinople took their law from the First Rome, their religion from Palestine, and their ciphering from Arabs. Some of their ceremonies came from Persia, and some of these trappings were Chinese.

My guidebook proposes that Bayazit Square is the center of Stamboul. But Stamboul is all circumference and the center is everywhere and nowhere. In Byzantine times when this was the Forum Tauri, a triumphal arch stood in the square, also a column adorned with reliefs like the Trajan Column in Rome. The reliefs celebrated the victories of the Emperor Theodosius. In the fourth century, he kept the Goths at bay. Officials like Roman *lictors* accompanied the sultan on his visits to Bayazit Square. They held up straws, a reminiscence of the *fasces* that went before the Roman consul. "Nay," said Lord Bryce in his stately history, "the intruding Ottoman himself, different in faith as well as in blood, long ago declared himself the representative of the Eastern Caesars, whose dominion he extinguished."

Istanbul gives antiquities the back of its hand but nothing gets wasted, and fragments of the Roman column are built into the foundation of the *hamam* or public bath. The soldiers in these fragments are still wearing their greaves and breastplates, but some of them are marching on their heads.

At the university, a friend of mine who doubles as a tour guide says that over the centuries since Constantine's time, the ground level of Istanbul has risen sixteen and a half feet. This is the height of three men standing on each other's shoulders. The men are Roman, Byzantine, and Turk. Under their feet, the past isn't layers of broken pottery but makes a lively presence. The Nika rebels who died in the Hippodrome not far away were buried where they fell, and their bones are still down there under the racecourse. Dry bones quicken in this city, Stamboullus can tell you.

On Whitsun Monday in 1453, Mehmet II gave the city to his

troops. "I give it over for you to pillage," he said, "to seize its incalculable treasures of men, women and boys." When the orgy was over, he made his triumphal entry, riding a white horse without reins. After the First World War, a French general with a flair for the dramatic did the same. There were no reins on the horse when General d'Espérey entered Constantinople. He thought he was laying the Conqueror's ghost.

We take tea and a plate of the Greek pastry they call *kurabiyes* in the outdoor teahouse beside the Bayazit mosque. Pretty girls wearing lipstick and young men in alpaca suits are drinking tea and smoking cigarets at the adjoining tables. Warmed by the company, Carstairs spreads himself. This jacket of his is like a bandolier and hung with pouches and pockets. From one of these pockets he selects an evil-smelling cigar. When Bayazit ruled the roost in Constantinople, smoking was taboo, and for a long time after this they were very severe on "the fetid and nauseating smoke of tobacco." However, the dikes went down, and in the seventeenth century an unhappy traveler has them all "puff-puffing in each other's faces and eyes." He says "they made the streets and markets stink." This is what Carstairs is doing. Summoning the waiter, he orders up vodka. You can't get vodka in a teahouse, but the omnipresent *odaji* scurries off and returns with a bottle. "A Thousand Bulls," they call it. Squeezing lemon in the vodka, Carstairs rolls it around on his tongue. "I'm all right, Jack."

The *chinar*, a giant plane tree, shields us from the sun. This is the Tree of Idleness. Above the tree are the minarets and the dome of the mosque. The minaret is a phallus, Carstairs explains, and he has an idea to suit for the dome. He likes to say what things mean, and everything boils down to its meaning. On the ground beneath the plane tree the *odaji* sits cross-legged, his hands folded on his crotch. He is looking straight ahead with his staring eyes like a blind man's. What he sees is mysterious. The Turk is pre-rational, says Carstairs puff-puffing, still back there grubbing for acorns.

In the square, the shoeshine boys are drumming up trade. They make a beeline for our table. Not all of these *boyajis* are boys. "I am hungry, sir," says one of them, but my shoes are shined already and I wave him away. Conscience nags at me, though, and he sees this. "I am sorry, sir," he says.

Taxis cruise by on the lookout for fares, horses clop past the *hamam*, and in one horse-drawn vehicle the driver stands erect and flicks the reins smartly. He is a charioteer from the time of Justinian, and in the Hippodrome the Blues and Greens are laying bets on the races. All hell will break loose if they don't like the outcome, and for these unruly Byzantines insurrection was always just around the corner. It isn't so long ago that they burned down old Sancta Sophia.

Gladiators in the Hippodrome hunted lions and leopards, and St. John Chrysostom called this place the Satanodrome. When the chariots were racing, the emperor came to his "Kathisma." This was the royal box, and below it in the northeast corner stood the four bronze horses of Lysippus. In 1204 the Crusaders sacked the city and took these horses away, and now they stand in Venice above the portal of St. Mark's. The packed earth of the racecourse ran for sixteen hundred feet. The Blue Mosque covers part of it, a public garden taking the rest. There are pollarded acacias on either side of the park, and along the *spina* or central line an obelisk and two broken columns. The classical arcade that used to ring the outer wall was pulled down four hundred years ago, and the masonry went into new buildings. On the serpent column, the serpents have lost their heads.

In the Hippodrome, the rival demarchs who led their demes or factions met to argue theology and the price of bread. *Demos* is "people." The Greens were lower-class people, also Monophysite, and the Blues were middle-class and Orthodox or true-blue. They sat to the emperor's right on the shady side of the arena, the Greens on his left in the sun. Blues and Greens were a scandal in Constantinople, always at each other's throats like Montagues and

Capulets, but their quarreling was lucky for the state. When they made common cause, the state tottered. "Nika" means "conquer," and in 532 the Nika rebels shook Justinian's throne.

On the steps of the mosque, street vendors are hawking prayer socks, cheap ties, and ballpoint pens. Against the bottom step a young man sits patiently, expecting his due. One of his trouser legs has collapsed below the thigh. His remaining leg, uncovered, shows as darkly mottled. It swells to a club with only the faintest indentation for toes, and he stretches it out for everyone to see. Beside him are his crutches and his cloth cap, upside down. This is for coins.

The muezzin or his tape recorder is calling to prayer from the minarets of the mosque. His chanting is tuneless and he likes it that way. In musical terms, he likes the monophonic line where the Word is unadorned and naked. Polyphony is his abhorrence. He thinks that if you clothe the Word in this muddy vesture of ours, you forfeit your meaning. In terms of theology, he is a Monophysite, like Coptic Christians in Egypt and some Orthodox Christians. The God he calls Allah has ninety-nine names but no lineaments or gender, and Allah doesn't wear a long beard.

After the Great Schism, Greek Orthodox Christians at the Council of Florence tried to patch up their quarrel with Rome. This was in 1439. But Latins liked to say that "the blessed see God," and Greeks couldn't abide this. Muslims can't abide it either. Their God is disembodied, all capital letters like these suras from the Koran the muezzin is intoning. "Praise belongs to God, the Lord of All Being, the All-Merciful, the All-Compassionate, the Master of the Day of Doom." Carstairs puts on his Chinese-water-torture face. "Sounds like Tarzan."

The world according to Carstairs resembles an old map, where "Terra Incognita" is lettered alarmingly at the edge of the map and the four puffing winds are bursting their cheeks in the corners. Land's end on this map is somewhere east of Calais. He pronounces this "Calis," and says that after you cross the Channel it is all a bloody ballsup. You are off the map altogether, after Bari. The "wily Greek, avaricious and plausible," lives out there. Carstairs, who speaks of "Greeks and Europeans," means to distinguish between them.

"*Charshi*" is "bazaar" and "*kapali*" is "covered." We enter the labyrinth from the Street of the Janissaries at the bottom of Bayazit Square. Olfactory-wise, says Carstairs, they would do better if they took off the roof. But the roof defines this enclave that is a city to itself. You can go to school in the Covered Bazaar, make your ablutions in the fountain or *shadirvan*, eat dinner, take tea, do your banking, use the toilet, or pray in the mosque. There is even a *turbe*, and someone is buried here too. If the little streets all ran in one direction they would run for forty miles. The four thousand shops and ateliers are caves and jars in the *Arabian Nights*. On the lids of the jars P. T. Barnum is sitting, cross-legged, sloe-eyed, and Turkish. *Mashallah*, and God save me from the evil eye.

"Hello, rich man. You want nice Turkish carpet?" I wouldn't buy the Brooklyn Bridge, not here in Istanbul. The Bosphorus Bridge is another matter, though, and I put my hands in my pockets and don't look right or left. This does little good. On either side of the long central colonnade, they are making exceptions in my favor. They want to sell me a wedding gown, matched alabaster vases, beaten metal trays, candelabra, brocaded vests, a tea urn, a soccer ball, an umbrella. Under my nose, a one-eyed Smyrna merchant is holding up black coral prayer beads. He jingles pendants and bracelets or proffers a tray of rings and cheap niello lockets. The incised surface is filled with black metallic alloy, and I have read somewhere that they made these lockets in Justinian's city. The more things change, the more they remain the same. I don't want a locket.

In the Covered Bazaar the goldsmiths have their street, also the haberdashers, the shoemakers, the ironmongers, and I narrowly avert the purchase of a cast-iron brazier. Selim the Grim has got hold of my elbow. In his right hand is a wicked scimitar. I cringe and he takes notice. He mistakes my meaning, though. If not a scimitar, then perhaps a Roman coin authenticated to the time of Septimius Severus, or a mess of potsherds from the windy plains of Troy. His shop is just around the corner.

Carstairs says that the Turk will sell you a hair from the beard of the Prophet. But Kapali Charshi isn't all Wardour Street where they doctor cheap furniture to look like Queen Anne and unwary Londoners take it for the real McCoy. If I want the real McCoy, I will find it in the Old Bedesten. The great domed hall in the heart of the bazaar is surrounded by gates. Having something to lose, they lock these gates at night. Over the Gate of the Goldsmiths a single-headed eagle spreads its wings in bas-relief. The old Turkish traveler Evliya Chelebi says what this emblem means. "Gain and trade are like a wild bird," according to Chelebi in his book of travels. If you tame the wild bird, it will lay golden eggs. On trays of brushed velvet, the antique jewelry sparkles demurely. The velvet nap is thick and soft, the jewelry isn't rhinestones, and these merchants can see at once that we are men of taste. Nothing here is going for a song.

Off the street of the Pearl Merchants, the third turning on our right leads into the New Bedesten, "new" as in four hundred years old. The twenty brick domes are carried on massive piers, and under the domes they are auctioning carpets and kilims. Carstairs calls for my wallet and extracts what he needs. He says I am casting my bread on the waters. The kilims are coarse-fibered, primitive but not crude, and Westerners like to hang them on the walls. The woven figures in the kilims make their meaning apparent but don't labor the meaning. Stick figures suggest a camel and his keeper, palm trees, a goat, a donkey, tent dwellings where the nomads live. The artisans who created these figures tolerated the world without caring very much to depict it.

On the floor the Turkish carpets are heaped up carelessly like bundles of rags, and in the half light of late afternoon they flicker like swamp light. There are carpets from Antalya down by the sea, and some from Kars far away to the east and north near the Soviet border. The design, repeating itself in a carpet from Kayseri, makes a *saf* or series. I see a *mihrab* or prayer niche in the *kible* wall of the mosque, where the imam kneels in prayer. But the "figure in the carpet" is my own idea.

The diamond-shaped lozenges in these carpets from Konya are called "Turkish triangles," Carstairs informs me. Running together, they simulate an arcade of ogival arches. Muslim architects like Sinan preferred these pointed arches. Sometimes the designer doesn't finish his design and the arches break off at the top. The designer isn't clumsy but his grasp exceeds his reach. Orange-red and purple flowers dyed with indigo and madder are blooming in the arcade. These flowers are stylized, substantial but not real, like the golden bird that sang in Byzantium. They look away from nature to art.

In this artificial world beneath the domes of the Bedesten, imitation of the natural world is under ban. They allow the arabesque, where floral patterns intermingle with geometric forms. At carnality they draw the line, and from their carpets all grossness has been purged. What looks like a turban in a carpet from Ortakoy might be an aorta, an artichoke, a kiosk, and is mostly unlocalized form. This form glows like fire and is as cold as ice. It shows itself in patterns of crystals and snowflakes. The figures in the carpet are identical and take hands like paper dolls. They march across the carpet but their progress is only linear, and they follow one another not because they have to but only because they do. Meaning is elusive, and Turks don't rack their brains to divulge it. They are men of Islam, where the word means resignation to the will of God.

Being ignorant of last things, they never made a Summa in Constantinople, before or after the Conquest. Turks and Byzantines have a lot in common. But the mind needn't rust if you are ignorant this way, and the carpet makers aren't throwing up their hands. They make chromatic melodies and geometric phrases, and the figure in the carpet leaves off where the selvage begins. If it weren't for the selvage, this figure would repeat itself forever.

Carstairs is cheapening a carpet from Anadolu and says it was loomed by machine. He knows better than this and they know that he knows. So the transaction gets done. *Yastik* is their word for the Anadolu carpets they use for pillows and pads. The serrated border is white like frozen fire and blue and white like their Turkish Mount Olympus. These figures of speech are only a convention of discourse, however.

Kilims, carpets, and churches have a common term, abstraction. Byzantines like Muslims held the world at arm's length. In Sancta Sophia as it used to be, the weightless figures on the walls spurned the world and looked beyond it with their cataleptic eyes. The Great Church is named for the Heavenly Wisdom. In Moscow and Rome they named their churches for Mary, a carnal woman, or they looked in the calendar of saints. Byzantines, when the idol-smashing fit was on them, set the spirit against the flesh. One of their patriarchs in Constantinople wouldn't allow that Mary was the Mother of God. This Nestorius was saying that there is no god but God, and the blessed don't see Him. But that is only half the story.

West of the Golden Horn in a dusty pocket beside the walls is the monastery church called St. Savior in Chora, and Turks know it as Kariye Chami. "Chora" means "in the country." When the city was young this church lay outside the walls, like St. Germain-des-Près in Paris or the London church of St. Martin's in the Fields. The inscription over the door that leads to the inner narthex promotes another meaning, however. "Jesus Christ," reads the inscription, "the Country of the Living." That is where you dwell if you walk before the Lord. The Psalmist says this, and the name of the Chora church puns on his saying. The mosaics in the narthex elucidate it for you, and they offer a guide to the Country of the Living.

This guide is peculiar, like the map of a labyrinth where the streets are dead-ended or return on themselves and your destination isn't obvious but your progress along the way seems important. To Christ on His throne, Theodore the donor presents a model of the church. The donor isn't a stick figure but wears an outrageous turban like a turbaned Turk. His sad eyes and the drooping mustache come from the East. However, his wrinkled eyebrows are Western and perplexed. The square brush of beard is stitched or glued to his chin. This bearded man is like a cartoon or a figure in a tapestry. But the brown curls tumble freely on the nape of his neck, making him lively or real. The designs on his gown have a life of their own, where the gold facing of the gown assimilates the kneeling figure to the gold mosaic background. He is color and mass, at the same time a tangible presence. The Pantocrator is Himself, noumenal or spooky, also real or incarnate. They show him as an infant, "Mewling and puking in his mother's arms." These workers in mosaic are full of anecdotage, the Scriptural story being too terse for them. Joseph in the first bay tears a passion to tatters. Having been away from home, he has come back to find his wife pregnant. It takes an angel of the Lord to convince this angry husband that he isn't a cuckold like a lot of other men.

The Country of the Living makes room for the dead, and mosaics on the domes remember the ancestors of Christ. In a side chapel vivid frescoes evoke the Worm. The damned are roasting in the Unquenchable Fire. But these Byzantine artists aren't using their colors to imitate the natural world. They are Expressionists, though hardly freewheeling, and in the school they belong to, Christ makes a pattern of blue and cherry red, where blue and yellow mean St. Peter and blue and claret red mean St. Paul. Still Christ and His disciples are recognizably themselves, and the linework declares the figure in the carpet. This figure is homely. On a soffit in the narthex, Mary, God's Mother, is only six months old but already she takes her first seven steps.

A thousand years separates the building of Sancta Sophia and the Suleimaniye. The church and mosque are a mile apart, one on the First Hill, one on the Third. From Sancta Sophia the cross is long gone, but the dome of the Suleimaniye is still topped by the *alem*, a bronze finial shaped like the crescent. The immortal antagonists make a composition. Rising like twin peaks, they send their signals to each other.

In the time of the Fourth Crusade, a Frankish chronicler wanted to level this city. He said Constantinople was "polluted by new mosques which its perfidious emperor allowed to be built." The emperor allowed this "to strengthen the league with the Turks." That was also Dandalo's idea. He was the Venetian doge who led the Crusaders, and he wanted an excuse. When he died a year later they buried him in the south gallery of Sancta Sophia. You can still see his name carved in Latin letters on the lid of the sarcophagus. HENRICUS DANDALO. The lid is broken, however. When they retook their city, Byzantines opened up the sarcophagus and threw the old man's bones to the dogs. A league between Greeks and Turks doesn't seem likely, but it lasted a long time. The parties to it were skeptics, denoting men who survive. They had their nice distinctions but didn't speak "from the chair" and their pronouncements weren't written in stone.

Sancta Sophia looks to the past, like a Roman basilica. But the flat roof has aspired and turned into a dome and two semidomes on the east and west. Columns running north and south divide the interior into three parts. Procopius, looking at this double colonnade, saw a line of dancers in a chorus. Separating the aisles from the nave, the columns are like those Roman termini or boundary gods that distinguished *meum* and *tuum*. Their capitals, decorated with palm leaves and acanthus, are surmounted by galleries, as wide as the aisles. Once upon a time, the vaulting over the galleries was crowded with mosaics. Seraphim looked down from the hollowed-out pendentives that meet at the dome. Their wings were peacock feathers. Scrolls of leaves and flowers blossomed in the pendentives, and birds perched on twigs among the leaves.

Like the walls and pavements, the columns are faced with rosy-red stone or the soft white marble from the island of Proconnesus, nearby in the Sea of Marmara. Where they used porphyry, the stone is flecked with silver crystals. The onyx stone is translucent like an alabaster vase. The builders of Justinian, opening a book, sawed the marble slabs in two. The book is full of designs, blood red, stark white like milk, crocus yellow. Though the colors have faded, if you work on your imagination you see a meadow decked with flowers in the revetments that cover the walls.

The nave by itself makes an enormous oval, and the aisles enclose the oval in a square. In the track of a ghostly procession, you follow the nave to the apse wall in the east. This is where the sun rises and the altar used to stand. Before the altar screen the tapered lamps were like trees. On the porphyry panels, stylized dolphins with foliate tails swam in an artificial sea. The red curtains around the altar showed Christ between Peter and Paul. A man of letters in Justinian's time remembered this figure woven in the curtains. His right hand admonished you as He preached the Word of Life, and in His left hand He carried a book. In this Book of the Divine Message, you could read what Christ accomplished "when His foot was on earth."

At the western end of the church is the vestibule or narthex. Through the nine doors, the people entered the nave. A lot of people have passed through here, and the marble thresholds are worn to concavities. They call the central door the Imperial Gate, and the door frame, they say, was made of wood from Noah's Ark. Above this door, Christ the Pantocrator sits on His throne.

"Peace be with you," He is saying, "I am the Light of the World."

Four great arches hold the dome. Beneath them, boxing the compass, are four irregular piers of ashlar stone bound together with lead. So the dome is a circle that sits on a square. At the base of the circle, the light comes in through little clerestories. They spring the dome from its foundation. It seemed to float on air, Procopius said, suspended by a golden chain from heaven. Michaelangelo's dome for St. Peter's is different, and you don't see it when you walk up the nave. It takes you unawares, and maybe this is a little tricky. When you enter Sancta Sophia, the dome is on you at once, a sustaining presence. The dome is a house or "domicile" where earth and heaven are fused. For more than nine hundred years, a Christian community lived here.

Then they turned the church into a mosque, tacking on minarets at the corners. This resembles the Suleimaniye where the four minarets thrust upwards, balancing the downward fall of the domes. The minarets are four "because" Suleiman was the fourth sultan to rule in Constantinople. Ten *sherefes* or prayer balconies encircle the minarets, Suleiman being the tenth sultan of the Ottoman line. That is how Ottomans made sense of the world. Christians in the older time were like this. They had their Holy Ghost come down to the Apostles fifty days after Christ rose from the dead. Noah's Ark, someone told them, was fifty cubits in breadth and it rode out the Flood and restored us.

At the southwest corner of Sancta Sophia on the site of the old baptistery Justinian built, the Ottoman conquerors made a *turbe*. Turks are buried in the *turbe* where Byzantines were christened. When Murad III died in 1595, his *turbe* wasn't ready, so they put the coffin beneath a tent in the garden. During the night, this coffin was joined by nineteen others. They held the surviving sons of the sultan, all but the first son, Mehmet III. Fifty years later, Turks buried their crazy sultan Ibrahim here. He liked to hide behind the latticed windows of the Parade Pavilion near the outer wall of Topkapi and pick off passersby with his crossbow. In this city snow falls in January, but a cherry tree is growing beside the smallest gray dome of the *turbe*, and even in cold weather it bears.

Ataturk, who didn't like mosques, didn't like churches either, and in 1935 Sancta Sophia became a state museum. Tourists gather in the narthex, and some of them are Arabs or Turks who live near Arab lands. Their women are dressed in black with shawls over their heads like the black wimples Catholic nuns used to wear. Both women and men wear baggy trousers. Sometimes a tour bus from the American Express in the Hilton Hotel rolls up before the mosque that used to be a church and is now a museum. It parks on the site of the old arcaded courtyard. Cameras are unlimbered and the tourists look in their Fodors. Then they go away, and in the kiosk beside the ramp that leads to the women's gallery the ticket taker shuts up shop and catnaps with his head on the table. A metal globe with a stopcock and an incandescent filament stands on the table, and the filament throws shadows and the butane fuel in the globe hisses softly.

If these tourists have sailed the seas and come to Sancta Sophia at the bidding of William Butler Yeats, they will likely be in for a letdown. In the nineteenth century the Fossati brothers, unlucky restorers, were brought over from Italy. Around the interior at the level of the galleries they hung eight huge medallions. These *levhas*, as they call them, are written over with gold calligraphy on a green ground. The calligraphy bears witness to the holy names of Islam, Allah, Mohammed, the first caliphs and imams. Like a bucket of eels, says Carstairs, a scornful witness. The wiggling inscriptions make a weird setoff to the apse mosaic, also restored. Slogans mock the Real Presence on the apsidal wall, where the Virgin holds the Christ Child on her knees.

Not much of the Real Presence is left in Sancta Sophia. The Great Church is like a theater where the people have all gone home. Justinian and Theodora, believing in the cloud of witnesses and the reality of the communion of saints, filled the church with mosaics. In the eighth and ninth centuries, the Iconoclastic emperors took them away. One of these emperors was called Copronymus. He soiled his baptismal water, and like an Arab he shunned the face of God. He said how the mosaics were "not worthy of us," being "made by human hands." The divine nature was seamless, and the makers of images patched it with our muddy vesture of decay.

In the ninth century the lovers of icons came back to the city, and every year on March 11 the Greek Church celebrates the triumph of these Iconodules. But six centuries later the Muslim conquerors of Constantinople, taking no pleasure in the representation of men and women and living things, whitewashed the images of God and His saints. I count half a dozen that remain.

Photius the Primate unveiled the apse mosaic on Easter Sunday in 867. Then, having broken the power of the idol smashers, he pitched into his famous quarrel with Rome. Latins used unleavened bread for their communion wafer, but he wanted his bread leavened. He said the Word was made Flesh, and the yeast in the leaven symbolized the human nature of Christ. Also he said that Latins tampered with the Creed. Like the Manicheans they divided God in two, or like the Neoplatonists they let us in for a ladder of heavenly Beings. Some essence you couldn't fathom created Father, Son, and Holy Ghost. Latins, Photius thought, were polytheistic. He thought like the East and stood against the proliferating of gods.

This quarrel with the Roman Church waned and flared up again, and finally they couldn't mend it. So Photius the hairsplitter bears a part in destroying the ecumenical communion. In his history of the Great Schism, Runciman says how every pious Christian must hope for the day when the Church of Christ will be united and whole. It is hard to quarrel with this, but in Sancta Sophia I find myself picking a quarrel. Some nice distinctions seem worth hanging on to, and the sacred art of Byzantium lives in detail.

Sancta Sophia shares the First Hill with Topkapi Palace. In the outer gardens of the Saray, the narrow road leads downhill from the Gate of the Watchmen of the Girls. This road is lined with sarcophagi, toppled columns and capitals. The capitals are branches that grow from the trunk of a tree. Set back from the road on the western slope of the old acropolis is their Archaeological Museum. The museum is chock-full of statues, one of them remembering the charioteer Porphyrios and his victories in the Hippodrome. The gravestones from Galata date from the Black Death. On a stele from the grave of Kefalo, this famous comic actor is playing a part. The part is indecorous, and his testicles dangle between his bow legs.

In a room on the ground floor the attendant warms his hands over the electric fire. The statue of the Ephebe wears a stone cloak. This boy is in his late teens. An athlete, he is resting after sport, says the inscription on the pedestal. He lived in Tralles, southeast of ancient Smyrna. Izmir, they call it now. Anthemius the architect, who built Sancta Sophia, came from this place, and both the boy and the architect died ages ago. The young Greek stands with his head down, a faint smile on his lips, and the lips are just parted. His legs are crossed in repose. You can see where he has folded his arms beneath the cloak. The hair is astonishing, as crisp as today. From the front his ears are flattened, but walk around him and they seem to protrude.

"God be praised!" said Photius, who had his hands on all the ropes. "The Russians have received a bishop and show a lively zeal for Christian worship." This was thanks to his friend Cyril, who ran the library in Sancta Sophia until he heeded the injunction to go out on the roads. He brought religion to the Slavs, and where they couldn't read or write he gave them an alphabet. When Gogol wrote *Dead Souls* and Pushkin wrote his "Bronze Horseman," they used the Cyrillic alphabet. This wasn't inevitable, and Cyrillic, being a vernacular tongue, might have gone the way of the dodo. The Pope in Rome said that Russians oughtn't to use it. The vernacular, sowing confusion, jeopardized the ecumenical thing. He told them to use Latin when they celebrated the Mass. Latin was the universal tongue.

These Russian tourists in Sancta Sophia have little to say about St. Cyril and his brother Methodius, and they aren't showing a lively zeal for Christian worship. What they think of the Great Church is anybody's guess. At a guess, another dreary museum like St. Isaac's in Leningrad or St. Basil's in Moscow. They have brought along their own tour guide, and he doubles as a cop, trying to see to it that they keep to themselves. "DAH-svee-DAH-n'yah," so long, goodbye. But this is a free country, and we walk the church together. From the nave we look up dutifully at the three mosaic portraits on the north wall, "sages in the fire." In the central niche there is St. John Chrysostom. This famous Greek saint was merciless to sin, a contemporary said, "but full of mercy for the sinner."

Ivan the Terrible was ruling in Moscow when they canonized their first Russian saints. Muscovites looked over their shoulders. From now on, they said, Russia "radiated piety like the Second Rome," and on the soil of "Holy Russia" the Orthodox Faith glowed "with the teachings of *our* Holy Fathers." When Greeks came from the Second Rome to purify the Russian liturgical texts, Russians didn't need them. "Coming here to teach us!" Their tsar in Moscow held the reins of the holy ecumenical church, said the monk of Pskov. He was the "one Orthodox Tsar of the Universe," and if you couldn't tell the difference between right and wrong he was willing to tell you.

In the Second Rome, one of their early patriarchs called himself "Pope of the East," a highfalutin title that never caught on. Gennadius, their last patriarch before the fall of the city, liked to lay down the law, and Latins who wanted union regretted his sharp eye for nice distinctions. But after the Conquest he made his peace with the Conqueror. The Oecumene was the world, and big enough to make room for all comers. He said how Christians and

Muslims might patch up their differences in a single faith. The church of Haghia Eirene means Heavenly Peace, and this patriarch was "irenical," a peace-loving man. However, he didn't muffle the difference between Christians and Muslims. Partly that is what "byzantine" means.

The Deeis in the south gallery of Sancta Sophia has been knocked about by time, and two-thirds of the great mosaic is gone. The faces remain, though, making a trinity, like the Dialectic. Mary is young but guesses at the future, and John the Baptist has looked into the abyss. They lean towards the Man of Sorrows, wanting Him to mend our fallen condition. He is willing to do this, and with His right hand He blesses the world. Russians have their own Deeis in their Smolensk church in Moscow. This grouping is conventional, and the Russian tour guide is spelling out the resemblance.

The triangular garden behind the Suleimaniye used to be Sinan's garden. This is where they put him when he died in 1588. Wisteria climbs on the garden walls, Persian lilac is banked against them, and in the spring blue-purple irises bloom around the marble *turbe*. The Royal Chief Architect was born to Christian parents in a village on the Anatolian plateau, and when he was young the Janissaries took him in their *devshirme* or military conscription. He lived for ninety-nine years, most of this time in the service of Islam, but was always throwing back to his beginnings. The Son of the Slave of God, he was "Sinan the Poor and Humble." This is the inscription he engraved on his ring, now in the Topkapi Museum.

For the plan of the Suleimaniye, Sinan went back to the beginning. Maybe it amused him to play variations on the work of Anthemius of Tralles and Isidorus of Miletus, the architects of Justinian a thousand years before. Half-cupolas support his dome, and the *avlu* before the mosque is like the old arcaded courtyard. This is the ancient aspect, but it touches a new mind. The new mind loves symmetry, and Sinan and Michelangelo are brothers under the skin. Like Giotto and his contemporary, the unknown master of the Chora church, they say how blood is thinner than the fraternity of craft.

The mosque of Suleiman doesn't overcome you like Sancta Sophia, and Suleiman whose name is Solomon wasn't out to beat King Solomon, like Justinian when he made the Great Church. In the Suleimaniye, mathematics is king, and the Light of the World is unrefracted. The proportions are flawless, the height of the dome being exactly twice the diameter. No aisles or dim passageways break the oblong space, no columns break the view. Where the Christian church was a clutter like the City of Man, the mosque is a seamless harmony like the City of God. Muslims live in this city, and they have opened up the vast interior, pushing back the supports of the dome and narrowing the galleries to balconies against the side walls. These balconies convert the mosque to a theater. From the painted heavens the royal patron looks over the scene.

The Suleimaniye doesn't promise much from the outside. This is like the Great Church where they made their walls of stone and brick laid in thick beds of mortar, and faced the surface with plaster or veneering. For the walls of his temple, Sinan chose the yellow limestone that comes from the quarries at Bakirkoy on the Sea of Marmara. Four hundred years later the walls have weathered to light gray, and the domes and semidomes above them impend like a sheet of gray water. Stamboul is built on Devonian rock, and the naked mosque is like the substrate.

The little shops on the Third Hill spill over onto the sidewalks, and the cobblestoned streets are piled with vegetables and fruit. Flies buzz among the raisins and apricot paste, settling on the beans and dried figs. The narrow streets twist and turn like the tail of a suckling pig. The Ford Fairlanes on Uzun Charshi Caddesi know better than to try to make it through here. Along the littoral at the foot of the hill, the tinsmiths are beating tin and the barrelmakers are hammering metal bands and wooden staves. Wet mud coats the cobbles like oil on a gun stock, and the carts that clog the streets smell of sour oil and rank cheeses.

But push through the heavy leather curtains of the mosque. Inside, the balconies cling to the walls. Calligraphic inscriptions say how "the God who looks down on all things" is also the Friend and Reviver. The Turkish arches are tulip petals, and blue carnations and white peach blossoms grow in a garden like no garden in nature. Lips are smiling in the faience, and the seeing eyes are there to ward you from harm. The dominant color is the deep tomato red that comes from the clay called "Armenian bole." Or these Iznik tiles make a harmony of blue and turquoise, shading to green, the holy color preferred by the Prophet. "Outside," in human time, the Blues and Greens made a discord.

Stained-glass windows in the east wall let in the light of day. These windows are lustrous but they don't tell a story like the windows of Chartres or Sainte Chapelle. Beeswax candles stand sentinel on either side of the *mihrab*, a white marble honeycomb, and the *mimber* or pulpit is carved from this Proconnesian marble. For the noon prayer on Friday, the imam climbs up to the canopied pulpit. The chair where he sits is inlaid with ivory and mother of pearl. Holding up the dome, the four "elephant legs" have a lot to do but don't look elephantine, and the intricate fluting brings your eye up with them as they rise.

Outside the mosque the temperature is falling, and the vendors rub their hands together. Inside, the floor is bigger than a basketball court but warmed and softened by small prayer rugs and large Turkish carpets. Most people are barefoot. There are no special socks for praying in Islam, though some old people wear *mests*, black or brown leather slippers. The vendors outside are enterprising, though, and they offer woolen prayer socks like après-ski slippers for foreigners who want to visit the mosque. My feet in their red and blue prayer socks are warm. But the mosque of Suleiman is cold.

The interior is stored with riches and empty like the desert. It belongs to Allah and asserts the triumph of pure form, where the human form is palpable and messy. Stalactites and lozenges are carved on the capitals. They cluster in the *mihrab* and fill the canopies above the doors—triangles, hexagons, cylinders, and squares, but no "human face divine." They don't invite your eye to pause as it ascends from the column to the impost that carries the arch. Over the uncluttered space broods the Logos.

In Sancta Sophia, at the end of the south gallery as you walk towards the apse, you see a portrait in mosaic of the Empress Zoe and one of her husbands. Christ, standing between them, looks astonished and no wonder. Above the head of the empress, an inscription honors "the most pious Augusta." But she wasn't pious, and when she lost her virginity at the age of fifty she found a good thing and didn't let it go. Zoe died in 1050, at seventy-two. Her hand shook with palsy and her back was bent with age. But even in age, says the old chronicler, "her face had a beauty altogether fresh." The portrait in Sancta Sophia still shows this.

Friday in Muslim countries is for public prayers, but whenever you enter the mosque of Suleiman men are touching their heads to the carpet. In Sancta Sophia also they prayed all day long. Their prayers began with the First Hour when they gave thanks for the light. At nine o'clock they remembered the descent of the Holy Spirit, and at noon and again at three the crucifixion and death of Our Lord. Mostly, they reserved these daily prayers to priests and deacons. Everybody prays in Islam.

They are standing or kneeling, facing the *kible* wall. The prayer niche in the wall points southeast from Istanbul to Mecca. Confronting it, the men pray alone. They have a priest but don't really need him, and the imam isn't a pastor like the Good Shepherd. He doesn't crowd in between the people and their God, and no communal ritual brings them together. The God they invoke is unacquainted with grief, not made in their image and likeness. The priest in Sancta Sophia broke the bread in his hands at the climax of their Greek Mass. He recited the words of Christ: "Take, eat; this is my body which is broken for you." Muslims are eclectic and make room in their pantheon for the God of the Christians, but they won't allow that He suffered. He was taken up to heaven without suffering, they say, and Judas was crucified in His place.

Like all the great Friday mosques, the Suleimaniye is a house of worship and something more. It forms the center of a *kulliye* or complex of buildings where any manner of business gets done. Public kitchens serve the mosque, and the domed *sebil* has a corner to itself beside the outer wall of the courtyard. If you are thirsty, they will pass you a cup of water through a grilled window in the *sebil.* In Islam they venerate theology and law, and the masters of those who know are the *mullahs.* Before Turkey became a secular state, the *kulliye* made room for these *mullahs* or teachers. On the north face of the Third Hill was their college or *medrese,* also cells where the students lived. Students still come here for religious instruction, like Sunday school back home. Unlike students back home they wear mandated uniforms, for the boys jackets and ties, for the girls white pullovers with a blue habit.

The old religious hospital still flanks the courtyard, but the doctors have departed and the military have replaced them. This building enclosed their *timarḥane* or Bedlam where lunatics were shut away. They didn't languish, however, and Chelebi tells of the musicians who came here to play for the sick and insane, "and so to cure their madness." In the *dershane* where the students meet for lectures, the *mevlevi* dervishes used to practice the *zikir.* Their dancing was formal.

Growing up in Salonika, Ataturk saw the dervishes in their flowing robes like women's dresses and their outlandish headgear, and he heard them shrilling on the reed flute they call the *ney.* Their bonnets were long and pointed, or trimmed with fur and rounded like the top of a woman's *turbe.* Some wore the *tark,* a cap shaped like a rose. This Arabic word means "abandon." Clashing their cymbals, they made an unholy din, and Ataturk said with disgust how the spectators shrieked and wailed and some of them fainted. When he came to power, he got rid of the dervishes or tried to, and he ordered his state radio not to play the old Turkish music. "Whining and wailing," he called it.

South of Ankara where the Gazi has his tomb is the city of Konya. St. Paul when he preached there knew it as Iconium. The dervish master Mevlana Jalal-ad-Din Rumi is buried in Konya, and his tomb is a national shrine. At the entrance of the tomb the words of the master welcome the people: "Come whoever you are. Our convent is not a place of despair." This thirteenth-century poet liked to whirl in the streets. Each year a million tourists visit his city in the steppes of Anatolia to watch the dervishes dance. Money talks, Carstairs says. Ataturk is in his grave, and tourism brings in a lot of money.

"Dervish" or "darvish" is from Persian, and the first syllable is the same as the English word "door." *Vish* comes from Persian *vihtan* and signifies begging, and the dervishes were mendicants who begged from door to door. But this exotic word is a portmanteau word, and *dar* also means "in" and *vish* can mean "thought." So the agitated dancer is a meditative man and looks for quiet at the heart of the storm. Where Crazy Ibrahim behind the lattice played his murderous game, and Dandalo the Christian doge ruined the great work of time, he made a spinning stasis. The world was sound and fury, and he danced to lose it and find his way out of life into art. In Constantinople, said an old poet in Justinian's time, "everything that was human had been set in motion." The end wasn't motion, however.

To music and poetry, the *mullahs* turn a deaf ear. They live in the mind and their orthodox religion is cold. Dervishes live in the body. In their *sema* or sacred dance they whirled round and round until ecstasy seized them, but they kept one foot planted on earth. The right leg was the "wheel" where the left was the "pillar," and to keep themselves from falling they fixed their eyes on the thumbnail of the left hand. This was a still point.

The dervish *tekke* in Galata goes back to 1492, a banner year in history. In this year the Jews and Moors were driven out of Spain. The *tekke* or convent is hidden from view at the far end of the courtyard, and one of their dervish saints is buried in the quiet *turbe* surrounded by marigolds and roses. You aren't likely to see the convent as you walk along Galip Dede Caddesi. Thousands of people who don't know it exists pass by here every day on their way to the tunnel underneath the Golden Horn. Most of these people want to get someplace fast. In a minute and twenty seconds, the underwater railway brings them from Galata to Stamboul.

A half-fence like a buttery-hatch, wrought in filigree, encloses the dance floor. To the right of the enclosure, stairs go up to the *mimber* or pulpit. The inner walls rise two stories and make an atrium in the center of the convent. The interior is mosquelike, but there isn't a dome and the walls don't lean inwards or aspire. A massive chandelier hangs from the flat ceiling, where it gathers and transmits the light. At the foot of Istiklal Caddesi, the traffic has got things all its own way. In this ancient house time collapses, and they haven't heard of the automobile.

The spectators on the upper level reclined on sofas and fur rugs, and looked down on the dance floor through a latticed screen. I see them, in the mind's eye, fingering prayer beads and smoking hashish in carved pipes. Bookholders like crossed staves stand at their elbows and hold the holy writings. The dervishes enter, sixteen men in file. They wear their tall hats like tombstones and the black gown or *hirka* that tells of the tomb. On the dance floor they sit like stones, their heads bowing low, and they are dead to the power of God. White-bonneted musicians make hypnotic music on the *ney* and the *rebab*, a single-stringed violin. Some of these musicians beat softly on the *kudum* or drum. A blind singer, accompanied by a shrilling solo on the *ney*, begins to chant in recitative. He sings of the One God and His Prophet. *La ilaha illa Allah wa Mohammed Rasul-Allah.*

The dervishes rise. They circle the floor three times in halting steps. This is the walk of life. Their cloaks fall away as they emerge from the tomb. Under the cloaks are bright white robes with full skirts that reach almost to the ground. Their witness is the Shaikh or Baba, and he and the lead dancer kiss hands. The Shaikh wears the green turban, a virile color. Their holy word *Hay*, meaning "the Living God," is denoted by this color. Folding his arms across his chest, the dancer hugs his shoulders, surrendering to God's will, and begins to turn slowly in a counterclockwise motion like the motion of the spheres. He wants to lose himself in God. Mevlana their master tells, however, of the bird in flight and how it rises above the rooftops but never reaches the skies.

One after another, the dancers take up the dance. They stretch out their arms, and the palm of the right hand faces up in the supplicant's gesture. But these dervishes are transmitting God's mercy to earth, and the palm of the left hand faces down. They are rotating now at different speeds, and effort is all gone into motion. Their tall hats incline slightly, their billowing skirts flame like Greek Fire, but the fire doesn't burn. Acting out a pattern, this formal movement makes their dancing creative. One movement begets another, and they go with the grain where the grain is the body. Carstairs, on a bargain-hunting expedition to Konya, has seen the dervishes dance. He says they can keep this up for an hour and a half.

TEST MATCH INONU STADIUM

MEN ARE calling *chay! chay!* and in the lounge most seats are taken, nobody wanting to be topside in this weather. Most ferries on the Bosphorus, unlike those on the Golden Horn, hug one shore or the other until they come to the chain of buoys below the entrance to the Black Sea. Then they turn around and take the same route back to Stamboul. Our ferry picks and chooses, criss-crossing the strait from Europe to Asia. This way, we see more for our money. The white-jacketed steward brings us our tea in glasses, sugar for me, lemon for her. Gonul is almost forty but slim and trim and hopes to keep it like that. To Turks this makes her uncomely, and the male eyes that look her over slide away without interest. She can live without this interest. On the upholstered bench that backs against ours, the young Turkish man and the girl from Down Under have struck up an acquaintance. He is all pomander, Levantine to the tips of his mustache. If she looks into his eyes for five minutes, he says, she will likely find herself pregnant.

Turkish men, Gonul says, will run their hand up your dress without a by-your-leave. When you tell them hands off, they wonder what ails you. Turks need to be taught a lesson, but half-measures won't serve. Take the White Eunuchs, who still made trouble in the harem even after their testicles were crushed or removed. However, the Grand Turk had their penises cut off, and the eunuchs left the harem girls alone.

As we ease out of the landing, I look back at the motes in air that compose Sirkeji Station. Beside the *iskele* underneath Galata Bridge, the fishermen in their yellow slickers have blended with their *kayiks*. Art imitates nature, also the other way round. Some cities seem obedient to the estimating eye of a painter. Rome is "the light that never was on sea or land," and in Rome they take their cue from Turner. Kokoschka should have painted the onion domes of Moscow where truth to nature is apparent but skewed. Istanbul is discontinuous-seeming. Truth comes in multiples like the names of Allah, and for this city the painter is Seurat. Light filters through scrim, shadows infiltrate the light, and the contours of buildings are like the dotted lines that make letters and shapes in a printout. The continuities are there, only blurred.

The crosscurrents off Sarayburnu are no match for the ferry but once they get hold of the junk in the water they don't let it go. Plastic containers, cigaret wrappers, and discarded animal parts from the slaughterhouses up the Horn jog in place and can't move to port or starboard. The Harpies who fouled the table of the blind king Phineus lived on the Bosphorus, but didn't hold a candle to Stamboullus. Offending ladies of the harem were drowned off the point in sacks weighted with stones, and the Greek renegade Ibrahim, the lover and counselor of the Emperor Suleiman, drowned his whole harem here, wanting a change. They had it both ways in Islam, Gonul says, and men relieved themselves impartially on women and boys. Rutting went by seasons. During the summer they let their desires incline towards young men. In the winter they turned to the women. The harem girls were handed over to the Black Eunuchs, who drowned them. The sack was tied around the neck but the head was left free. Not so long ago, a diver went down to the bottom. He saw the harem girls standing upright on the floor of the sea. After this, Gonul says, he was never the same.

At Istanbul University, Gonul is writing her thesis on Ataturk and the Emancipation of Women. Progress is slow, Ataturk being like the elephant explored by a college of blind men. How you "see" him depends on where you take hold. "Availability," he said, when they asked him what quality he most admired in a woman. But in his new civil code, he legalized divorce. In the twenties at a ball in Smyrna, he had them play Western music and made the men get up and dance. He began the dancing himself, a fox-trot with the governor's daughter. Never before in Turkey had a Turkish woman danced in public with a man. His wife, Latife, read Byron aloud to their guests, also Victor Hugo. Nobody understood her but he wanted Latife to do this, being proud of his educated woman. On their honeymoon in Anatolia he had her strip off the veil and show her face to the people. When he divorced his wife, however, he went back to Muslim custom and put her away. "Leave the house," he said, repeating this three times.

To keep herself in pocket, Gonul gives guided tours, also lessons in Turkish to people like me. Her illustrated books for children have a modest but steady sale. She is partial to titles like *The Sick Man of Europe?* and *Rambles in Old Stamboul Town.* Her head is stuffed with facts and figures. The bridge across the Bosphorus is 1,074 meters long between the piers. This is seven meters longer than your George Washington Bridge across the Hudson.

"*Bismillâh!*" The water turns rough when we pass the headland, and Valentino behind us is invoking his Maker. "O gracious and compasionate God!" This is what they say when setting out on a voyage, also when they ejaculate sperm. In his *Natural History*, Pliny says that "the sea Pontus evermore floweth and runneth out into Propontis but the sea never returneth back again within Pontus." The Black Sea is Pontus or Pontus Euxinus but doesn't look black, and it keeps up a running feud with Propontis or the Sea of Marmara. The currents run two ways at once, never mind what Pliny says. All the way to the Hellespont, they battle each other. I don't see how the Argonauts made it through here. Before the Hellespont stood the Symplegades. Some ancient writers say this, but most have these islands guarding the Black Sea. If they saw a ship coming, they clashed together like cymbals. Byron has a couplet that remembers these waters.

There's not a sea the passenger e'er pukes in,
Turns up more dangerous breakers than the Euxine.

Uskudar on the Asian shore is our first stop. A long time ago, the Rifais or Howling Dervishes practiced the *zikir* in this place. They came from Iraq, and unlike the Whirling Dervishes they sobbed and gnashed their teeth. *Ya Allah!* these dervishes cried, and in the *tekkes* of Uskudar they stabbed themselves with cutlasses and licked red-hot irons. They did this in remembrance of their master Ahmad Rifa'i, who put his legs in a burning basin of coals. *Gül* or "rose" was their word for the instruments of torture they used to mortify the flesh. The use they put them to was like the odor of the rose to these voluptuaries of pain. When the savage dance was over, the Shaikh rubbed their wounds with his spittle. People say this cleansing made them whole.

When Uskudar was still Scutari, Florence Nightingale came out from London to care for the British soldiers in the Crimean War. She arrived in November 1854, ten days after Balaclava and the Charge of the Light Brigade. Evidently this famous charge was a mistake. Her hospital stood on a steep rise near the Selimiye Barracks. I make this a quarter of a mile in from the water. There weren't stretchers enough to go round, so the walking wounded dragged the others up the rise. Four miles of beds with just space to walk between them crowded the barracks, and the walls were crowded with vermin. Sewers and cesspools lay under the rotten flooring. This hospital had no basins, soap or towels, mops or brooms. The men got fed somehow but not on plates, and they did without knives, forks, or spoons. When the London *Times* appealed for help, the money poured in, but the British ambassador in Constantinople said that British soldiers didn't want charity. He told them to spend the money on the new Protestant church in Pera.

Forty-two percent of the men who came to Scutari died of their wounds or diseases. Florence Nightingale brought this down to twenty-two cases per thousand. It took her half a year, working night and day from her little room off the enormous gallery. The labor used her up. She said her nature was "passional" and being a normal woman she had a young man in her eye. However, she said, "I have a moral, an active nature which requires satisfaction, and that would not find it in his life." Gonul, telling me this, is approving.

Behind the landing stage stands an ancient *hamam*. According to tradition, this public bath is the work of Sinan. A modern entrepreneur has got title to the *hamam* and has built a supermarket in the shell. Stamboullus embarking for the picnic grounds beside the Sweet Waters of Asia stop at the market for the soft drink they call *Fruko* and the creamy thick Silivri yoghurt that has the consistency of cheese. If they can afford it, they buy a bottle of Binboga vodka. Empty bottles stick in the muddy foreshore where the Sweet Waters flow into the strait.

The Bosphorus is Ox-ford and named after Io, who swam across it in the form of a heifer. Jove loved this woman but Juno sent the gadfly and drove Io to frenzy, and her wanderings on three continents were like a lasting storm. For these Stamboullus, the Bosphorus is Bogazichi. This is how they render the Byzantine word *stenon* or strait. Across the strait, defying you to make up your mind, is Dolmabahche Palace, stupefying, grand, pretty good, okay. "Dolmabahche" means "filled-up garden," where the garden is made out of the sea. The first Sultan Ahmet, who lived in Shakespeare's time, began to fill in the harbor. After this, says Chelebi in his book of travels, every ship that tied up in Constantinople had to load with stones and dump them before the royal garden.

The water usurps on the long marble quay or the quay usurps on the water, and the blinding white façade tells of iced sherbet and the harem girls of Abdul Mejit, who built this pleasure dome in 1853. Sometimes the entire harem assembled in the gardens, and the girls vied with each other to catch the sultan's eye. All their charms were focused on one man alone. The sultan threw a handkerchief to the girl of his choice, and none of these girls ever said no.

In the low white wings that flank the central building, they have a crystal staircase and an alabaster bathroom. This is incredible but Dolmabahche doesn't bear looking into. The echoing halls are faced with marble, like a cenotaph where the dead have departed. On the ponderous furniture, the ormolu decor looks like gold. However, it is only pretending, and in the huge throne room the trompe l'oeil ceiling is pulling the wool over your eyes. Crystal chandeliers from Czechoslovakia hang from the domed ceiling. They shimmer in the light from the fires that light this pile at night but never make it warm. In the half-light, the dripping chandeliers resemble stalactites in the pendentives of the Suleimaniye. The resemblance is only superficial, however, a pale reflex of the past or the past deferring to the present, and it hints at a failure of nerve.

On the night of November 10, 1938, Ataturk died in Dolmabahche Palace. For three days his body lay in state, and the people came to bid him goodbye. Then they bore the body up the hill to Pera and down the hill to Kasim Pasha beside the Golden Horn. Crossing Galata Bridge, the military band played Chopin's Funeral March. Ataturk, dead, went by ship out of the Bosphorus into the Marmara, then by train from Izmit for burial in Ankara, the new capital in the east. Stamboullus remember, and in Dolmabahche Palace all the antique clocks are stopped at 9:05 p.m. Day and night in Taksim, two armed sentries patrol before the monument the Gazi shares with his soldiers. "*Mehmetchik*" is their word for the Turkish Tommy Atkins, and Ataturk said that in Turkey "the greatest monument is *Mehmetchik* himself." His soldiers were food for powder. In his wars he used them up in their thousands and tens of thousands, but in the War for Independence one of them said, "It is for today that our mothers gave birth to us."

About Ataturk, there are plenty of Turks who aren't sure. Gonul is one of them. She says the Gazi is to Asia as Garibaldi was to Europe, but the Gazi in power became the "Gazoz Pasha." This derisive title means fizzy lemonade. He lost his temper with "those who create confusion in the innocent mind of the nation." Some of them he shot. One of his associates remembered him saying how "mercy, pity, and sentimental morality" were luxuries he couldn't afford. His name is ill-omened for Ottoman Turks. When Suleiman sent the mutes with their bowstrings to murder his first-born Mustafa, a pretender called "the false Mustafa" rose up to vex him. Mustafa Kemal, as he was called before he became Ataturk, is like the dead son of Suleiman. In his death "he has not ceased to exist." Major Gurjan said this. He led the failed putsch of 1963, conducted in the name of the Gazi.

Marx protested once that he wasn't a Marxist, and you can't blame Ataturk for the crimes and follies they do in his name. He wasn't a "Kemalist." The *Cumhuriyet* he established in 1923 means "Republic" in Turkish, and he took it to mean "Chose Publique." In the 1930s his party boss proposed that they take Fascist Italy for their model. "You'll do all that after I die," said Ataturk. After he died the generals revolted, and their General Gursel went to Ankara and wrote in the book of honor in the Gazi's yellow limestone mausoleum, "Great Father, approve us, and permit us to follow in your footsteps." This approval meant different things, contradictory but not exclusive. After seventeen months of military rule, the generals restored democracy to Turkey.

"Maybe," I tell Gonul, "this will happen again." She is skeptical, and who knows what General Evren is thinking? The dictator keeps his own counsel. "Forty foxes go round in his head, and the muzzle of one fox never touches the tail of the next." Gonul, who appeals to progress, prays on Fridays in the mosque, but not for General Evren. She is a Shiite Muslim and belongs to their Hurufi sect. Her religion is a reticule like a woman's handbag. Like many women and most Muslims, she makes room in this handbag for miscellaneous things. She numbers Christ among the prophets, and hunts clues for daily living in the Bible as well as the Koran. The Book of Revelations is her favorite stalking place. Every morning at breakfast she checks her horoscope in *Milliyet*, the independent paper. Around her neck she wears the *muska*. The letters in this amulet are Arabic and written on parchment. Each letter of the Arabic alphabet has its servant appointed by Allah, she says. You can invoke these servants in case of need.

"*Huruf*" in Arabic is the science of letters, and letters have their temperament like you and me. In the four elements there are twenty-eight letters, divided into four classes. Seven letters combine to make the word "fire," and all the letters that do this are hot. Viz., *a, h, t, m, f, sh,* and *dh,* and each has its mystical number. *A* is 1, *h* or *heh* is 600, *t* is 400, etc. Numbers are auspicious or ill-omened like names, and Gonul's Science of Calculation shows her the essence concealed in the name. To discover the essence, you add up the numbers assigned to each letter. The sums are good or evil by fiat. 666 stands for the Antichrist or Beast of the Apocalypse, and Gonul would like to see General Evren in this number. However, he doesn't add up. He is Kenan Evren, no *h* or *heh* in his name. Even if you throw in "General," you still have a long way to go.

The general comes across as a fatherly figure, and the coup of 1980, some people say, was a case of the righteous father taking his errant child to the woodshed. "Spare the rod and spoil the child." Students say that since the September coup they can get on with their studies, and businessmen say that they don't feel oppressed but more free. At Martial Law Court No. 1, though, the trial of the Revolutionary Left is beginning. The Askeris have rounded up almost eight hundred suspects, and the charge is wanting to abolish the system. For ninety of these suspects, the military prosecutor is asking the death sentence. This seems hit-or-miss. But Turkey, says General Evren, has been going through a mortal sickness. "Sometimes cancer surgeons are forced to cut normal tissue as well."

Gonul is squeamish when it comes to violence. The Dev-Yol Terrorists don't see the trees for the forest, she says. This is why they find it easy to kill. However, she takes their point. "You can't make an omelet without breaking eggs." Maybe Socialism à la Russe is the wave of the future. How can she say this, there being no freedom in Socialist Land? I get the full treatment from her snapping black eyes. Have I ever thought how it is with the peasant woman in Turkey? Rising in the dark, she works until dark. She bears her children one after another, and they all live together in a one-room tumbledown with her father-in-law and mother-in-law. Once or twice a month she gets to take a bath. At night her husband beats her, and this happens every night. Under Socialism, does this woman gain or lose?

In the little park at Chengelkoy old men feed the pigeons or finger their rosaries. The *yalis* stand over the water on piles. These wooden country houses look like Swiss chalets, and both shores of the Bosphorus are like a seedier version of the Rhine. But in spring along the foreshore color shades into color, purple larkspur, yellow mustard, and the red and yellow of snapdragons. In the gardens of the wooden houses, the gingerly tracing of the redbud makes an unexpected harmony with the pink of cabbage roses. On a rainy day in winter, this promise seems remote. The storms that come down from Russia have bent the ancient plane trees, and they mourn grotesquely beside the water. But the fine rain is a kaleidoscope, changing things before your eyes, and the umbrella pines against the skyline recall the landscape of Rome.

Along the shoreline at Beshiktash, fingers of wisteria twist around the magnolias that glisten in the rain. Even in winter, the curling leaves of the magnolias are green. Beshiktash means "cradle stone," and St. Helena, the mother of Constantine, brought this stone back from Bethlehem and housed it in a shrine above the water. But when the Crusaders sacked Constantinople, they took the cradle stone away. We get down to stretch our legs. The fierce-looking young men, Alaric and Athaulf, two barbarian kings who need a shave, also a bath, reach out a helping hand. They greet me like a brother, *Was gebt?* and words to that effect. At a glance, they can see that I come from over yonder, and they want to show off their German. Over yonder everybody speaks German. These men are on their way home from who knows what indignities in some factory abroad, but they aren't going home by choice. Abroad, the job is finished, though, and their visas have been canceled. They are part of the great migration from the East to the West. Unlike their ancestors who came from the East, they don't want to burn the house down. They want a job but nobody can use them.

This town on the water is sports crazy. The best eleven in Istanbul wears the colors of Beshiktash. Carstairs says this, and though Beshiktash is at best mediocre these days, the patch on his anorak still declares his allegiance. Beneath the black letter B, the white star and crescent on its red shield is like an old battle flag. He wouldn't flaunt these colors in Emirgan or Yenikoy, soccer being for Stamboullus a matter of life or death. On alternate Sundays they lock horns at Inonu Stadium. Minor-league games are played at Sheref Stadium just above the water outside the grounds of Yildiz Park. You can pick up the bus that runs along Chiragan Caddesi. Abdul Hamid II, their last absolute ruler and an amateur chemist, lived on the hill at Yildiz with his menagerie and his cracked retorts and Bunsen burners. He cut a comic figure in his oversized fez that almost covered the eyes, and his clothes that hung loose on his body. The "Great Assassin" stirred up his people to massacre Armenians in Constantinople. Also he practiced fretwork and sailed the lake at Yildiz in a little clockwork boat. The park was a fortress where the sultan lived in a blaze of light so nobody could get near him. Stamboullus being suggestible, he wouldn't let them put on plays that showed the violent deaths of princes. This included Shakespeare.

After Kandilli the ground begins to rise. The Bosphorus pinches in, narrowing to a width of seven hundred meters. Across these narrows the Great King Darius built a bridge of boats, and from a throne on the high ground he watched the Persian army cross over into Thrace. The hill behind the village is covered with bracken. Though the meadow lands are cultivated, wild poppies are growing in with the maize. The Sweet Waters come in here, two effluent streams. You can bathe at the mouth of these streams, if you want to.

Anadolu Hisar looms up on the right. Behind the bridge the little hamlet has wedged itself into the fortress. Six hundred years ago, the first Sultan Bayazit built this fortress. He was the Lightning, *Yildirim* in Turkish, who wanted to cool his fires in the Golden Horn. But Timur Khan and the Mongols came out of Asia and defeated him in a battle near Ankara. They put him in a cage and paraded him round until he dashed out his brains. Marlowe in his *Tamburlaine* tells the story.

On the European shore, across from Anadolu, is Rumeli Hisar. They called it the "throat-cutter," *bogaz-kesen*, "*bogaz*" meaning "throat" and "Bosphorus" too. Mehmet the Conqueror picked out the site himself and kept a keen eye on the construction. He scoured Anatolia for lime slakers and masons. Three thousand men worked from April through August to get the job done. This was in 1452. Mehmet meant to surpass Julius Caesar, he said, also Alexander and Xerxes.

Muslims ban pictures, but the Sultan, disregarding this, had

Bellini come over from Italy to paint him. Two portraits by the master survive. The face is valanced with sideburns, a tuft of beard, and black mustaches. A Turkish poet said that the mustaches were like leaves enfolding rosebuds. The overbite suggests avidity, and below the plucked and arched woman's eyebrows the nose curves like a tapir's. In one likeness the eyes are dull pebbles, hooded and cold. They look out of Asia, the ancient home of the Turk. In the other the eyes are wet, almost beseeching until your back is turned. This Levantine merchant keeps a catamite on the sly. His plans, locked in his head, are his own. "If a hair of my beard knew them," he seems to be saying, "I would pluck it out."

When Mehmet built his throat-cutter, he was twenty years old. He wrote poetry, he knew philosophy and science, and he liked to read in the literature of Greece and Islam. Scholars and poets were his chosen companions. He spoke fluent Greek, Arabic, Persian, and Hebrew. A year before this, his father, Murad, had died of an apoplectic fit. When his father's widow left the harem to congratulate the new sultan, he sent his servants to smother her son. After the Conquest he rode through the ruined city of Constantinople, and the desolation moved him to tears. "What a city we have given over to plunder and destruction," he said.

Rumeli Hisar makes a rough triangle in a green bowl of hills. Where the triangle peaks, a tower with a sea gate overlooks the water. This tower flies the red flag with the crescent and star. On the ramparts an ancient cannon rusts in the salty air. Gonul, who knows where she is going, leads us uphill along the cobblestone path from the wharf to the northernmost tower. The rain has stopped falling but we slip and slide on the cobbles. Oleander, rain-wet and heavy, slaps against our legs. Lizards and scorpions hurry to get out of the way. In Byzantine times the church of St. Michael the Archangel occupied this rocky ledge, but Sultan Mehmet knocked it down and used the building stone to build his Castle of Rumelia. Some of the material went unused, however, and the broken columns and capitals suggest a Gothic "ruin" disposed inside the walls for the innocent pleasure of the people who lived here.

From the bases of the triangle the walls run downhill for two hundred and fifty meters, and the width is half the length. The hills have been cut over and the sequoias are mostly gone, but conifers grow on the high ground. These provident Turks have replenished the walnut groves, walnut being a cash crop. Two towers dominate the high ground, confronting each other, and a curtain of walls bisects the steep valley between them. These walls are immensely thick, almost three meters. However, their purpose wasn't defensive.

Knowing his protocol, the Byzantine emperor sent a pair of ambassadors to complain about the building of the fort. Sultan Mehmet cut off their heads. The Italians who traded on the Black Sea weren't persuaded by this, being courageous, foolish, and greedy, and in November a Venetian grain ship coming down from the north ignored the great cannon on the seaward tower. When their ship sank, the Venetian sailors swam to shore. Mehmet had them all beheaded. He had their captain impaled, and left his body unburied by the side of the road. Death by impaling was the method of execution preferred by his contemporary Vlad Dracul, known as Dracula. Mostly, Mehmet preferred sawing in half.

In Constantinople they read the writing on the wall and said, "These are the days of the Antichrist!" The sultan was the Antichrist but so was the Pope in Rome, and as between these iniquities some Byzantines called it a tossup. Their Grand Admiral of the Fleet said he would rather see the Turkish turban than the Roman miter in Constantinople. He was Lucas Notaras, known as the Megadux. When the city had fallen, Mehmet came to visit him. In the house the admiral's wife lay sick in bed. "Greetings, Mother," said the Sultan, wishing her a quick recovery. Notaras had a beautiful boy of fourteen, and Mehmet wanted this boy for his harem. The father refusing him, father and son died together.

In 1953, when Turks celebrated the five-hundredth anniversary of the Conquest of Constantinople, they spruced up the fortress at Rumeli Hisar. They demolished the little village and the mosque that lay inside the walls. A piece of the minaret marks the circular cistern where the mosque used to stand, and today this cistern functions as a theater-in-the-round. In the summer months Shakespeare's plays are produced here. A tattered flyer on the hoarding that stands beside the sea gate announces a performance of *King Richard III*. The guns of Sultan Mehmet poke out above the barbican, half hidden in a tangle of fire thorn and locust. Stone cannonballs are lying at the foot of the tower, some of them weighing six hundred pounds.

Beyond Rumeli Hisar, the villages on the upper Bosphorus run together for me. The baroque mosque at Emirgan has its appeal but isn't up to the best of Sinan, and along the water at Yenikoy the *yalis* please the eye but aren't anything special. Near the gulf at Istinye, Daniel, a holy man, lived on top of his pillar. Byzantines made a lot of these pious stylites who lived only to die. Alypius the Paphlagonian was a favorite saint of theirs. He stood on a pillar for fifty-three years until paralysis made him lie down. Byzantines and stylites have gone where Saturn keeps the years, and there being no reason to stop at Istinye, our ferry turns around and heads back to Stamboul.

On Cumhuriyet Caddesi, vendors with sticks of roast corn patrol the sidewalk, bootblacks squat hopefully under the trees, and in the hotels the men who wait tables have come up from the slums or the country. Behind the commercial buildings fronting the street, the crazy wooden houses are roofed with red-brown pantiles. The people who live in the houses set out thyme and sweet basil in pots on the window ledges. You see nothing of this unless you walk west, and Cumhuriyet Caddesi is like a façade in Disneyland.

Crossing the wide thoroughfare, you are on your mark, get set, go. It angles north from Taksim, and the bus that runs down the middle is protected by an iron palisade. There are openings in the palisade every so often. In the shops, the Turkish carpets are displayed behind glass. The *zerde* is good at the Divan Hotel, rice pudding with saffron, and their melon or *kavun* is the best in Istanbul. The airlines have their offices on Cumhuriyet Caddesi, the travel agencies too. If you are hoi polloi and can't manage the airfare, they will put you on a bus all the way to Kabul.

"Taxi, mister, you look tired," the cab driver says, but we carry on by foot to the little *lokanta* Gonul has appointed for lunch. Music of the fifties blares from a victrola, Sha Na Na tunes and "You Ain't Nothin' But a Hound Dog." The uncluttered restaurant is like a taut ship where they are calling to battle stations, busy, pared down, and efficient. One Speaks Turkish Here. Hypothetically, this is all to the good. However, as Gonul doesn't hesitate to tell me, I am an indifferent scholar and I begin to see why.

Ataturk and his colleagues wanted to make Turkish a rational language, and in 1928 they worked out a new orthographic system. They wanted an equivalence between each letter in the alphabet and the sound of each consonant or vowel. The grammar book I am trying to master reflects this. It tells me that spoken Turkish is clear like running water, one sound for each letter. Also it says that you vocalize each letter. But this is taking the wish for the deed.

Turkish is all slurring. Where letters on the page look delimited and hard, they turn soft when you say them and run into each other. Foreigners rub elbows in the cosmopolitan city but keep their identity, Russians, Americans, Arabs, and French. In Turkish this identity tends to dissolve, and their plural *lar*, pronounced *larsh*, makes an alphabet soup. *Ruslarsh, Amerikalilarsh,*

Araplarsh, Fransizlarsh. Turks are peripatetic, and they have lived on the Nile, also on the Oxus and in the deserts of Tartary. The old historian Ducas, who spied for the Genoese in Galata, says that before the Conquest more of them were living in Europe than in the Anatolian homeland. The language of the tribe remembers where they have been. Take the Janissaries, Christians who fought for the Sultan. These *Yenicheri* or New Soldiers have something in common with the Russian river Yenisei. But this "New River," rising in the highlands of northern Mongolia, flows into the Arctic Ocean, a long way from Istanbul. Yenikoy on the Bosphorus, meaning "New Village," is their version of suburbia. But "to" and "koy" make East Village, and Yenikoy and Tokyo must have their connection too.

Our waiter is Uğur but answers to U-ur. The "*yumushak*" ğ in his name is silent, and the vowels before and after it are produced in one breath. Would we like the anchovies for starters, he wants to know. However, this isn't a question. His voice is uninflected, the signals are all wrong, and questions don't imply themselves in Turkish. Syntax is where you lose yourself to find yourself. Sometimes they drop the verb or hide it until they get to the end of the sentence. Words and phrases are thick with meaning, like old barnacled scows in their dry dock on the Horn. This is hard unless you are sealed of the tribe. When you speak Turkish, you must fine-tune your ear. Otherwise the trails of meaning and the echoes that come down from the past will betray you.

The menu, written in purple ink, is all cedillas and umlauts, and Gonul orders for us both. She starts us out with a glass of *raki,* a colorless distillation of grape mash and aniseed, and a plate of *meze* or hors d'oeuvres. After this comes "bridal soup," a lemony concoction, and we go on to the *imam bayildi.* "Imam" is priest, and when he tasted this chopped eggplant cooked in olive oil, "the priest fainted" with joy. Sometimes they stuff and fry the eggplant "split-belly" style. Either way I don't like it, and I ask for the meatballs with rice. The rice is in the meatballs, and this entree, called *kadin budu*, means "woman's thigh." Elsewhere on the menu I find *kadin göbeği*, "woman's navel." Carstairs says that the Turk is anatomically perverse. He has his privates in his belly, like the men in Shakespeare's play who have their heads beneath their shoulders.

For dessert we can choose from "beauty's lips" or "grand vizier's finger" or a pastry made with pistachios and shaped like a nest. I need a cup of coffee. Gonul settles the bill and points us across the street to the groomed and shining compound where the Hilton Hotel looks over the Bosphorus to Asia. Off the lobby, a trio in peasant costume is playing for cocktails, and the Turkish man who holds the microphone pretends he is Maurice Chevalier. "When love comes in—And takes you for a spin—O la la la—C'est magnifi-que."

The shop windows in the long arcade are mostly denuded, a rope of pearls, a diamond pendant, a tea rose gown draped carelessly across a chaise, and a single spot that illuminates it subtly, a bolt of cloth from Savile Row. Inside there is a tailor who will make it up for you. If you want an Oriental carpet, they ask that you listen first to a tape-recorded lecture that tells about their carpets. The tearoom on the water is Louis Quatorze, and they seat us at a table before the plate-glass windows. The white table linen could double as a bedspread, carnations are swimming in a white cut-glass bowl. The auspices are good, and crossing my fingers I ask for a cup of coffee. The waiter opens his hands, an international gesture, and looks aggrieved for us both.

Coffee, said an Arab poet back in the beginning, is "the negro enemy of sleep and love." In Istanbul the wheel has run back to the beginning. The same killjoys in the older time who got rid of alcohol and tobacco saw much evil in coffee, and the muftis pronounced against it in their *fetvas* or legal rulings. However, these rulings were honored in the breach, and everybody knows how the Turk and his coffee are not to be parted. A cup of coffee, says the proverb, is worth forty years of friendship. The generals who run the city have made foreign exchange their first priority, though, and in Istanbul today you can't buy a cup of coffee.

Sipping our tea, we look out and down on "the garland of waters." Asia is out there just over the water, and the bridge at Ortakoy will take you across. This is the fourth longest suspension bridge in the world, Gonul tells me. Boats are moored on the far shore, mosques define the skyline. Below them march the phalanxes of new housing. East is East and West is West, but here where the Bosphorus makes a seam between continents, East is East and also West and the eye can't tell them apart.

Going east in Anatolia, you might be back in Thrace. This is true until you come to Bursa. In the mind of every tourist, Mount Olympus stands for Greece, but Turks in Anatolia have their Mount Olympus too. It hangs over Bursa where the Ottomans came from. The highway that brings you there runs through fruit orchards, gnarled olive trees, tangerine and peach, and the leaves on the cherry trees are yellow. You recognize the persimmon by the bright orange globes. The mulberry is a "dirty" tree. Wherever it grows, its fruit litters the ground.

In the Hilton Hotel we are sitting on the mountain, like the Chinamen who stare "on all the tragic scene" in Yeats's poem "Lapis Lazuli." But this scene doesn't look tragic. Fishing smacks dot the Bosphorus and the Sea of Marmara, and the pleasure boats aren't much bigger than the life boats that hang from their davits. They float on the glassy water like toys in the bathtub. A Russian light cruiser of the *Kynda* class lies at anchor near the old cannon foundry called Tophane. The morning edition of *Milliyet* carries a story on this goodwill voyage into the Bosphorus, and an interview with the captain of the *Admiral Golovko.* Fraternal greetings to the sovereign people of Turkey, etc. The Russian visitor is flying the Hammer and Sickle, also the Turkish flag, and except for the red bands on the funnels, it glistens from stem to stern with white paint. The twin funnels are raked. Stepped forward of each funnel where the masts ought to be, enclosed towers carry radar. Pairs of missile launchers are mounted fore and aft, but the cannon on the fo'c'sle are shrouded in canvas, and on the stern the helicopter pad is empty.

In the late winter of 1453 before the city fell, the war fleet of Sultan Mehmet assembled off Tophane. There were two-masted triremes, single-masted biremes, and the swift longboats known as *fustae*. The *parandaria* or transport vessels carried the soldiers, and the larger vessels carried cannon. Around the beleaguered city, the mullahs repeated the *hadith*, a traditional tale they ascribed to the Prophet. "Have you heard of a city with land on one side and sea on the two other sides?" The disciples having heard of this city, the Messenger of God spoke again: "The last hour will not dawn before it is taken."

But the Byzantines blocked the Horn. They stretched a boom across the entrance, and the Turkish sailors were on the outside looking in. Wooden buoys supported the enormous bronze links. You can still see this chain in their Turkish Army Museum in the Harbiye district north of the Hilton. No marker remembers the boom. But I have paced off these streets around the cannon foundry, and I reckon that it began near Gumruk Sokagi. This is just in from the water, and the Russian cruiser is tied up just "outside."

By the middle of April, the Turks sitting down before Constantinople were almost ready to call off their war. Then the sultan had his idea. He collected timber at the Double Columns, the name they gave the quay where Dolmabahche Palace stands. He made cradles for his ships and metal wheels for the cradles, and built a road up the hill like a launching pad or a primitive tramway. He greased this road with tallow. Then he brought in teams of oxen and yoked them to the ships. At first dawn on Sunday, April 22, the fleet began to move. They hoisted sails and flew their battle flags. Kettledrums were beaten, trumpets shrilled, and the rowers rowed in empty air.

The ridge above the water rises two hundred feet, and up the steep valley came the seventy triremes, biremes, *fustae*, and *parandaria*. Like the funeral cortege of Ataturk, the uncanny procession took in the soccer stadium and the grounds where the Hilton is. It crawled along "Republic Street" until it came to the site of Taksim. Turning left, it moved downhill past the British Embassy and the Crimean church to the low ground beside the water. Kasim Pasha, Turks call this, and Byzantines knew it as the Valley of Springs. Then the Turks were in the Horn and inside the boom. Christian sailors in the harbor and watchmen on the harbor walls saw the fleet coming on, and there was no way to stop it. Over these walls, on 13 April 1204, the Crusaders entered Constantinople.

Before the Crusaders came, a million people lived in Constantinople, but when Mehmet besieged the city only fifty thousand were left. A poet in their Greek Anthology, remembering the death of Troy, said how Time's tooth was in to the lot. The Turk administered the coup de grace, and that is a way of reading the Fall. One man's decay is another man's quickening, though. At the end, the ancient city began to put out fresh shoots. After the Latin Conquest the church of St. Savior was a tumbledown place, but Byzantines restored it. For this Chora church, Theodore Metochites had them create the frescoes and mosaics that make you feel when you see them that you have come home. He was the Grand Logothete, a high civil servant and learned in the art of the past. But the art he brought into being, though it speaks to the past, looks to the future, and in the last years of Constantinople new life was encroaching on death.

Constantine XI, the last emperor, made a census of his soldiers, and the tale was bleak so he kept it hidden. He had five thousand Greeks, including monks, under arms, and two thousand foreigners who said they would stay. These foreigners were Italians, Catalans, and renegade Turks loyal to their prince Orhan, an Ottoman pretender. Outside, the sultan's army numbered eighty thousand men. Swelling this total were the irregulars called *bashibozuks*, like locusts on the land. Across the Horn Turkish soldiers waited behind Pera where the Genoese kept quiet, hoping for the best, and now a crude pontoon bridge brought them over the water and up under the walls near the old palace at Blachernae.

Twelve thousand Janissaries camped around the sultan where he pitched his tent on the hill at Maltepe. The tent was red and gold, flying the seven horse tails. The horse tail or *tug* was the ensign of the Ottomans, and before they left Central Asia they had the tail of a yak for their ensign. Governors of provinces flew one, two, or three *tugs*. Only the sultan flew seven. Holding the center, he faced the gate of St. Romanus, less than a mile away. This gate looks towards Edirne on the western edge of the city. Against it, the sultan trained his great cannon. A Hungarian renegade, loyal only to his bread, made the cannon, and the length of the barrel measured twenty-six feet. He said that no wall "in Byzantium or Babylon" could withstand it.

The Army of Anatolia lay on the sultan's right and held a line that ran down to the Sea of Marmara. On the left was the Army of Rumelia, anchored on the Horn. By Rumelia they meant their European possessions, Macedonia and Thrace. But this word was thick with meaning and deep down it meant Romania or Rome. A few years after this, when Trebizond, the last Greek city, fell to the Turks, balladeers sang mournfully how "Romania has passed away."

In Constantinople men wrote their recollections. The skies were falling, and it seemed important to set down the details. Barbaro, a Venetian doctor, kept a diary of the siege, and after it was over, Leonard, a priest of Chios, and Phrantzes, a Byzantine, wrote about it. They remembered how things were in the dying city, and how the emperor said goodbye to his men. He asked them to pardon him where he had failed. Then the men embraced each other, being about to die. Gibbon didn't like Greeks and said "the nation was indeed pusillanimous and base," but he granted their last emperor the name of a hero.

A man should be ready to die for his faith and his country, the emperor told them. He spoke of the ancestors, ancient Greeks and Romans, and reminded his people where they had come from. The Turk wanted to exalt his false god in their temples, and to prevent this Constantine made his bad bargain. At the eleventh hour, he agreed to union with Rome. But it did no good. Now they stood alone in Constantinople with only Christ and His Mother and St. Constantine to help them.

This city that began with Constantine, called the Great, ran its course of eleven centuries, ending with another Constantine, the eleventh emperor to bear the name. In the New Rome they made a new beginning, and their first emperor had his vision of the Cross in the sky. His soldiers wore the Christian monogram called the labarum. This city was a reliquary. It housed the True Cross, the Staff of Moses, and King Solomon's Throne, and the Second Rome was also the Second Jerusalem. "The eye of the Christian faith," said a Greek Christian thirteen hundred years ago, and he said how an attack on the "God-guarded city" endangered the preaching of Christ's mystery "to the ends of the world." In the last days, the Byzantine emperor, having defeated the tribes of Gog and Magog, would hand over his power to God. The Kingdom of Heaven was only a better version of Constantinople, where the Basileus, a king touched with divinity, ruled in God's name.

However, the Turks took the city. They used a new broom, sweeping Christ from the temple. In His place they exalted Allah. They ripped the icon of the Mother of God from its setting. This was the holiest picture in Byzantium, brought to the Chora church when the siege was beginning, to inspire the men on the walls. The Janissaries hacked it to pieces. The Great Church was barred against them, and the upper and lower galleries, the sanctuary, the choir, and the nave were crowded with refugees waiting for a miracle. But they broke down the doors with axes. Inside, they took the altar cloths to caparison their horses, and on the altars they raped boys and girls. "God Is One," they said, "and has no son as companion in His government." So they took down the crucifix and crowned the dead Christ with a Janissary's cap. On the walls of public buildings, they replaced the double eagle with the crescent and star. For almost five hundred years, Ottomans governed the city. Mehmet was their first sultan in Constantinople, and their last was also Mehmet, the sixth of that name.

At the end of May 1453, roses were blooming in the city gardens. May 28 fell on a Monday. It dawned bright and clear, and the sun shone in the faces of the men on the walls. In the early evening, however, the rain began to fall, and shortly after sunset the bells of Sancta Sophia called the people to Mass. When their emperor decided on union with Rome, Greek Orthodox Catholics left the Great Church in droves. But five months later, all bitterness gone, they came back to Sancta Sophia, and Greek and Roman Catholics celebrated the liturgy together.

They lit the silver lamps that hung on chains from the dome and hung from the colonnades that ran along the nave. The wicks floated in burning oil, the light playing on the gilded bands that encircled the columns and on the gold mosaic background that outlined the Cross in the dome. Gold candelabra flamed on the altar. Perfume from the swinging censers lay heavy on the air. In the semicircular apse where they kept the patriarchal throne, Cardinal Isidore sat with Greek Orthodox priests who deplored him. He was the Metropolitan of All Russia until he went over to Rome. "There exists only one true Church on earth, the Church of Russia," his successor told the people, and they banished the apostle of Union. Over the altar, the solid gold orb and the gem-studded cross stood for the Oecumene. Nielloed designs reflected the light in the cone-shaped ciborium. This canopy covered them all.

For the ecumenical service they brought out the sacred vessels, wanting on this occasion to set the table right. This meant gold spoons and patens, and gold chalices and ewers encrusted with pearl. The silver vessels were gone, melted down to make bullets. They poured water from the ewers, a rite of purification, and at the Washing of the Hands the congregation sang the words of St. John Chrysostom: "I love this house, Your dwelling place, and the abode of Your glory. Link not my soul with the lost ones, nor my life with men of blood." A thousand years earlier, a court official in Justinian's time said how the lighted church, rising over the dark acropolis, cheered the sailors in their ships on the Bosphorus and the Sea of Marmara. Out there were the Turks, their fleet enclosing the city on three sides.

At one-thirty in the morning, the last assault began. The Turkish ships in the Horn were brought close inshore, eighty biremes in a line between the Wooden Gate and the Beautiful Gate. Alongshore, five hundred Christian archers and slingers awaited them. Notaras the Megadux commanded at Blachernae, and Giustiniani, a Genoese who fought like a lion but broke and ran in the end, held the gate of St. Romanus. Here the emperor joined him, having left the last service in Sancta Sophia. Church bells rang the warning. From the Great Church, says Ducas the chronicler, rose dark laments. *Kyrie eleison! Kyrie eleison!* "Let us say with our whole soul and with our whole mind: Lord, have mercy!"

The *bashibozuks* came first. They were driven in with rawhide whips and iron rods. Flares lit their way. They clashed cymbals and shouted their battle cries. As they advanced, the pipers spurred them on with wild skirling music. They threw javelins and shot arrows, but most of these irregulars filled the ditch before the stockade with their bodies. When the first wave broke, the men on the walls looked for a breathing spell. Then Mehmet sent in his Anatolians and Rumelians. These regulars wore armor, they carried scaling ladders, and their lances were tipped with hooks to pull down the earth-filled barrels on top of the walls. I know how they looked to the men on the walls, having "seen" them in the Ordu Museum.

Turkish "*ordu*" means "army," and this gives us our English word "horde." Violent images wait for you in the Army Museum. Bad Delacroix, some glare from paintings of the Battle of Varna, where Turks massacred Hungarians and Hungarians did the same for Turks. Men are lying on their backs with their faces upturned and being trampled by cavalry horses. The fetlocks of the horses are flecked with red paint. *Sipahis* wave scimitars, and these cavalry soldiers are black-bearded and heavily mustached. Their breastplates are glittering and their white and red turbans are spiked. The Ordu Museum goes in for verisimilitude, and the three-dimensional figures in the museum are like gory wax figures in Madame Tussaud's. The auxiliary cavalry they call *akinjis* wear the fez. Though they look like comic-opera Turks in their extravagant sashes, they mean business. The *azaps* or foot soldiers wear baggy trousers. Their headgear resembles the old Russian helmets you see in the Kremlin Armory in Moscow. Behind these Russians and Turks looms a common antecedent, and the Mongol presence is vivid in the Army Museum. This is "Asia," a state of mind.

Late in the afternoon, a Janissary band gives a concert in the lobby. The men in the band are dressed in red tunics and blue trousers. The white woolen cap with its pendant like a sleeve is their emblem, and the old story tells how a dervish saint gave this cap and a name to the Janissaries. "Be the name of this new host *Yenicheri*," said the *hodja*, flinging the sleeve of his robe over their heads. "May God the Lord make their faces white, their arms strong, their swords keen, their arrows deadly, and give them the victory!"

As they play their martial music, the Janissaries move. They advance two steps forward, then take a step back. Some of them are chanting the name of Mohammed, and the chant rises to a scream. These are men, and love war even if it kills them. They use the old instruments, the double-reeded hautboy and a vented woodwind like a shofar that makes the whining noise of the pipes.

They shake red-tasseled rods that hold little silver bells and are tipped with the crescent. Their cymbals and steel triangles shatter the air, and over the din rides the thrilling sound of cornets. Under the eerie music is the deeply stirring and affrighting pulse of the drums, elephant drums, camel drums, mule drums, and the rat-tat-tat of the snares.

Faulkner says somewhere that for every Southern boy it is still the first of July, 1863, and the fight at Gettysburg can go either way. The fight for Constantinople is like this, no matter how often you read over the tale. The odds were long but not insuperable. Had they remembered the unguarded postern in time, if Giustiniani, wounded, had not quit. . . . Tuesday in the early hours, May 29, 1453, and the fate of nations and peoples hangs in the balance.

Like the *bashibozuks*, the Anatolians and Rumelians broke against the walls, and as the night wore on to morning the defenders of the city still held. "In that fatal moment," says Gibbon, "the Janissaries arose, fresh, vigorous, and invincible." They came in at the double, keeping perfect order, and out on the Bosphorus men heard the wild music. Along the stockade they fought hand-to-hand with the exhausted defenders, and little by little they breached the walls. The city fell at dawn, and chroniclers say how the crescent moon still shone in the sky. The Emperor Justinian wanted to flee this city in the time of the Nika rebellion, but the Empress Theodora kept him at his post. "Purple makes the finest shroud," she said. Constantine, the last Emperor, when he saw that everything was lost, charged the enemy, his sword in his hand. No one saw him after this, and his shroud was Constantinople.

The emperor had a brother Thomas who ruled a despotate in Greece, and this brother got away and fled to Rome. He brought away with him the head of the Apostle Andrew, the patron saint of the Byzantines, and he sold the head to Pope Pius for an annuity of six thousand ducats. But he died soon after, the annuity unspent, in Santo Spirito close to St. Peter's. Zoe called Sophia was his daughter, and she went to Moscow and married Tsar Ivan III. So the claim to the throne of Byzantium passed to Russia. In Moscow they took over St. Andrew, making him their patron saint. He was St. Peter's older brother, and this put Rome itself in the shade. Also they prophesied that one day the Russian race would reign in the God-guarded city. Their Empress Catherine the Great renamed a gate in Moscow "the Way to Constantinople." Napoleon was aghast when Tsar Alexander wanted to seize the city for Russia. "Constantinople," he said, "that is the empire of the world."

In the right foreground below us, Stamboul and its minarets drift in a golden haze. Smog builds towards sunset, when the wind drops. The Russian light cruiser is contributing its bit, and the puffs of smoke from the raked funnels are Rorschach blots on the air. From our perch aloft, we can't make out what they are doing, only that they are doing something. I expect that on the quayside men are freeing the hawsers from the capstans, and the *Admiral Golovko* is getting ready to cast off.

The Cistern lies in darkness beneath the First Hill. Turks call it Yerebatan Sarayi, meaning Underground Palace. Justinian stored water here for his Great Palace, and Muslims used the water for the gardens of Topkapi. However, time passed and they forgot about the Cistern. It disappeared from view, like the hiding place of the Once and Future King. People in the neighborhood knew that something was down there, and when they wanted water they lowered buckets through the floors of their houses. Sometimes they drew up fish. Byzantine engineers made this fabulous place, and the columns they raised are still standing. The Underground Cistern is an image for Constantinople, its unquiet past and its future, still dark. What the darkness hides is anybody's guess. The past is always prologue, maybe a spirochete, or yeasty like leaven in dough.

After their Revolution, Turks in Constantinople tore and canceled the bond of the past. When Ataturk & Co. sent away the last sultan, they meant to mark an ending and a new beginning. Russia, a hopeful country, was sending them signals. Five years before, Nicholas, the last Russian tsar, read the signals and abdicated his throne. He did this in Pskov, a provincial town north of Moscow, and that is one of those ironies too gross for art but acceptable to history. In Pskov five hundred years ago, Philotheus the monk had his vision of the Third Rome where history ends. The new rulers in Moscow, wanting to abolish history, got rid of the tsar and his ecumenical Church. They looked to the future. But the Revolution handed on the past to the future, and the new moon was cradled in the arms of the old.

Russians and Turks, who share a common border, have in common their image problem too. The eighteenth century, an era of good feeling, tidied up the image of the malignant and turbaned Turk, and Mozart in his *Abduction from the Seraglio* is taking his cue from the time. Pasha Selim in the opera burns with love for his Christian captive, but she doesn't reciprocate. He is a man of feeling, though, and dismisses her to happiness with the young man of her choice. The opera ends with a chorus of Janissaries who applaud this: "Pasha Selim, long may he live!" But when the music stops, the savagery starts up again. The unquiet past still lives in the present, and if they know what is good for them the tenor and the girl will clear out of Constantinople.

For a long time, Turks and Greeks have fought over Cyprus. The island is blood-drenched and the blood hasn't stopped flowing. When the Turks took the island four hundred years ago, they tortured the governor, cutting off his ears and nose. They tied him to a yardarm and ducked him in the harbor, then flogged him and skinned him alive. They quartered the body, exposing the parts on their cannon, and stuffed the flayed skin with hay. Janissaries sat the effigy on the back of a cow and paraded it through the camp. Afterwards, they smoothed out the skin, pickled the severed head in a vat of salt water, and sent these objects to their sultan. He was Selim the Sot, the fifth Ottoman after the Conquest.

Ottomans came from the borderlands that stretched eastward from Bithynian Mount Olympus. In the fourteenth century, they starved out the old Greek city that used to be Brusa and is Bursa today. They made the city their headquarters, and this is where they sowed the whirlwind. Osman their first dynast dreamed of a tree that sprang from his loins, overshadowing heaven and earth. The Crescent topped the tree and dashed against the Cross in Constantinople.

This warrior-race of the Osmanli or Ottomans has left its residue in the "Green City." The residue is surprising. In Ottoman Bursa the past, though still lively, isn't virulent but tamed. Six hundred years after the Ottomans took the city, travel agents want to book you there for your vacation. Most days in summer, tourists are out in force, looking at the classical mosques. Huge peeling sycamores and ancient horse chestnuts shade the *turbes* where the Ottomans are buried. The *kervansaray* in the covered bazaar resembles an old English innyard. *Kervansaray* is their word for a stopping place in the country. In Istanbul, this same place is called a *han*. Arches, enclosing the innyard, support a hostelry on the upper story. Merchants traveling with the caravans along the Anatolian trade routes broke their journey in this comfortable place. There were shops on the upper story, still open for business.

The Green City makes a harmony where new and old exist side by side. Justinian built the public bath or *hamam*. Turkish men and women still soak themselves in the thermal water. The sudatory in its building plan resembles Sancta Sophia, and the same intelligence created them both. The water coming out of the ground is heated to a temperature of ninety degrees centrigrade. Before it enters the baths, they must cool it.

All year round, snow lies on Mount Olympus. It looks like a picture postcard, and you can climb the mountain or visit the house where the Conqueror was born. The tombs of his ancestors are built over what remains of a Christian monastery. On the tessellated floor rest the Ottoman sarcophagi, surrounded by Corinthian columns. Turks who took these columns from the monastery church didn't know what they were looking at or they liked their little joke, and the columns in the *turbes* stand upside down. When Muslims conquered Egypt, long before the Turks, they stripped the pyramids of their limestone covering. It went to face the new mosques. This seems a reasonable way to deal with the past.

West of Bursa is the town of Gebze where Hannibal killed himself, having come to the end of his tether. Many centuries later, Mehmet II gave up the ghost in Gebze. Someone gave him poison and he died in great pain. This was on the third of May in 1481 at the hour of the afternoon prayer. Old chroniclers note that this hour was governed by Mars. Like his ancestor Bayazit, the Conqueror meant to stable his horses in St. Peter's. But his dream of world conquest went glimmering, and Mehmet was only forty-nine when he died. They returned his body to Constantinople for burial in Fatih Chami, the mosque he built over the Church of the Holy Apostles. Hannibal in death had no place to go back to. When the Romans took Carthage, they sowed the ground with salt. So Hannibal is buried in Gebze. His tomb is still standing not far from the road. People who live there appear not to know this, and if you want to see the tomb you must look for yourself. Gebze has forgotten the violent men who died in this dusty corner of Anatolia.

Sometimes the dead are still quick in their shrouds. This is when history brings in its revenge. Istanbul is a city where the past is mostly rubbish to be bundled away. Stamboullus, who think history is like this, still pay usury on old obligations, however. In 1182 Greeks hunted down Latins and killed them. Then Latins did the same for Greeks, and for more than fifty years they made a violent order in Constantinople. Greeks took back the city in 1261. Michael Paleologus was their leader. He called himself the Basileus, Christ's vicar on earth. This Michael had a rival, the boy emperor John. He blinded the boy and seized the throne for himself. As time flies, it was just the other day that Turkish mobs roamed the city, beating Greek merchants. September 6, 1955, and the battle cry was Cyprus. Before this, they were killing Armenians. April 24, 1915, was the day the Young Turks chose for their genocide. "Armenians Never Forget," reads the legend on a wall in the Old City of Jerusalem, and off the East River Drive in Manhattan the red letters announce "Death to Turk Assassins!" Underneath is the inscription "April 24, 1915."

To please their Arab friends, Turks have downgraded relations with Israel. But you can fly out of Istanbul to Tel Aviv, if you don't mind a detour through Athens. The Israeli carrier El Al has its office on Cumhuriyet Caddesi. A policeman admits callers one at a time. In the interior, the lights are turned low. A year ago in this office, the manager was killed by a bomb. But after the glass breaking, things quieted down. Turks, who have their truths, are ignorant of Truth, and they will send you to the stake but not for your opinions. In the mosque at Eyup, you see them praying in silence before the Window of Help. The latticework in the window is brass and highly wrought, and the Star of David has a place in the lattice.

The old city is still a reliquary. When the black bile is flowing, it seems to me that only God changes, where man remains the same. In Topkapi Museum, the Mantle of the Prophet is preserved under glass. Their first sultan named Selim, known as the Grim, brought this relic back from Egypt, together with the Prophet's footprint, one of his teeth, and hairs from his beard. Islam is a religion not notable for pity, and in the mind's eye the Prophet's mantle is stained with blood. But it covers a multitude of sins, and if you want shelter they will offer you a piece of the mantle. If you are poor, you can count on a handout. They don't ask for your credentials when they pass you a cup of water in the *sebil*.

Living in a fallen world where light and darkness swap

back and forth, Turks have a painter's feeling for nuance. Their skepticism is total. Luther, the contemporary of Suleiman the Magnificent, detested them for this. He said the Grand Turk was Antichrist, and his presence on the stage of history meant that history was ending. This optimistic point of view isn't native to Turks. A proverb of theirs goes "Until you have crossed the bridge, you should call the bear your uncle." After the Conquest they tolerated the Greek Orthodox Church in their city, and the people still had a patriarch. One of these patriarchs was a Calvinist in secret. Preferring a world of primary colors, he said how East is East and West is West. Turks threw him in the Sea of Marmara.

Exclusiveness has its virtues, though, for example the fierce clarity of Lenin. You can't make a revolution unless you honor this virtue. With the Russian Revolution, said the poet Andrei Bely, the last great battle against Antichrist begins.

A little to the east of Justinian's Cistern are the great churchly monuments of Christian Byzantium, the Heavenly Wisdom and the Heavenly Peace. I keep going back to Haghia Eirene, the "peaceful" church, hoping they will let me in. So far, nothing doing. Something archaeological is going on inside, and Turks, unlike Italians, don't look the other way if you press a tip in their hand. The old church, enclosed within the walls of Topkapi, makes a hybrid, part Muslim, part Christian. Both Muslims and Christians sprinkled it with blood. Three thousand people died here when Arians and Orthodox brawled in the courtyard, arguing the merits of the new Nicene Creed. A lot later on, Haghia Eirene became a military storehouse. The ancient marble column to the left of the entrance supports an artillery shell, and in a corner of the garden stands a modern field gun, bearing the legend KRUPP-1914. The first church on the site is long gone, destroyed by Nika rebels.

Yerebatan Caddesi on the First Hill runs north and west from the square before Sancta Sophia. This was the nerve center of the Byzantine city, shared by the Great Church and Justinian's Palace. On your left hand, a few feet along the street, is the inconspicuous building that admits you to the Underground Cistern. To get into the Cistern, you go down a flight of thirty-nine stairs. The great columns stand in water, cypress trees in a swamp. The columns near the platform at the base of the stairs are washed with electric light from unshaded bulbs. The Corinthian capitals remember the Roman thing, and over the capitals are imposts that carry little brick domes. If you screw up your eyes, you can make out the herringbone pattern on the domes. Twenty-eight columns form a rank or row, and more than three hundred columns support the vaulted ceiling. Only the first few ranks are visible, however. Mostly the colonnade recedes in darkness.

When the Janissaries broke into Sancta Sophia only a stone's throw away, the priests at the altar went on chanting until the last moment. Then they gathered up the sacred vessels and stepped through the sanctuary wall. It closed behind them, and priests and vessels were never seen again. That is how the story goes, and pious Christians believe that they are still down there beneath the First Hill, waiting for time to come round.

In 1921, Turks and Greeks fought two battles at Inonu. They met on the high ground southeast of Bursa, first in the snow of winter, then in the mud of spring. Each time the Greeks were beaten. The Turks came on "steadily and lumpily," said young Ernest Hemingway who covered this war, and it was the first time he saw "dead men wearing white ballet skirts and upturned shoes with pompoms on them." Ismet led the Turkish army. He was the Gazi's right hand, and when the fighting was over he changed his name to Inonu. The soccer stadium on the hill above Dolmabahche Palace glorifies this man and his battles.

In Carstairs' opinion, Inonu Stadium is the best of Istanbul. He spends a lot of time at the discotheque in the Etap or at the blackjack tables in the Hilton casino, but the stadium is his home away from home. Cab drivers still call it by its former name, Mithat Pasha. Whatever they call it, it has a great view across the Bosphorus to Asia. If the game is boring, there is always this view. Carstairs doen't think the game will be boring.

The horde pours out of the ferry from Asia at the *iskele* below the Dolmabahche mosque. Flowing uphill, it covers the hill like locusts on the land. The men are waving soccer flags, chanting hoarsely, and beating little drums joined together like bongo drums. They wear colored hats and sashes, maize and blue for Fenerbahche, black and white for Beshiktash. The stadium has seats for forty thousand people, and every seat is taken. Outside, ten thousand men are trying to get inside, or they are craning their necks where the ground rises and looks over the wall. The Askeris push these men away with their illuminated sticklers that look like cattle prods. In the milling crowd, I don't see a single woman.

For the first thirty minutes, the match is uninspiring. Nobody strikes a goal, and we admire the view. The vendors are doing a land-office business. They come through the stands armed with doughy rings of *simit*, bags of chick-peas, pistachios, and roasted pumpkin seeds, and they carry iced sherbet and tea on brass trays. The trays are hung on chains, looped around the vendor's neck. On the field, play is rough. Fouls interrupt the free flow of the game. The referee, saluted by catcalls and whistles, penalizes three men of Beshiktash. The roaring crowd is a fire fanned by the wind, and the stands shake when the men stamp their feet. Beside me, the hairy man who wears the colors of Fenerbahche throws his arm around my shoulders, pounding on me like a side of beef. His grin is golden, all caps and fillings.

In the fifty-ninth minute, Fenerbahche goes ahead. The move is inititated by their left winger, who finds his teammate unmarked. Carstairs, interpreting, wants me to note the intelligent "cross." Six minutes later, Beshiktash equalizes with a "header" from a thunderous free kick. Play after this is mostly defensive and I agree that it is sweet to behold. Goalkeepers for both clubs manage daring saves. Avni Riza, defending for Beshiktash, is a hero of our time. A bold run on the right flank gets the crowd to its feet. This is followed by a dangerous "inswinger." But Riza is equal to it. He dives full length, and Fenerbahche is denied.

Five minutes from the whistle, though, a knee-high free kick is taken by their right winger. Beshiktash tries to check him but he finds a gap in the line. His header rattles the upright, and a long sigh like a bellows collapsing comes from the partisans of the black and white. Riza in the nets puts his hands to his face. 2–1, and this is the ballgame.

The city buses go by us, throbbing with Turks, and the men in the buses are hanging on outside the doors. We walk back towards Galata with the Bosphorus on our left. On our right is Tophane, the cannon foundry the Conqueror built. In the fading light, the eight domes are towers in the Magic Kingdom. The mosque of Kilitch Ali Pasha, built by Sinan near the end of his life, stands on the corner of Kemeralti Caddesi, just outside the old walls of Galata. Kilitch Ali Pasha, for whom the mosque is named, was an Italian, born in Calabria. He converted to Islam and became Lord High Admiral, a great Ottoman grandee, also very rich. A good sailor, he adjusted his sails and kept on the windy side of care. Selim the Sot gave him his name Kilitch or Sword. Even in old age he couldn't renounce the pleasures of the harem, and he died at ninety in a harem girl's arms.

The mosque, making a little replica of Sancta Sophia, has a projecting apse and a narthex. This has been a puzzle to some. Mostly, Sinan left the Great Church alone. A good Muslim, he kept faith with his own tradition. One of his daughters was named for the favorite wife of the Prophet. The architect was thrifty, though, also accommodating, and like a good carpenter he used what he had in the shop.

ROME

FELLINI IN ARCADY

MY ROMAN FRIEND Giordano likes doing things that pop into his head, *che salta in mente*. On organized excursions he turns a dead eye. "*Chi me lo fa fare?*" he wants to know, when we make a trip to the Vatican, a miracle of organization. "Who got me into this?" The last Sunday in the month they let you in free, but Giordano isn't grateful. He has his own way to cope with Rome. Like an old Quaker asking the Bible to give up its truth, he opens the book of the city and puts his finger down at random. Sometimes this lands us up in Deuteronomy, but that is part of the story.

The stringy black hair falls away like a mop on either side of his high domed forehead, the head of a Medici. Cheap wire-rimmed glasses belie the black estimating eyes. Where his long nose, a ski jump, turns up at the end, the heavy undershot jaw ends in a fist. However close he shaves, he has five-o'clock shadow. A dusting of black mustache softens the hard line of his lips. The tapering, expressive fingers, always working, suggest an artist or an executioner.

When Giordano was born, just after the War, men coming back bet on life against death. His father, a left-wing Socialist and a friend of Pietro Nenni's, named him for Giordano Bruno. This free-thinking priest stood for life. In 1600, the Roman Inquisition burned him at the stake in Campo dei Fiori, a working-class district. His statue, enveloped by market stalls, looks across the Tiber to Vatican City. Sometimes they put a red flag in his hand.

A degree in civil engineering is the goal that beckons for Giordano, who wants to build better bridges and roads. I hope he will do this. Just the other day, a bridge over the A2 outside Anagni fell without warning, crushing a motorist. They had the contractor up on the carpet. "*Ho sbagliato*," he said. "I made a mistake."

Giordano studies part time in the engineering college, the central branch in Piazza di San Pietro in Vincoli. "Vincoli" is chains, and in the church in the square they have the chains that bound St. Peter. The church is noble but cursed by yesterday and today. A new pavement of travertine marble, restorer's work, gilds the lily, like the "Oriental" carpets you can buy in the market at Porta Portese. Michelangelo's Moses, a Trojan horse, came in through the front door four hundred years ago. All day and every day, busloads of tourists, many of them Japanese, roll up Via Terme di Tito and into the square. Moses wears a set of horns, provoking a buzz of speculation. A mean-looking priest with his hand out guards the *portone*. "*È mio*," he says, don't forget your humble servant. The Prophet, holding the Ten Commandments, has come down from the mountain. On the plain, his wretched countrymen worship the Golden Calf. His eyes blaze, and the knotted veins in his hands and forearms are full of malediction. Giordano warms to the rage in Michelangelo's Moses. However, he says, these famous chains in San Pietro are like pebbles on the beach at Ostia. A lot of other churches have them too.

Half days in the working week and all day Saturday, he works in the body shop or *carrozzeria* on Largo Corrado Ricci, nearby at the foot of Via Cavour. The owner of the body shop is known behind his back as "Signor Saltimbanco." Like "saltimbocca alla Romana," veal so tasty it jumps into your mouth, this Signor jumps up on a bench. He is also proprietor of the salesroom next door, where they sell and rent Lambrettas, Alfa Romeos, and Fiats. I rent my Fiat from Signor Saltimbanco, who would think better of me if I rented an Alfa Romeo. Over his office door hangs a framed inscription: *"Ogni volta che vedo passare un Alfa Romeo, io mi levo il cappello."* "Every time I see an Alfa Romeo go by, I tip my hat." This saying is ascribed to Henry Ford.

The proprietor smells of grappa and makes a lot of noise. "*Cretino*!" he shouts, buttonholing his men. "*Scemo! sciocco! stupido!*" Being Roman, he puts an *h* between the *s* and the *t*. When I ask him if this Fiat will get me where I want to go, he turns cagey, however. "*Direi*," he says indifferently. "I guess so."

"Once a week," says Giordano, "even Saltimbanco rests." This being Sunday, *riposo settimanale*, we open the book of Rome and put down a finger on Via di Porta San Sebastiano. Modern Rome, the ancient city, and the medieval city mingle their spurs around the Street of the Gate of St. Sebastian. This doesn't make it special, and that is why the random method works for Rome.

Just before the piazzale where the street begins, Santi Nereo ed Achilleo half hides itself in trees. Fashionable young Romans who want to get married have made this church a place to go to. It vies in popularity with Bernini's little church of Sant' Andrea on the Quirinal Hill. A wedding is in progress and we take a seat to the rear.

The old church is like an old house where people have been living for a long time. Tastes change, but these people are thrifty. Nothing gets thrown away, and the furniture shows this. The Bernini church, a Johnny-come-lately, is exclusive like a good work of art. Its harmony is studied, the common term being whimsical-baroque. Inside the church, the human comedy is playing. Cherubs watch from the domed ceiling, their fat dimpled legs hanging down into the nave. In Santi Nereo ed Achilleo, the play mixes different genres. Also it lacks structure, like those medieval pageants that began at three a.m. and went on until midnight. Everything gets its innings, and the self-conscious artist takes a back seat. A porphyry pedestal from the Baths of Caracalla holds the medieval pulpit. On a cornice, pagan faces look out of the sculpted foliage.

The church commemorates the *fasciola*, a bandage St. Peter used to ease the sores on his leg when they chained him in the Mamertine Prison. Fleeing from prison, he dropped the bandage, and that is where they built the church. They said something off-handed like "Let us have a church that remembers the bandage." The early soldier-martyrs for whom it is named are buried in a catacomb not far away. Saints Nereus and Achilleus sound like Homeric heroes to me.

The bridegroom wears a white silk suit, a shirt of robin's egg blue faced with frills like the paper sleeves you put on pigs' trotters. The girl is vivid with mascara, her eyes larger than life. A Donizetti heroine, she hangs on her husband's arm like the Daughter of the Regiment. Children dressed to the eyes pelt the two of them with flowers when they come down the nave. Outside the church doors, kibitzers are crying "*bravo!*" As the wedded couple emerges, they wink and applaud, congratulating themselves. The men of the regiment, honoring their own, have turned out in their parade-ground regalia. Like West Point cadets, they line the walkway to the limousine, a black Mercedes gay with streamers. "Medals will be worn." The engraved invitation will have said this. Also the men wear pleated cummerbunds, canary yellow sashes like a pectoral cross, gilt-topped swords, and plumed hats. Giordano supposes they are *carabinieri*. I say they are supers from the opera house on the Viminal, hired by the impresario who has this production in charge.

My friend, if he gets married, won't tie the knot here. Sundays in the Campidoglio, a civil servant who wears a decent frock coat performs weddings in the Municipal Hall. He keeps the fuss to a minimum. Also, says Giordano, there aren't any priests.

In the emptied-out church, the Virgin above the altar acknowledges the glad tidings brought by the angel. Up there on the arch, our Divine Comedy is playing and the happy ending is already written. The glittering figures turn away from the world, waiting for the moment when the God of Revelations will wipe away all tears from their eyes. In the meantime, Roman artisans have their conventions. In these old Roman churches, the same twelve sheep approach the Lamb of God, the same elders of the Apocalypse offer Him their crowns. Their figures are rigid and reprieved from human time. Giordano, not a lover of mosaics, is reminded of the Wax Museum in Piazza Esedra. A God-fearing man who doesn't go to church, he is like that fierce Moses who broke the Golden Calf. The upright heart comes first for him, before idols and temples. I take his point, a good one. But a Latin tag, remembered dimly, is moving around in my head. "*Domine, dilexi decorum domus tuae.*" This inscription, lettered in gold, is set into the coffered ceiling of San Francesca Romana, a sumptuous old church in the Forum. "Lord, I have loved the beauty of Thy House."

You can see the mosaics in Santi Nereo ed Achilleo every day except Friday and except for siesta. Affixed to the door, a printed notice says this. Whatever it says, the church is always closed unless a wedding has been scheduled. Giordano has a name for churches like this one, legion in Rome: Santa Maria Sempre Chiusa. "Chiusa" is closed. A little priest in a brown cassock is closing the doors. His bare feet are shod in sandals, a gray stubble of beard on his chin. Coughing politely, he points to his watch, then folds his hands prayerfully and lays them under his chin. It is time for siesta.

Leaving the church, we cross the roundabout, no man's land. Rome, going down towards the Appian Way, smells of hot rubber and exhaust fumes. Also, says Giordano, it smells of the rich. Their villas beside the road turn away from the traffic. Descending from the city, it pours into the wide thoroughfare that passes the ruined Baths of Caracalla. Shelley, pensive on the grass, wrote poetry amid the ruins. The roundabout is a centrifuge, Piazzale Numa Pompilia. The stream of traffic, tiny particles fleeing the center, emerges from its close confinement and shoots into Via di Porta San Sebastiano.

Within the Aurelian Wall, the Street of the Gate of St. Sebastian is another name for the Appian Way. No one knows for certain if the great cardinal ever lived here. But a house on the street is called after him, Casa del Cardinale Bessarione, and if his luck held this was where he spent his last years. Along the front of the house, frescoes adorn the roofed-over arcade. The elegant windows beneath the loggia put a frame around the world. A vertical strip, dividing the window panes, slices up reality in pieces you can deal with. Festooning the walls on the other side of the mullioned windows, garlands hang from brackets like ravens' beaks. The garlands are artificial and the corbels that hold them are a painter's cunning illusion. This house is worth loving, it being unreal.

Growing up in Trebizond on the Black Sea, the last Greek city to hold out against the Turks, Bessarion converted to Rome. This meant a life in exile. He was one of the *fuorusciti*, men gone outside. Italians gave this name to defeated Guelfs and Ghibellines who fled their native place when the other side took over. For these exiles, however, the wheel kept on turning, and likely as not they got to go back again. Bessarion, like Dante, never went back. While the world was burning, he collected Greek texts and translated Aristotle into Latin. An impersonal labor, it reprieved him from the flesh. He was far away when the Turks entered Constantinople, and lived another twenty years after the city fell.

In the garden behind the house, the dark green boxwood is trimmed in formal shapes. Broken classical sculptures stand among the parterres, and a small fountain plays over a terra-cotta urn. Terra-cotta is "cooked earth," but even in the Roman summer it is cool in Bessarion's garden.

Next door on the right, if you stand with your back to the street, the church of San Cesareo lives up to its name. "Saint Caesar's" is a hybrid. Romans who are thrifty are superstitious too. They take the stone the builders rejected and make it the headstone of the corner. The old rejected thing is an antidote and powerful, like the hair of the dog. This impure art gives offense to some Romans, Horace, for instance, a fastidious poet in their classical age. He told them not to put antipathies together. The torso of a beast and the feathers of a bird make a monster, he said. But Rome is full of monsters. When Aeneas Piccolomini, their humanist pope, came to St. Peter's throne, he called himself Pius II. Pope Pius I was there before he was, also Virgil's Pius Aeneas. Why not have both?

San Cesareo is medieval but much restored in modern times, modern meaning for Romans four hundred years ago. The Cosmati, medieval craftsmen who worked in mosaic, made the choir, pulpit, and altar. They came from different families but a lot of their young men were christened Cosmate, and that is how the guild got its name. Veneering the altar, the round of porphyry is flanked by oblong panels, a geometric pattern that communicates repose. Around it, the mosaic border trembles on vertigo but just keeps its balance. This formal art, making room for chaos, persuades you that its form is true.

Not far from my pension on Via Capo d'Africa, the mosaic over the old gateway is signed by Master Jacobus and his son Cosmate. On the gold ground of the mosaic Christ is picked out in stone, beside Him two men, one of them black. "Head of Africa," maybe. The men in the mosaic are slaves ransomed by the hospital that stood on the other side of the gateway. Across the Via Navicella, there is still a hospital on the Caelian Hill.

Piecing together tiny fragments of marble, the Cosmati wove

stone tapestries alight with bits of gold. They liked a white marble surface where colored disks break the polychrome mosaics. Swirling, the mosaics form up again in patterns. For the colored *tesserae* they wanted, red, purple, and green, the Cosmati picked over the ruins. When they found what they wanted, they sawed it up in different sizes and shapes. On their friezes and writhing columns, monstrous creatures out of old mythologies confront you, sphinxes, chimeras, griffins that are both beast and bird. Often, not always, these craftsmen put their names to what they made. Sometimes they added a pious sentiment in Latin: "Glory to God in the Highest." Mostly, however a signature is all they give you. Glory belonged to God and they rendered it freely, absorbing themselves in their craft. The craft they practiced is called after them, "cosmatesque."

Poking around behind the altar, I discover sea monsters cavorting on the tessellated floor. These monsters are left over from some long-ago classical bath. Being indifferent to the company it keeps, San Cesareo has hitched itself to the ruins. This might have given scandal, some Christians wanting to make a fresh start. Giordano, a free thinker, is like these scandalized Christians. The only revolution worth having, he tells me, is a total revolution. Otherwise, the past, a virus waiting to break out again, lives in the present. Wanting to lay the town flat, he despises the men of half-measures, "*tagliatelle* Socialists" who bungle the job. *Tagliatelle* means spaghetti, flabby and weak. Also it means me. Where Noah shut his ears and sailed off in the ark, I would have admitted my friends. "*Vecchio Tentenna*," Giordano calls me, Old Shilly-Shally.

Walking the Appian Way within the Wall, a long walk, we save our breath to cool our porridge. Down the road and across it, an arrow points us up a flight of stairs to the tomb of the Scipios. In republican Rome they were consuls, soldiers, and orators. Scipio Africanus, the greatest scion of the house, cut a great figure in history. He defeated Hannibal two thousand years ago. Cato the Elder, an angry old man, told them in the Senate that Carthage must be destroyed. "*Delendam*" was his word, meaning total destruction. When the Romans defeated Carthage in the last Punic War, they didn't leave a stone on a stone. For Scipio Africanus, the famous victory turned to ashes. He wanted glory but the full measure escaped him. Embittered, he went into exile and never came back to Rome.

The modest house where the *guardiano* lives and sells us our ticket sits beside the tomb at the top of the stairs. A Roman house lies beneath it, perhaps the house of the custodian who guarded the ashes of the dead. Beyond the tomb the ground rises, turning into a park and playground. This is the Orti degli Scipioni, a dusty, neglected place littered with garbage and public pronouncements. Mostly these *avvisi* go unread. Men sitting in their pony carts wait for our custom, others want us to buy their *gelati*. The lovers on the grass have no better place to go. They throw discretion to the winds, and in this Catholic country no one pays them any heed. Meanwhile I read how back in Islam, lovers in the park have been arrested for committing *khalwat*. This includes holding hands.

Avoiding the lovers, we cross the park, descending the hill on the other side. This brings us to Via di Porta Latina, a private preserve. Running parallel to the Appian Way, it ends where the Latin Gate pierces the Aurelian Wall. High walls, insulating the villas of the rich, come down to the road. In the tops of the walls, shards of broken glass are embedded. As we walk further, towards the Latin Gate, the sidewalk narrows to a catwalk. We have to hug the walls to avoid the Fiats and Cinquecentos that barrel along the road.

St. John the Evangelist is a vivid presence here. I call him the patron saint of writers, remembering the Gospel according to St. John: "In the beginning was the Word." Just inside the Latin Gate, a tiny chapel is named after him, San Giovanni in Oleo. Boiling in oil was the fate they intended for this disciple. But he surprised his tormentors, emerging from his ordeal "as from a refreshing bath." I think the hagiographers mean us to take their story in figurative ways. St. John was a writer, not the life of Riley. The hard going restored him, though, and the Word that got his attention is still current. No one knows where he died, perhaps a dusty town in Asia Minor.

Around the corner and a little in from the road, a twelfth-century campanile humanizes the empty sky. I tug Giordano's elbow, wanting him to notice. Being Roman, he is apt to take his city for granted. Classical pillars face the church of San Giovanni a Porta Latina but aren't there to overawe us. The portico, making a simple horizontal, is bisected by a solitary pine tree. Long feathery branches sweep the ancient well or *pozzo* in the courtyard. Inside, moonstone windows soften the light. If you rue the day, a visit to San Giovanni will change this.

Giordano says bitterly that the Catholic Church has gobbled up the best real estate in Rome. The land occupied by San Giovanni is prime, also a charge on society. Priests are like mendicants who don't toil or spin. Where they live in idleness, you could put up low-cost housing for the poor.

When Nero was emperor in the first century A.D., he carved out a huge rectangle butting on the Forum. It extended from the Palatine to the Caelian and beyond, almost to St. John Lateran, and north to the Esquiline Hill. On this common land he built his Domus Aurea, a "Golden House" nobody needed. The poor, living hereabouts, protested, saying angrily how "Rome will become a single house." But the poor are always with us, and the emperor had his way. In his dining rooms the fretted ivory ceilings slid open, raining flowers on his guests. Hidden sprinklers dispensed perfume. Sea water ran from the taps in the baths, and over the stairway an artificial waterfall cascaded. Tacitus, up in arms at this conspicuous consumption, sounds like Giordano on the R.C. Church. Nero's pleasure dome, gratuitous, isn't just the same as San Giovanni, however. The church is gratuitous, but like grace you can't do without it.

Seven huge water tanks supplied the Golden House, their ruins hidden behind a wall off the Oppian Hill. The wall encloses the gardens of Palazzo Brancaccio, private property. Romans, hating Nero's memory, still follow his lead. High above the Tiber, where the Garibaldini died for Rome in the Year of Revolutions, the Janiculum Hill belongs to the rich. Keats, dying in Rome, strolled the Pincian Hill with his friend Severn, but couldn't do this today. Pauline Bonaparte, a princess and a great beauty, used to walk on the Pincian Hill too. Her descendants are still welcome there, only you don't see them. On Via Porta Pinciana, outside the walls that fence the villas, you have to pick your way with care through the dog droppings and the overflow from the trash cans.

Public trash cans, like the buses, street lamps, and manhole covers, bear the legend S.P.Q.R.: *Senatus Populusque Romanus,* the Senate and People of Rome. The municipal government, whose legend this is, still sits in the Campidoglio that used to be the Capitol. But these modern Italian senators, Giordano says, are *menefreghisti,* men who don't give a damn. Public space is filthy space in Rome. There are little oases, and the store fronts along the streets are all spit and polish. Women in tight skirts are on the street bright and early, polishing door knobs or washing shop windows. A few years ago, these women wore heels like stilettos. Now they wear flats, this being the latest fashion. Roman women are barometers of fashion and taste, and their eye to personal appearance never sleeps. In the coffeehouse on the corner, the man behind the bar puts a shine on the liquor bottles. Next door, the proprietor of the pricy *bottega* sweeps the rubbish from his territory into the street. It stays there. Private property is worth taking pains with, *vale la pena.* Romans could teach something in Socialist Land, where this kind of caring is a lost art. However, public property is nobody's business.

Two churches are named for St. Sebastian in Rome. Most people know the one on the Appian Way. This church is very old but spruced up in the baroque style. Always open, it is popular with tourists, being one of the seven basilicas of Rome. Catholics who make a pilgrimage to these basilicas are promised a plenary indulgence. All their sins are forgiven and their time in purgatory is excused. The 118 bus lets us off at St. Sebastian's, and you can board it by the Scipios' tomb. We pick it up, however, at the *fermata* outside the gate. Making haste slowly, it stops for the little chapel where Christ appeared to St. Peter, a fugitive from Rome. You can still see the jail where they kept him, under the Capitoline Hill. "*Quo vadis, Domine?*" said Peter to Christ. "Where are you going, Lord?" This was all the Lord needed. "I am going back to Rome," he said, "to be crucified a second time." Taking the point of this, the Apostle turned back. Rome in the early sixties was a bad place for Christians, Nero needing a scapegoat for the Great Fire of 64 A.D. Some believe that the emperor, fiddling while Rome burned, set the fire himself. St. Peter, a convenient scapegoat, was in the way.

At his own request, they crucified him upside down. His gruesome death gave Caravaggio the subject for a painting. It hangs in a side chapel to the left of the altar in the church of Santa Maria del Popolo. St. Peter, in the painting, half raises up on his cross. He is mostly naked, where his executioners are clothed. Shadows spread from the tucks in their clothing. This saint isn't plaster but a physical presence. Bushy white hair fringes his chin and temples. His face is lined but vigorous, his belly is flat, and the thighs below the loin cloth are muscled. The man about to die looks down at the spike driven through his left hand. Struggling to lift the cross, three Renaissance Italians have lashed a rope to the foot. One of them, straining with effort, has got the rope across his back. This man wears green britches, his assistant a red coat and white shirt. The man beneath the tilting cross makes the difference for the painting. Where the rope extends upwards, his arms extend down. His fingers and the heel of his hand push off from the earth, his toes, gripping the earth, dig for purchase. The bare feet are soiled with grime. This rough-cut man is only doing his job.

Dominating the painting, his broad inelegant bottom thrusts up towards the cross.

Caravaggio, coming to Rome around 1589, painted shadows and the press of flesh, and nobody before him saw the world with its warts on. Mostly his paintings are Christian, this being the subject matter that got him commissions. He painted the Virgin with dirty feet, an epileptic St. Paul on the road to Damascus, a squeamish boy Jesus with his heel on the head of the serpent. Tender or violent, his subjects live in a real place and time. They aren't waiting for God to wipe the tears from their eyes. If a better time is coming, Caravaggio doesn't say. Painting things in their quality, he makes them important, however. St. Peter, dying on the cross, is important, Caravaggio having got his colors and masses right. Romans skimp on electricity, and the chapel in Santa Maria del Popolo is almost always dark. But a coin box by the altar rail takes fifty-lire coins, and this illuminates the painting.

Between the Quo Vadis chapel and the church of St. Sebastian, the old Roman road divides. The right-hand fork brings you south and west to Fosse Ardeatina, gloomy caves where German soldiers massacred the innocents in the Second World War. These innocents were three hundred and thirty-five Italians, shot in reprisal for something they didn't do. Hostages to fortune, their bad luck was to be in the way. On the afternoon of March 23, 1944, partisans in Rome, filling a rubbish cart with bombs, blew it up in the Via Rassella. They killed thirty-three German soldiers, riding in a lorry, and such Italians as were passing in the street. Not like the death of Heydrich, a butcher of Czechs, this killing was meant for provocation. Their best way to power, Italian Communists thought, was to provoke the Germans to come down hard and harder. Some of the people who died in the caves made a brave end but none wanted to die. I don't like to go to Fosse Ardeatina. If what happened there had meaning, only God knows.

All this is reverie on the way to the tombs. On to the tombs, across the fields from Fosse Ardeatina. Early martyrs are buried here, evoked by pathetic scratchings on the walls of St. Sebastian. Giordano, raised a Catholic, explains. The fish symbolizes Christ the fisherman, who draws us up from the water and carries us to heaven. Christ is also the great fish, taken by the fish-hook of God. His flesh nourishes the world, and the water He lives in cleanses us from sin. The whale that swallowed Jonah and belched him up again tells of our death and resurrection. The Christian dead in the catacombs were waiting, says Giordano, like Jonah in the belly of the whale. The bodies have moldered a long time ago, and the caves are empty now, like the Lavra Caves in Kiev.

"Let the dead bury their dead!" Giordano, like his namesake, is on the side of life. Also his feet are pinching in their narrow Italian shoes. "*Prepotente!*" A slave driver is what I am, and Saltimbanco doesn't have a thing to teach me. Chilled by the damp of St. Sebastian's, we emerge on the Appian Way. Outside in the Roman twilight, the air is soft. Across the road on our left, the Trattoria Archeologica, a potent restorative, awaits us. For dinner they suggest the *seppie con carciofi,* squid with artichokes. The restaurant is full and we dine out in back in the garden.

They brown the squid in oil and garlic, sprinkling in salt and pepper. This done, they add thin slivers of artichoke hearts. Growing between the flagstones in the center of the garden, the red sedum looks like itself, dragon's blood. At the base of the wall, sweet alyssum flows around the ilex, shiny green with red berries. It being *tramonto,* the hour of sunset, a fine rain begins to fall. In the restaurant they are ready for this, and the *cameriere*, his arms full, is coming towards us to set up our umbrella.

"We aren't in Naples, eh?" Fumbling with the dead bolt, the *portiere* says this, also *pigro*, *lazzarone*, other hard words. For the past five minutes, the young man has been banging on the double doors of our pension. *Non siamo a Napoli?* Being in Rome, we might be in Naples, land of the *burrino*. The pounding continues. "*Ma*," says the *portiere*, "*che cosa si può fare?*" But what can you do? *Niente*.

The pension, up three flights of stairs, faces Via Capo d'Africa on the skirts of the Caelian Hill. In the center of old Rome, the Seven Hills are armies drawn up in line of battle, the way you see them on a military map. Next in line from the Caelian Hill is the Palatine, on the other side of the Colosseum, then the Capitoline, anchoring the left flank. To the rear, the Aventine, a reserve corps, has its foot on the Tiber. Confronting these hills, as the eye moves from left to right, are the Quirinal, the Viminal, and the Esquiline. Looking down on the Forum, neutral territory between the lines, they don't advance or retreat but palaver.

From the pension windows, the green space over the way invites my eye. Public buildings take most of it, priests taking the rest. The *ascensore*, when you can find it, accepts ten-lire coins. People coming and going omit to shut the doors, and mostly this elevator is stuck on an intermediate floor. In the street from early hours, the Roman carnival storms the senses. It dies down for siesta, then heats up again. Not far away, however, the Palatine Hill is the eye of the storm. Up there you are in Arcady, an idyllic place invented by poets, now a byword for peace and quiet.

Rome, a real place, lives partly in the mind. A privileged traveler, I shuttle between the two cities. In the mind I climb the Palatine, haunted by old gods. Pales, a divinity who protected shepherds and their flocks, gave his name to the hill. This etymology, romantic, is a plus for tourists. The foul goathead and brutal arm, poking up from the ruins, are intimidating, though. On the southwest slope, traces of the Iron Age city survive, and the shed-like dwelling with its ancient cistern is billed as the house of Romulus. To the north and west, the sunken palace evokes the memory of Tiberius Caesar. Implacable and secret, a Roman Stalin who settled old scores, he makes the flesh crawl. Some historians give him high marks. But Tacitus, an artist among historians, wrote the guilty epitaph people remember, and whatever good this emperor did is buried with his bones.

Pagan Rome was born here but doesn't have the hill to itself. In a corner to the northeast, tucked away behind its wall, the church of St. Sebastian speaks for Christian Rome. The church that isn't much more than a chapel goes back a thousand years and had another life before that. On this site were the gardens of Adonis, laid out by the Emperor Domitian. Adonis is like Christ, dying of his wounds and reviving every year in the spring. He comes up as a flower, the anemone.

Where the gardens of Adonis survive only in the mind, the church garden is visibly present. The date palm, first among equals, is surrounded by roses, orange trees, and showy purple wisteria. The wisteria, a parasite, would like to throttle the grapes and take over the arbor, but the parish priest or his gardener sees that this doesn't happen. Tradition says that St. Sebastian died here, a victim of the persecuting emperor Diocletian. In the odd way of art, his violent death has been attractive to painters. Feeding on violence, they turn it into something else. In their paintings, they show the martyr pierced with arrows and expiring sweetly. In fact, he survived the arrows and was cured of his wounds by a pious Roman lady. Later, when he died, his body went to the catacombs. But this is only matter-of-fact, and what the painters "saw" is what people remember.

The Palatine is for constitutionals, the easygoing kind, not the bracing kind you take on shipboard. This is where I walk in the late afternoons. Towards the end of her life, Napoleon's mother Letizia, a sad old woman more Italian than French, did this too. She paced the Belvedere, a cantilevered terrace jutting over the southeastern corner of the hill. Her famous son fluttered the dovecotes in Rome. Like a natural force, he redrew the map of Italy, abolishing laws and kingdoms. He sent Pope Pius into exile. The Pope, who wanted to die here, "could die anywhere," they told him. Being his own Pope, Napoleon crowned himself with the Iron Crown of the Lombards, made from a nail of the Cross. "God has given it to me," said the self-made man. "Woe to him that touches it!"

From the Belvedere, the city abides your question. The Colosseum behind you is a familiar view on a postcard. But the view is beguiling, and down there is the bestial floor. Unpurged by the Cross in the arena, it smells of cat piss. As the daylight goes above the Baths of Caracalla, the Roman sky turns deep blue. The umbrella pines on the horizon are a darker presence against the sky, green shading to indigo. These Roman pines are crooked. Being alive, they lack the perfect symmetry of moribund things. In the foreground, the last rays of the sun are caught by the modern glass temples of FAO, the Food and Agricultural Organization of the UN. Its headquarters are in Rome, a great modern capital. The modernistic-looking sculpture that stands in front of FAO is the obelisk of Axum. Mussolini brought it back from his African war.

Some cities make sense when you see them in outline. Moscow is a spider's web and New York a giant grid. Rome is a jumble of ancient and modern, all the cities of the plain lumped together. Under the skin, this jumble sorts itself out. The lines reticulate, making a pattern, but not the way they do on a map. Old Rome on the map is a near-parallelogram, bent out of shape. Inside is most of the city you can't dispense with, the "eternal" city of many pilgrims. Face north on the Belvedere and the Circus Maximus is at your back. Boyhood memories of Ben-Hur come alive in the circus. Beyond it in the far distance sprawls the new city Mussolini built. EH-OO-AIR, they call it, Esposizione Universale di Roma. The Forum is in front of you, to the west the whited sepulcher named for Victor Emmanuel.

Near the Victor Emmanuel monument, in Piazza Venezia, Mussolini harangued the crowds. He stood on the little balcony that sticks out from the façade of the palazzo, on your left as you look at the Via del Corso. You can follow the Corso that used to be a racecourse all the way to Piazza del Popolo just inside the Aurelian Wall. On the other side of the wall, the Corso turns into Via Flaminia, the Roman road tramped by the legions on their way to Ravenna and the north. The legionaries were foot soldiers, *mascula proles* who made the old republic march. From their service abroad, they brought back a taste for *luxuria*. Their ghosts are still lively on the Flaminian Way, only they wear different faces. On holidays like All Souls, the day of the dead, this road is bumper to bumper.

From your point of vantage on the Palatine Hill, you can only see so far. In the mind you see farther, having an eagle eye and the wings of the dove. The Pincian quarter outside the wall comes into focus, above it Parioli, a bedroom suburb. People live there as they might be living in Brooklyn Heights. An oblique line, running east and south from Piazza del Popolo, ends at Santa Croce, the church of the Holy Cross in Jerusalem. This emptied-out quarter between the railroad stations looks a little like downtown Detroit.

Rome is a ragbag, like its old churches. Take San Lorenzo, a dogleg away to the east and north. Plunked down in an industrial wasteland, it hearses the bones of an early Christian martyr. Summoned by the prefect to hand over the treasures of the Church, this St. Lawrence assembled the poor. Romans, taking offense, roasted him to death on a griddle. Funereal cypresses loom over San Lorenzo. Crowning the brick bell tower, twelfth-century work, the tiled roof has grainy texture, like the hair of your head. These red ochre tiles, seen from above, give Rome its peculiar color and shape. Arching on top, they fit down over flat tiles whose edges are raised. The cloister, stuck all over with scraps and orts of the past, says how the ruined past is prologue. Catholics who die in Rome are buried in the Campo Verano, a huge necropolis lapping the church. The stalls of the flower vendors across the street are full of color, and in the church porch

Alcide de Gasperi, a Roman hero, is buried. After the Second World War, this prime minister brought the city back from chaos. Vintage scenes in low relief decorate the classical sarcophagus near his tomb.

The basilica of San Lorenzo is *"fuori le mura,"* outside the city walls. The eye, returning to the walls, follows the bounding line west and south to Porta San Paolo, the southernmost gate. St. Paul followed this route to his death. The Tre Fontane monastery where they cut off his head is down in EUR, Mussolini's new Rome. This modern suburb is too far for the hardiest walker. If you want to go down there, you can choose between a bus and the subway. Close by is a station, but the ceiling, resembling crushed paper coffee cups, has begun its slow descent to the platform. When I go to Tre Fontane, I take the 23 bus.

At Porta San Paolo, the First Rome and Second Rome meet again. The donjonlike towers are the work of Belisarius, Justinian's great general. Having defeated the Nika rebels in Constantinople, he came to Rome, a nest of provincials, and took back the city for the world. The pyramid, older than the towers he made here, rises above them. A wealthy Roman praetor who died before Christ was born is buried in the Pyramid. From Via Marmorata, it is only gray mass. Closer up, however, this Pyramid turns white. Keats lies in its shadow, in the Protestant cemetery enclosed by a wall. A vertical slit in the wall, the first one you come to as you walk towards the entrance on Via Caio Cestio, frames the poet's grave. In despair, Keats said his name was written in water. The pathos of this grave, glimpsed for the first time, meets you like a blow. A lyre is cut into the gravestone. Outside the cemetery and around the corner, a plaque tells of Persichetti, a young partisan killed for Rome in the Second World War. Tourists assume that this is Persichetti the composer.

Westward is the Tiber, shallow, swift-running, and prone to meanders. It passes Trastevere on the far bank. This bohemian quarter has come down in the world. A port of entry in the medieval time, it no longer smells of the sea. Silt chokes the river mouth. In the narrow bore between the banks, modern vessels can't navigate, drawing too deep. The church of San Francesco a Ripa, "on the bank," is embarrassed by its shabby piazza. The austere façade, plain as the Alamo, needs an opulent foil and doesn't have it. Bernini's statue of the Blessed Ludovica is in the chapel to the left of the altar. Modern Rome wears the image and likeness of Bernini the way modern London celebrates Sir Christopher Wren. But where Wren speaks for the verities, classic and assured, Bernini has his doubts. His young Roman nun, her eyes closed, her lips parted erotically, is swooning into life. Smiling cherubs look down on the Blessed Ludovica, their expression both cynical and tender.

I think Bernini thought she was kidding herself. An irreverent man, he may have been wrong, and his powerful art has lacunae. Across the river, in the Cornaro chapel of Santa Maria della Vittoria, his St. Teresa languishes in ecstasy. Members of the Cornaro clan, seated in theater boxes left and right of the chapel, assess this doubtful performance. "If that is divine love," said President de Brosses of France, "I know what it is."

At Porta Portese where my parallelogram goes over the river, the flea market draws big crowds on Sundays. The church of San Francesco is just across the road, a trolley line separating the piazza from the market. In this open-air emporium, as vast as St. Peter's, everything in Rome is up for sale. Old icons are on display, painted overnight and heavily varnished. *Caveat emptor*. But if you have a feel for texture, you can buy somebody's jacket made of antelope skin for thirty thousand lire, about twenty dollars.

Eastward on the Tiber is Castel Sant' Angelo, the terminus of Vatican City. An angel stood on the roof once, signaling to Pope St. Gregory an end of the plague in Rome. The Pope, leading a procession through the streets, nearly empty, saw the angel in a vision, sheathing his sword. This last segment of the parallelogram, taking in the papal fortress that was once an emperor's tomb, brings you back to Piazza del Popolo on the north.

Using public transport, efficient in Rome, you can travel the bounding lines in a matter of hours. Buses and trolleys are packed to the gunwales, though, a hundred-lire thrill. Roman men since the Renaissance being flamboyantly heterosexual, this isn't a problem for them. For women, however, hat pins are in order. The subway, still building, offers more room for maneuver. But the little orange cars that look like Lionel trains, when they don't go underground, mostly go the way the crow flies. What the crow sees in outline, it misses in detail.

Most Romans, having an eye for detail, stop, look, and listen, except on the highway. They like to turn things over or look at things in the round. The food they put on the table says this. So does their elegant clothing. Go to Via Condotti and see for yourself. Disputing is an art where thesis meets antithesis, a colorful standoff. Little gets resolved, fender benders, for instance. "Your mother is a *puttana*," says one aggrieved party. "I have just come from sleeping with your sister," says the other.

On a synoptic view, okay for cartographers, the cities of the plain merge in a single city. Look closer, however, and you see how the city is all clutter and edges, like their Roman roof tiles. Italian language, impure in the grain, shows this clutter. Spendthrifts of language, generous or slipshod, Romans when they talk to you upend the horn of plenty and dump it on the table. They never had a French Academy to tell them what to say. Achille Starace, Mussolini's "cultural person," tried to tell them. He wanted them to use archaic *voi* for *lei*. Some aristocratic Romans used this form until he told them they had to. Most Romans, eclectic, like to have it both ways. *Qui* and *qua* are both "here," *lì* and *là* are both "there," *comunque* is "however" but so is *però*, and for "then" they say *allora* and *dunque*. Picking and choosing makes things clearer but does this by leaving things out.

Saying goodbye to the cartographers, I mean to put things

back in. The bounding lines of the city, apparent from the hilltop, are only bare bones. Fleshing them out involves coming down from the hilltop, however. This is hard on the feet, Roman streets being paved with cobbles cut from volcanic rock. If you go on foot, you will want to wear sensible shoes. Crepe soles are best, except in high summer. Roman women who ignore this, summer and winter, are made of sterner stuff than me.

Fitted out in my Wallabys, I head for Porta Maggiore, away to the southeast. The great gate in the wall is a nodal point, also itself. The road beneath the double arches leads to Palestrina, Roman Praeneste. Etruscans lived in Praeneste until the Romans put their city to the sword. Just outside the gate, a donkey on a tomb frieze makes the baker's mill go round. The baker who is buried here died when Rome was a republic, not the modern republic, the one before the Caesars. Round stone ovens are sculpted on his tomb.

Where the brick railway embankment juts into Via Prenestina, a door opens on the underworld. Inside the doorway, workers stand on scaffolding, chipping out a broader passage to the basilica fourteen meters below the street. You must crawl on hands and knees through the dust and rubble to get down there. The votaries of a mystery cult met in the basilica. They believed in the transmigration of souls where one image begets another. Something endured, they thought, conveying this on the walls and the ceiling. Above the ceiling are the tramlines and the tracks of the railroad. Leaving Stazione Termini, the Rome-Naples express shakes the ancient foundation, now reinforced by concrete. In 1917 ballast from the railroad fell into the nave, a lucky accident. After two millennia, it brought the basilica to light.

Fellini in his movie *Roma* has a similar story of things lost and found, but his ending salutes the darkness that wants to take the city back. Excavating for the subway, Fellini's Roman workmen are trailed by a camera crew, impudent *paparazzi*. The car they are riding in passes a necropolis, then stops at the far end of a tunnel. The drill, punching through the tunnel wall, reveals a Roman villa, pristine but empty except for bright frescoes two thousand years old. For a moment the past is lively, seen through the eyes of the crew. Then the colors fade and the villa begins to crumble.

In the Basilica di Porta Maggiore, however, the low stucco reliefs are still fresh. Children, frozen in time, are playing ball on the vaulted roof of the nave. Sappho in the apse dies for the love of Phaon. This boatman of Mytilene was ugly and old, but for one good thing he did, Aphrodite gave him back his youth and beauty.

Ascending the stone stairs, lit dimly by a votive candle in a filigree wall bracket, I emerge in the piazza before the Borgia Tower. The public lecture in the Institute is scheduled for noon: *"Il Cinema di Federico Fellini."* Giordano, though a movie buff, will let this lecture go by. Like the young activists in Fellini's *Roma,* he wants his politics up front. Fellini doesn't oblige and this peeves him. With the trouble in the depths of our being, Fellini says, no public celebration or political symphony can cope. On the poster thumbed to the *portone,* a photograph of the maestro shows him in a felt hat and sheepskin collar, his eyes squinched against thought or the sun.

The Salita dei Borgia, tunneled under the palace, brings you up to the piazza from Via Cavour. On a June night in 1497, Cesare Borgia dined with his brother in the palace garden, then stabbed him and threw the body in the Tiber. Everybody knows about the Borgias, devils incarnate. Before their time, however, a Roman woman killed her father in the gloomy passageway. *Vicus Sceleratus,* old Romans called it, a street accursed by crime. Overhead in the Istituto Centrale Restauro, they are making reparations.

Restauro is restoring. The Institute, where they do this, is closed to the public except for special occasions. In drafty rooms of the palazzo beside the Borgia Tower, old men who wear green eyeshades and smell of sizing and pigment are repairing the ravages of time. Time beginning to dull the luster of Caravaggio's *Madonna of Loretto,* the priests of Sant' Agostino brought this painting to the Institute. Between their church and the palazzo, the connection goes back a long way. High-class courtesans used to frequent Sant' Agostino's, among them the mistress of Cesare Borgia who had her own chapel there. Caravaggio's painting being the glory of the church, the priests were anxious to have it restored. The restorers in the Institute respect their limits, however, and Caravaggio still looked like himself, not "better than ever," when the church got him back again.

In what was once the saloon of the palace, rows of folding chairs face the movie screen and the lectern. The antique trappings are long gone but the air is still chilly with neoclassical pomp. Admission is free and most of the seats are taken. The speaker in his pince-nez and shiny black suit is beanpole thin but has a lot of register, like an electric guitar. Cicero without a toga, he is addressing the conscript fathers. His wigwagging hands send messages in semaphore, and when he speaks he sprays the front row.

"*Per quanto riguarda il cinema moderno poi si potrebbe parlare a lungo.*" This is true and makes a self-fulfilling prophecy. "Regarding the modern cinema, one could speak at length." Americans being taciturn, the silent film is their medium. Gary Cooper never needed to open his mouth. If talkies didn't exist, Italians would have to invent them, the Italian thing being to say little in much. "How are you?" I ask Giordano. "*Ebbène, insomma, venire al dunque.*" Okay, in sum, to come to the point.

Fascinated, I watch our speaker peeling his onion. There is nothing underneath. His monologue is all adverbs, conjunctions, interjections, *dunque, comunque, ovunque.* The interjections don't translate, *Beh, Boh.* Questions are rhetorical, less than meets the eye. *Che c'è da dire?* What is there to say? Where we want food for thought, he gives us old chestnuts. *Tanto è vero!* So true! The lecture is worth the price of admission.

However, there is the camera, worth a thousand words. A black priest's hat, sailing from the dome of St. Peter's, blots out the screen and the city. We hear how Fellini's education at the boarding school in Fano, run by Carissimi Fathers, "did much to shape his anticlerical ideas." In his art of film, the angry young man is getting his own back. That is what the speaker thinks. The ideas themselves are inert, though. If you are lucky, they quicken with life in ways you can't anticipate, dragging reality with them. Fellini, vindicating his cast of misfits, has this kind of luck. His camera's eye retrieves the city, conferring the gift of life. The taxidermist behind the lectern is stuffing dead animals or eviscerating live ones.

Fellini's little truths and pieties are everybody's business. Not everybody rides the 23 bus from the Pyramid of Caius Cestius to St. Paul's Basilica outside the walls. Via Ostiense seen from the bus window is a montage of gas works, dingy sheds and warehouses, railroad tracks, open-air markets where you haggle over pennies, the sour dwellings of the poor. This is Fellini country. In the *spiazzo*, a cleared-out place before the basilica, the empty buses wait. The bar is shuttered, the outdoor toilets are locked, and in the little park no one rides the carousel. All by his lonesome, an adolescent boy is kicking a soccer ball. A fat girl pushes a pram. On the patchy grass, old pipe-smoking men wear ragged sweaters in the cool of late afternoon. These men are playing *bocce*, a lazy game of bowls. Against the sky they have their clarity, and Fellini lets you see this. "Humility before the camera" is how he puts it.

Hungry, I quit the palazzo and make a beeline for Nerone's, around the corner on Via Terme di Tito. The minestrone is thick enough to eat with a fork. I dunk my crusty white bread and wash it down with a glass of house wine, Frascati from the hill towns *di fuori*, outside. Eugenio is my waiter. Greeting me by name, he wants to know about the state of my liver, not a perfunctory question for Romans. Mostly, though, he keeps mum. His quick fingers, setting the table, don't grudge what they are doing. Waiting on tables is a man's occupation. For siesta, Nerone's closes and they turn out the lights. Eugenio, cradling his head in his arms, goes to sleep on the table. He doesn't lock the doors, and in the darkened *ostaria* old men from the neighborhood sip wine and study a chess board. These men are widowed, their children grown or moved away. Nerone's is their club.

Fortified by a *doppio,* black coffee double strength, I settle my bill. In the park the Domus Aurea, Nero's Golden House, awaits me. Across the street, the Colle Oppio is bordered by a chain link fence and a row of lamp standards that light the park until midnight. The wire fence is the upright for the pickup soccer game that goes on here all day and well into the night. Bouncing off someone's head, the black and white soccer ball comes flying over the fence and lands at my feet. I try to kick it back again but it squirts away to the side. This elicits the Roman equivalent of a Bronx cheer.

The little street, named for the Baths of Titus over the way, runs into Via Nicola Salvi. In the eighteenth century, this architect made the Fountains of Trevi. Ekberg, in Fellini's movie, went wading in the fountains, and Marcello Mastroianni watched her with lust in his heart. "You are the first woman on the first day of creation," he tells her.

Time warps in Rome and the present re-creates the past. Sometimes, like Dante in his *selva oscura,* you don't know where you are. Roots, tentacular, drag you back and down, and your contemporaries are dead men. Fellini's Ekberg is a water nymph, the virgin Trivia, long dead, who showed the thirsty Roman soldiers where to drink. The aqueduct called Acqua Vergine brings this water to the city from outlying springs. Some Romans, valuing its softness, keep it on their windowsills in bottles and jugs. Giordano says, however, that the waters of Egeria are best. They rose behind the high box hedges of the Villa Celimontana, on your route as you go down to the Appian Way. Numa Pompilius, the second king of Rome, used to meet the nymph Egeria beside the springs. A bottled mineral water remembers this nymph, lissome like September Morn. Advertisements on the bottle testify to its quality, sovereign, says Michelangelo, for constipation and liver disorders.

The Goths cut the aqueducts, knowing how water is life's blood for Romans. In the dying city, people left the high ground for the marshy lowlands around the Tiber. Down there they sickened and the population fell. In Rome, where death waits to take back the city, old disorder battles civilization. *Scarabocchi*, angry slogans scribbled on the walls, summon the *cittadini* to another battle, the wrong one. *La Lotta Continua* reads the slogan on the façade of San Martino ai Monti, just outside the Colle Oppio. "The Fight Goes On." Left-wing sectarians who want to hoist the red flag paint this slogan on church walls and railway embankments. In the night, other sectarians come with their buckets and paint it out. They cover the walls with the letters MSI, *Movimento Sociale Italiano*. At their rallies these "Meesee" sing the Fascist Party song, *Giovinezza*, "Youth." Sometimes left and right, meeting in the Colle Oppio, knock heads. The fight for Rome that matters is remote from these shenanigans. Fellini, having something to say, has no message, and the old men in the Institute aren't scribbling graffiti on the walls.

Viale della Domus Aurea, traversing the park, brings me into the garden beneath the wall of Trajan's Baths. Crocus, violas, and euonymus are growing in the garden. Ancient Romans, the Germans of their time, classified where they didn't conquer. Like Adam in the Garden who saw the essence in the name, they named plants for their qualities, not botanical but moral. The euonymus, literally "of good name," is a plant of good omen, growing over an ill-omened place.

The rheumy old man who has the Golden House in charge

lives behind a dark door, a ferryman by the stygian waters. He spends a lot of time in his garden. Nero's underground palace, ruined and shut away, isn't popular with tourists, and most Romans are like New Yorkers who know Grant's Tomb is there. This solitary man is Papageno in *The Magic Flute,* his lips sealed with a padlock. Free of the padlock, he has things to say. Nero, he says, was a pretty piece of flesh but pustular and had a bad smell. His neck was squat, his legs spindly, and his belly stuck out before him. *Per Dio,* however, his liver was sound as a baby's.

Driving a chariot on the Appian Way, Gnaeus Domitius, Nero's father, whipped up his horses and ran over a boy in the road. Suetonius, the Roman historian who tells this story, has a moral: Like father, like son. Dying at thirty-two, the emperor filled his short life with incident. He liked to prowl the streets at night, attacking men on their way home from dinner. If they resisted, he stabbed them and dropped their bodies down the sewers. His sexual tastes were catholic. He raped a Vestal Virgin, and castrated his favorite Sporus, hoping to turn him into a girl. An English poet made great poetry from this. With his mother Agrippina, Nero committed incest when they rode together in their litter. You could tell, says Suetonius, from the state of his clothes. However, his mother palled and he killed her. He kicked his wife to death, she being pregnant and complaining. The theater was his passion, and when he gave a recital the gates were kept barred. Men wilting from boredom and wanting to leave the theater shammed dead and were carried away. Just before he took his life, Nero muttered through tears: "Dead! And so great an artist!"

In the Golden House, says Papageno, the emperor showed the state of his art. The pillared arcade ran for a mile, and the statue that stood before it, Nero's, not Jupiter's, was one hundred and twenty feet high. Like carious teeth, bits of the ruined portico, once covered with gold, stick up in the Forum. But time and the vegetation that grows wild in this forgiving climate have dragged most of it to earth. As you pick your way about the ruins, wild fennel and asparagus, clematis and viburnum tangle your feet.

After Nero died, fire gutted the Golden House, and the emperors Trajan and Titus hid what was left of it beneath a new palace and new public baths. Rome, the modern city, is like this ruin, only the tip of the iceberg. As I walk the city, I see where time has been there first.

The Basilica of St. Peter's stood in the Borgo across the Tiber for a long time. In the summer of 1505, Pope Julius, wanting to build his new church, knocked it down. He shattered the ancient columns and dug up the tessellated pavement where a million pilgrims had knelt, Charlemagne among them. The pavement went to the dustbin, and the bones of the ancestors, lifted out of their sarcophagi, went into the crypt. Like Trajan and Titus, Pope Julius let bygones be bygones.

His monument, a little cold, is the pilgrim's first glimpse of Rome, seen from the Campagna or the crest of Monte Mario. St. Peter's, a sign or flag, says that Rome is eternal. But the Goths and Vandals have been here before, and I feel how someday the new church will go the way of the old. "New" St. Peter's, like the rest of Rome, induces detachment. Already it declares its own dying.

Back in the Golden House, Papageno hands me a flashlight. He unlocks the door and we descend the stairs together. Nero, incarnate evil, is down there. Romans, being prudent, might have left this place alone. A pest house, says Giordano, who gives it a wide berth. Who knows what infection it carries? In the Age of Discovery, however, when Columbus, a Genoese, was exploring the new world, Romans turned inward, exploring the old. Under a vineyard near the Baths of Trajan, they found the Laocoön. It stood in the Golden House once. Raphael, a spelunker among painters, had himself lowered down on a rope. What he saw by torchlight did great things for his art.

First-century painting in Rome, a time of horrors, is tranquil. Fruit trees flower on a blue-green field, pomegranate, quince, and lemon. Songbirds fly above the field or perch on the branches.

They reprove the emperor Nero who liked to quote the Greek proverb "Unheard melodies are never sweet." In the bucolic landscape on the walls, men and women are resting. Making a stir is the last thing on their minds. Out there in Rome they were killing Christians, "a sect," says Suetonius, "professing a new and mischievous religious belief." The production line of busts and statues in the Vatican Museum shows you what these Romans looked like. Jowly, pinched, or hard-featured, they lived on the surface. But this delicate art is inward.

In the dark gallery, the walls are cut with niches. Playing my flashlight over the ceiling, I see where Raphael has scratched his name, still there. "*Non c'è male,*" says Papageno, having seen these magic letters before. "Not bad."

The books they read in the Golden House were shelved in this gallery, he tells me. So the devotees of violence wanted food for thought. They read Virgil, Horace, and Livy, classics of the age before them. In a famous passage schoolboys used to get by heart, Virgil promised eternity for Rome, no fixed period of years, no bounds to Roman dominion. For a time after he died, the empire, fulfilling his promise, kept growing. Its longest north-south axis, from Hadrian's Wall in Britain to the edge of the Sahara, extended for 1,600 miles. This about equals the north-south axis of the United States from Canada to Mexico at the mouth of the Rio Grande.

Horace, Virgil's friend, wrote political poems but his art is mostly personal. He said his powerful rhyme would outlast the bronze and marble of the Caesars. Livy, in more than one hundred and thirty books, retrieved the early history of Rome, otherwise unremembered. However, of the books he wrote, only thirty-five remain. History, he said, records the infinite variety of human experience, set out clearly for everyone to see. If you have eyes to see, you can find in the record examples and warnings for your country and yourself. In the fifteenth century, when Rome recovered the Golden House, Alfonso of Naples, a romantic scholar-king, was making up his mind to go to war against his neighbors. But Cosimo de' Medici, preferring peace to the sword, bought him off with a priceless manuscript of Livy.

Going *piedi,* the legionaries would have got there before us. Under the tomato red hood of the Fiat, the water in the radiator is turning to steam. Giordano watches the needle on the temperature gauge. Another nudge upwards and Saltimbanco will need a new block. Crossing our fingers, we cross the Tiber, our Rubicon, by the Milvian Bridge. On the Via Cassia, the clot of traffic begins to dissolve. The needle, wavering, recedes, and we leave the legionaries in our dust.

I am on the track of the *marmorari romani.* These Roman marble workers glorified the old abbeys in the country north of Rome, a wilderness on the doorstep and much of it remains. Progress is alert to its business, however. After centuries of sleep and dream, the wild country won't keep itself to itself for much longer. Outside Rome in the Campagna, round shepherds' huts used to dot the marshes where water buffalo lived. Their milk made mozzarella cheese. Today in the Campagna, canals move the stagnant water along. On the recovered land, new towns burst their seams. Rome's population doubled, thirty years after Mussolini drained the marshes.

Between Rome and Nepi, the past lords it over the present. In this solitude of stony valleys and plains, the stream beds have gone dry. Pasted to the hills, the little villages aren't picturesque. Trees, when we see them, poke up like gnarled fingers among the ruined tombs by the roadside. Glimpsed from the car window, a peasant on a mule appears and is gone. The modern highway runs parallel to the Roman road, where dark basalt paving-slabs still show their honeycomb pattern. Over the wide Tiber valley, Monte Soratte looms like the Pyramid in Rome.

Claustra Etruriae, Romans called this country, the keys of

Etruria. It took a long time before they possessed the keys, Etruscans being here first. No one knows where they came from. Flowering superbly, they had their time in the sun, then disappeared forever. Death was their familiar. Like Caliban to Setebos, they prayed their gods in fear. Thunder, rolling from Monte Soratte, called them to prayer. In their museum beside the Tiber, named for Pope Julius, a grinning Medusa sticks out its tongue like a Mexican idol. A warrior, sword in hand, turns back to face the adversary who is preparing to destroy him. His eyes, already dying, look death in the face.

In Tarquinia, to the west, Etruscans built their necropolis between the empty sky and the sea. Demons in the tomb paintings threaten the dead with serpents, or hold hammers, poised to strike. But the flute player on the tomb walls, a Pied Piper of Etruria, is a jaunty presence in the dust. The winged horses, their nostrils flaring, aspire to heaven in the local museum. On the lid of a sarcophagus, the young married couple has outwitted time. Dying young, this bride and groom are still as young as they were.

The hills around Tarquinia, storm-buffeted, are bare. Inland, this changes. Our route north from Rome, sticking to the interior, brings us through forested country. Near Ponzano Romano in wooded hills by the Tiber, Sant' Andrea in Flumine keeps the wilderness alone. The church has a signed ciborium, not grand like Bernini's for St. Peter's in Rome, but after eight hundred years it covers the altar. Civita Castellana, an infernal landscape, stands above its gorge on the site of old Roman Falerii, still girt with ruined walls. On the weathered façade of the church portico, the inscription tells us that Master Jacobus, a citizen of Rome, and his "beloved son Cosmate" made this work, Anno Domini 1210.

Castel Sant' Elia, the gain of sleep and dream, isn't far from the Etruscan town of Nepi. The Cluniac monks who had their priory here came out from Rome by the Via Flaminia. A Benedictine abbey housed them but is gone. In the volcanic gorge, sunlight filters through clumps of trees. A noisy stream breaks the silence. Between the high cliff face and the ravine below, the church clings to its narrow rock shelf. From above, the roof is half hidden, and down below, on one side, a grove of dark cypress hides the wall. We get down there by descending more than a hundred steps, taken with caution.

Blind arcades relieve the plain façade, arches surmounting the doors. Two of the doors are nailed shut with wooden planking, a rusty padlock bars the third. The crudely lettered sign tells us that Sant' Elia is closed for restoration. This is ominous. Where Americans demolish, Romans restore. The result is, however, the same. A wooden fence or a sanitary cordon goes up around the building and doesn't come down until the work is finished. In Rome it never comes down. Appearing out of the ground before the façade, the caretaker is jingling his key ring. A ragged shadow, if he turned sideways we wouldn't see him. Giordano, proffering a bill tactfully, hopes he will drink a *mezzolitro* for us.

In the echoing interior, the roof timbers are exposed. Narrow windows like slits in a fortress cut the rough masonry walls. Defining the nave, the antique columns make a double arcade, lifted from a vanished pagan temple. The *marmorari* have been here. Their floor mosaic, still luminous, has rosettes and six-sided crosses. In the simple ciborium over the altar, columns with sculptured capitals support a gable roof. The beauty is in the structure.

Saracen invaders, coming up from Sicily, burned Sant' Elia, but St. Odo of Cluny restored it. In the tenth century, Romans did these things better. This was the time of Otto III, the Holy Roman Emperor and a patron of churches like this one. His mother was a Byzantine princess, his father a Saxon king, and he made Rome his capital and had a palace on the Aventine Hill. Half monk and half barbarian, he dreamed of reviving the lost world of the Emperor Justinian. When he went to Aix-la-Chapelle, he opened the tomb of Charlemagne and took the scepter from his hand.

In Rome, however, Crescentius was there first. The emperor defeated this republican hero and hung his body on a gibbet atop

Monte Mario. Pope John XVI, running from the city, was taken in flight. They cut off his nose and ears, put out his eyes, and mounted him back to front on a donkey. Rome in the Dark Ages was like this.

Where Otto's palace stood, orange trees are growing and there is a piece of wall for *scarabocchi.* Someone has written SEX PISTOLS on the wall. The Holy Roman Empire was gone in everything but name when Napoleon gave it the coup de grace. But the emperor's likeness in bas-relief survives on a wellhead in his Roman church of San Bartolomeo. This church on the Tiber island is built over a temple sacred to the god of healing. The wellhead, scored by the ropes that drew up the buckets, opened on the healing waters below. Otto, in his marble likeness, holds the imperial scepter. Ottone Terzo, Romans called him, but they rose against their foreign master and drove him from the city. He died of fever at twenty-six near Civita Castellana in the shadow of Monte Soratte. This was in 1002.

Time has spared the frescoes on the apse wall of Sant' Elia. Christ, beneath a blue sky, raises His right hand in admonition or blessing. In His left He carries the scroll of the law. The lower tier of the apse, a sight for Doubting Thomas, rivets my attention. Enthroned in the center, the Roman emperor wears a foliated crown. He holds the orb in one hand, his long scepter in the other. It is the man on the wellhead in St. Bartholemew's church, Ottone Terzo. Like Schliemann with his mattock, having stumbled on the ruins of Troy, I am shaken, exhilarated too. In their old church art, there is nothing like this. Christ the Pantocrator takes center stage, never a secular king.

Behind us in the transept, the caretaker gives signs of pricking my bubble. He holds up his right hand like Christ on the wall. With his index finger he swipes at the fresco, unseaming the emperor from the waist to the chops. He shows me the offending finger that has done this. It is covered with chalk. "Fellini," he says cheerfully.

Enjoying his sensation, the caretaker explains. I remember the scene in *Roma* where the *paparazzi* find the fresco in the underground villa? This is where they find it and watch the colors fade, Sant' Elia being "on location." Triumphant on the apse wall, the fresco isn't real but made up, like the movie.

Giordano, thinking back, can guess how the trick was done. They run the camera forward slowly, beginning on the left where the lower apse panel is empty. As the camera moves, the fresco in the center comes into focus. Just for a moment, you see it close up. Then focus blurs and they leach the colors slowly, simulating the corrosive effect of the air. Before your eyes the grainy image appears to dissolve, fading from something to nothing. Now you see it. Look again, and the fresco is gone.

DONEY'S SUNDAY MORNING

"BIGLIETTO," he says, and I fish for my ticket. *Non c'è niente.* Sneering, he might have guessed. What do I mean, I can't find it? Tongue-tied, I grin sheepishly, unable to manage a word. Turning up the volume, he asks me again. In the crowded bus, they are all ears and eyes. Xenophobia looks out of their eyes. I am *straniero,* a foreigner bilking the state. Like the open-air market or the neighborhood bar, this bus is their theater. Connoisseurs of emotion, they like a good hanging or a quarrel in the streets.

Most city buses are automated, a coin-operated machine replacing the conductor who used to sit in the back. Romans, if they are honorable, feed the machine. This inspector, boarding the bus on the Corso, wants to make sure. Showing me his back, he addresses himself to the others. All honorable men, they produce on demand. He goes from seat to seat, taking the left aisle first, then, with deliberate steps, returns to the rear.

Awaiting his second coming, I yank at my trouser pockets,

pulling them inside out. Reproachful eyes watch me do this. Except for tissues, a box of matches, and pieces of lint, the pockets are empty. Under my arms, I feel the sweat begin to prickle. My fingers, scrabbling in the old corduroy jacket, discover that the lining is torn. Through the hole in the lining, I retrieve the missing ticket. This is an epiphany.

Cymbals crash, a drum rolls. The spectators applaud me. Where I was the villain, I am now the hero. Pride going before a fall, the inspector becomes the villain. Like Milton's busy bees, my fellow passengers expatiate and confer. Surprise, begetting consternation, then compassion, turns to outrage. The inspector is its target. He is the banker in a top hat, a *pezzo grosso*. "Big shot!" I, however, am *simpaticone*. Making a clown of myself, I have brightened their day.

Shaken, I leave the bus in Piazza del Popolo. The frayed ends of the afternoon need knitting together. The old church in the square serves nicely for this, gratifying my taste for old bones. Like the Capuchin fathers who live with skeletons in their church on the Veneto, I feel life more keenly down among the dead men. Cesare Borgia's murdered brother, fished out of the Tiber five hundred years ago, is buried in Santa Maria del Popolo, in the chapel to the right of the altar. After the horror, he sleeps well.

Old Roman churches, sanctifying horror, draw the venom and leave a residue of peace. In San Pietro in Montorio, up on the Janiculum, the discreet carpet in front of the altar hides a grave. Beatrice Cenci, her agony and hot revenge all gone into dust, is buried under the carpet. A felon, she killed her incestuous father, paying for this with her life. Shelley in his romantic tragedy makes her a heroine. The sacristan, if you ask him, thinks this can hardly be so. San Pietro in Montorio isn't Catholic for nothing, however. A little shamefacedly, it makes room for old disorder.

Piazza del Popolo, a focal point always humming with activity, serves different functions. Market stalls outside the square sell mass-produced clothing, cheap but stylish. One of the stalls offers women's skirts decorated with the onion domes and towers of Moscow. You can choose between a red Kremlin, cheerful on a blue ground, or a blue Kremlin on red. Romans, exchanging gossip, crowd the Canova Bar. Girl-watching is popular, tables on the sidewalk catering to this. In the last century, a scaffold or stage went up at need in the center of the square. This was for public executions. In 1825 the Pope hanged two freedom fighters in Piazza del Popolo, Targhini and Montanari.

It being late afternoon, the traffic is building. A monstrous growth in a petri dish, it hides the great square that is really an oval. Self-appointed custodians tend the parked cars. Spear carriers in this theater-in-the-round, some wear caps and long dusters. Guarding the obelisk, make-believe lions spit water. A prop for *Aida*, the obelisk is also three thousand years old, older than morality, like these theatrical Italians. Neapolitan tenors want me to believe that Italians are happy-go-lucky. I agree that they have a lot of brio.

Looking back at the Corso, I do a double take. The twin baroque churches at the base of the square are oddly concave, perspective drawings backing the stage. Pulling in their bellies, they lead my eye away out of the square. I see in the distance a three-fingered fan of streets, like a trompe l'oeil vista on the wall. In one of these streets, the Via del Babuino, art dealers have their shops. They sell machined copies of Piranesi engravings, nests of lacquered tables from Alinari's in Florence, leather elephants, Roman portrait busts, modern paintings and old prints. In Moscow, where memory is long but selective, I combed the city for a print of St. Basil's. All I found was kitsch. However, the print I wanted turned up in the Via del Babuino.

The Porta del Popolo opens on the square at the opposite end. This is the proscenium arch. In 1655, the College of Cardinals, coming down to the footlights, bowed the Queen of Sweden through the arch. A great prize in her time, this Protestant ruler converted to Rome. When she came to the city, the Pope rolled out the carpet. He let her fire off the cannon in his Castel Sant' Angelo. She didn't fire in the air but hit the Villa Medici at the foot of the Pincian Hill. They still have the cannonball in a fountain before the façade.

The Pincian Hill, banked with flowers, overlooks the action in Piazza del Popolo, like Bernini's theater box in the Cornaro chapel. Ramps, stage left and right, bring you up. Beneath the hill in the northeast corner, Santa Maria del Popolo, an ancient of days, denies its antiquity. Over the church wall beside the ramp, the designer has fitted a neoclassical shell. In his illusionistic theater, nothing discrepant spoils the mise-en-scène. Martin Luther, visiting Rome in 1511, lodged in the monastery that used to adjoin the church. He said he fell on his knees, held up his hands to heaven, and cried, "Hail holy Rome." Later he changed his mind.

In the piazza, the *cittadini* are still posturing. Patrons and players both, they turn life into art. The composition they make is formal, a bohemian scene but arranged. My living room at home, a defensive redoubt, has its harmony too. It comes complete with stereo, fireplace, and a pitcher of martinis. Gratefully, I go there at the end of the day. In Rome, with the rest of the world, I go out. The piazza is my living room, an alfresco entertainment. Donizetti's balloon, a great coup de théâtre in his opera *The Elixir of Love,* is due to come down from the flies any minute.

Awaiting this event, Italians go about their business. Merry as sin, they like a good time. "Let us enjoy the papacy," said Pope Leo X, "since God has given it to us." Gregorovius, a German historian who wrote a history of the city in the Middle Ages, called this Medici Pope a pagan. He wasn't pagan, however, but pagan and Christian together. Rendering to Caesar, he rendered also to God. Descendants of the people who sat in the Colosseum, Italians take their pleasure where they find it. Speculating on this, I let my mind walk up and down. Not far away, mailed gladiators fight to the death. They do this in old mosaics in the Borghese Gallery, on the other side of the wall. Some of these gladiators, unlucky, are marked with the first letter of the Greek word *thanatos,* death. Not caring to save them, the crowd has turned thumbs down.

The Villa Borghese, like Gorky Park in Moscow, is a world to itself. In Piazza di Siena, where they hold the Horse Show in May, joggers run the perimeter. My friend Giordano runs there twice a week, early in the morning. He is that rare bird, a Roman athlete. Mostly his fellow joggers are out on parade. Models, not joggers, they wear blue and white running suits from La Rinascente. Preserving their *bella figura* is important, but doing this they never break a sweat. Stone pines, more trompe l'oeil, deepen the sky around the hippodrome where the grass, scuffed by many feet, has worn thin. In early spring, the city fathers fence the hippodrome, put up wooden stands, and seed the piazza. For a little while, the grass is green. Then the fence comes down and Giordano resumes his biweekly.

Playing soccer on the grass, the men and boys grimace horribly. An elderly eccentric has got up a game of croquet. Pony carts on the walkways mingle with pedestrians. Children, shy but pleased, stand in the carts, eat *gelati,* or ride the merry-go-round. All these children are dressed to kill. The wooden horses go up and down to the tune of a ricky-ticky jazz band. Real horses gallop on the Galoppatoio. Preparing for departure, the Arizona Express, an electric wagon train, toots its whistle. Passengers hurry to fill the last seats. Goethe, on Viale Goethe, surveying the scene, takes a dim Teutonic view. At the foot of his statue, Faust and Marguerite gesture theatrically. Where he is importunate, she can't make up her mind.

On the upper edges of the park, the zoological gardens pull an appreciative crowd on the weekends. Queuing up for the World's Biggest Exhibit of Poisonous Snakes, parents and children stand goggle-eyed before the vipers, cobras, and boa constrictors. The coral snake, whose bite is instant death, is a favorite. In the House of the Carnivores, young men and their girl friends divert the big cats. Pretending to catarrh, they imitate the deep cough of the leopard. Hanging from the cage, the sign says PROIBITO, but school children hit the leopard with popcorn.

In the park, Byron, self-absorbed, recites the lines from *Childe Harold*, inscribed on the base of his statue:

Oh Rome! my country! city of the soul!
The orphans of the heart must turn to thee.

The grandiloquence is right, Rome being hyperbole, a refuge and "my country." But it isn't a city of the soul.

Back in the piazza, I have a cappuccino in the Canova Bar, waiting for the sacristan to unlock the doors of the church. Bread and wine means for Romans the body and blood of Christ, as in the mystery of the transubstantiation. Also bread and wine are themselves, and no meal in Rome is complete without both. Chunky bread washed down with wine induces drowsiness, though. Closed for siesta, Santa Maria del Popolo reopens in the late afternoon. A parish church or *populus*, five hundred years old, it occupies the site of earlier churches, the first of them sanctifying the tomb of Nero, a monster. Like the *oecumene* of the Byzantines, the parish embraces the world. This argues disorder, or say a wild civility.

Santa Maria del Popolo finds its order in disorder. The austere façade is early Renaissance, the interior baroque and gorgeous, and there are even stained-glass windows, rare in Rome. Evidently a Frenchman has been here. Appealing to a lifelike harmony, the *populus* is stuffed with miscellaneous treasures. Pinturicchio, a tender painter, composes his difference with Caravaggio, a bravo. The Madonna over the altar, Romans say, is the work of St. Luke. In the chapel behind the altar, the ceiling accommodates Christian saints and pagan Sibyls. Coming down from the ancient past, the Sibyls, resident in Rome before the saints and their new dispensation, present the dark underside, our moiety of shadow. This underside, rank and steamy, still bears. The same mouth, said Pope St. Gregory, couldn't praise Christ and Zeus. Santa Maria del Popolo says he was wrong. The *populus* isn't "tolerant," a modern idea or shibboleth, but comprehensive. Sometimes what it comprehends gives me gooseflesh.

Satyrs' heads and stone lizards adorn the marble tombs beside the wall. Sansovino, a Renaissance sculptor, made these tombs for two great princes of the Church who rendered to God when they had to. The dead men on the tomb lids have seen it all. Worldly-wise, used to coping, sybaritic but hard, they look like sleeping Etruscans on the tombs in the Villa Giulia.

Once in New York, an insular town where you meet the true provincial, I leaned over the ramparts by the Battery to Brooklyn Tunnel, eavesdropping on two kibitzers. "Ever been down there?" one wanted to know. "Who goes to Brooklyn?" said the other. Hunkered down in their *rioni,* Romans don't go to Brooklyn. I have heard an old man in Trastevere say that he has never crossed the Tiber. Proud of his insularity, he turns his back on the rest of the world. Bridges over the Tiber run in two directions, though, and the world doesn't leave him alone.

Each year in July, Trasteverinos celebrate their boisterous holiday, "*Noiantri.*" This gives the popular café its name. I took an English novelist to Café Noiantri once. He was studying to be Evelyn Waugh. "A lot of wogs," he said. It wasn't true then and still isn't. Trastevere is for tourists, their Roman version of Washington Square. Providing local color, Romans live there too, but keep in the background, like the Anvil Chorus.

Piazza di Santa Maria is the heart of Trastevere, duplicitous, very old, but still throbbing. Water, a Lorelei, sparkles in the fountain, magnetizing the crowd. On the day Christ was born, pure oil bubbled from the earth where the fountain is now. All day long, it flowed into the Tiber. Via della Fonte d'Olio, leading out of the piazza, remembers this. Appraising the crowd, hucksters, Romeos, and tour guides lie in wait by the fountain. Their eyes are avid, full of fierce love. They want to sell me a package tour, a wind-up monkey with cymbals on his fingers, a plastic replica of the church of Santa Maria, genuine simulated gold. It lights up inside when you plug the cord in the wall.

In front of the church the cicerone marshals his charges, German students thumbing guidebooks, middle-aged American widows well left, two young Frenchmen wearing T-shirts stenciled with cannabis leaves, me, a free-loader listening in. Following their leader, the young men don't hear him. Each holds a Sony Walkman, the mind's best defense against thought. Faintly from the ear plugs comes the tintinnabulation of rock.

The cicerone, short but barrel-chested, plants his flag and calls for attention. A half-cartridge Mussolini, he has jaw enough for two. Saying nothing distinctly, the tour guide's forte in Latin countries, he thrusts out his jaw and stands with arms akimbo. "*Ecco! i disegni, le figure, gli oggetti sacri, i colori.*" His taste runs to sublimity, the gilded ceiling by Domenichino, Fontana's elegant porch, the Renaissance tomb where Cardinal Stefaneschi is lying. The last of the Stefaneschis, he had Veronica's Veil, the *Volto Santo,* in his keeping. "*Bello,* eh?"

Outside the piazza, the little brick campanile is almost hidden by the buildings around it. It belongs to the ancient church of Sts. Rufina and Seconda. The medieval bell tower stitches earth and heaven together. In the guidebook, it gets a footnote. Coming on this campanile is a rare privilege, though, and my heart is perturbed when I see it.

Rome, a hundred cities, comes down at last to two, the City of God and the City of Man. This division is St. Augustine's, but his labels are misleading. The City of Man, like the borough of Brooklyn, is famous for churches. Some, like St. Peter's, cut the people down to size. In the City of God, the relation goes the other way. No. 12 Via Anicia, a street in Trastevere scoured by sun and years, has a brown door in a blank masonry wall. On the other side of the wall, Genoese sailors built their hospice in Rome. This goes back a while. Sage, thyme, and marjoram still grow in the courtyard, also *prezzemolo*, crisp green parsley just tart enough so you smell it. In summer, swags of jasmine soften the old *pozzo*, a marriage of January and May. This Genoese hospice, secular, not sacred, is a version of the City of God.

You can tour the Heavenly City on foot or let your imagination do this for you. Today, fortified by images, I travel in the mind. Below the Palatine Hill, I look in at San Giorgio's. A medieval dwelling place built to human scale, it brings the people up to its level. Named for the dragon slayer who rescued maidens in distress, the little church is functional. The iron gates before the portico stand open in the dog days. A spot of color on the wall of the apse punctuates the interior, cool, gray, and dim. Neighboring the church, the neo-Gothic building looks over the square on one side, across the road to the Tiber on the other. Neo all the way, it suffers by comparison with the real thing next door. Like wax flowers to real flowers, close but no cigar, it is only a copy and shows this. Claretta Petacci used to live in the building. Mussolini's mistress, she stuck by him to the end. Everyone remembers the grisly news photos of Claretta and the Duce, hanging upside down like sides of dressed beef in Piazzale Loretto, Milan.

Between Claretta's villa and St. George's church, the arch of the money changers, *Argentari*, crumbles against a hillock. Hubert Robert, who painted ruins, had a subject here if he knew it. Like old money, the arch is silvered and black. Caracalla, a monster of note in this city where no one takes notice, is sculpted in low relief on its face. The emperor in the relief is only a boy, his dagger still muzzled, and the brother he murdered later is shown with him. On the hillock behind the arch, a single lemon tree is blooming.

Another arch, named for Janus, stands over the road in the hollow called the Velabrum. Janus is two-faced. Not a hypocrite but catholic, he looks in different directions. Maybe St. Augustine, coming here from the provinces, found his trope of the two cities in Via del Velabro. When Alaric and the Visigoths sacked Rome in 410, he gave up on the City of Man. His famous book tells the story, and I read it for the first time in Rome, late at night, the indelible time. It still smells of cheap grappa, an impure drink made of the lees of grapes.

The City of God, less arresting than the other one, is like the thatched house with a flitch of bacon on the rafters where Baucis and Philemon had the gods to dinner. Also it lies off the beaten track. Tracking from the Colosseum to the Lateran church, I climb the hill above the neighborhood market, not an arduous climb when you do it in the mind. The abbey fortress of the Quattro Coronati disclaims attention, and most tourists who come this way pass by, unseeing. In the marble cloister, the English grass is never sere. Shoots of bamboo grow taller than the grass. The four-sided arcade has double columns, slender but strong. Roman masons, whose names go unrecorded, made the cloister. Water from a fountain trickles into the pond where goldfish swim lazily, their economical motion pared down to the flick of a tail. Otherwise, this walled-in place fills up with silence. Sunlight, moving as the day moves, warms the inner wall of the arcade, and on the second story the nuns have hung out their underclothes to dry in the sun.

Up the road but light-years away, the giant statues on the roof of St. John Lateran, Roman candles poised for flight, gaze across the Campagna. Respectfully I pace the nave, guidebook in hand. The Mother Church of Christendom, asking me to notice, makes its presence felt. Big Roman churches are like this, a lot of riches in a lot of room. Down in EUR, St. Paul's Basilica takes me by the lapels. Across the Tiber, St. Peter's does the same. In the eighteenth century, Piranesi, an engraver with an eye for detail, put St. Peter's in perspective. He did this from his station on the Aventine Hill, in the Square of the Knights of Malta. Behind the door in the square, a jeu d'esprit of Piranesi's decorated with obelisks and old military trophies, is a state within a state, the Cavalieri di Malta.

These Knights Hospitalers gave aid and comfort to Christian pilgrims in the Holy Land. When Muslims took Jerusalem, they moved on to Rhodes. In 1522, Suleiman the Magnificent, capturing the island, made them persona non grata. Resettled in Malta, they had to clear out when the British, a Protestant people, came in. This was after the wars with Napoleon. Their story of forced marches has a happy ending, though. Up there on the Aventine, the Knights can die in Rome if they want to. Below the Spanish Steps, they own a palazzo, extra territorial. For my Roman pied à terre, I would like this palazzo on Via Condotti. Preferring the more salubrious air of the Aventine, the Grand Master of the Order lives in the Knight's Priory on the other side of the wall. Leading to his residence, the locked door has an intricate keyhole.

Across the river in the Leonine City, the Pope is a temporal sovereign, too. An ebullition of Titans, his great dome, disdaining earth, challenges heaven. This is the familiar view, visible from the promenade behind Santa Sabina where the palace of Ottone Terzo used to stand. Piranesi's creation, the view through the keyhole reduces St. Peter's to scale. Infinite riches in a little room, the church is smaller than the aperture that frames it.

Gigantism, running wild in the Empire, went underground when Rome fell. Dormant for a long time, this Roman virus broke out again in the Renaissance. "They knew how to build then," Mussolini said, walking the corridors in the Vatican Palace. "What a lot of rooms, and how big they are." In one of these roims, the Sala Rotonda, I look up from under, a traveler from a distant land, at the giant porphyry basin. As the Tsar of Bells in the Kremlin is to any old bell, this basin is to basins. It says how the Empire, growing to a pleurisy, died of its own muchness. A Renaissance Pope who thought that bigger was better brought the basin to the Vatican from Nero's Golden House.

Borromini, restoring St. John Lateran, left it looking like the Palace of Versailles. Unimpressed by pomp but delighting in circumstance, most Romans leave "Versailles" alone. They go to the Lateran for big public occasions like the one in Holy Week when the Pope comes to the church to wash the feet of the poor. If they need to pray, a private matter, they go elsewhere.

Okay for weekends, the grandeur that was Rome is hard to accommodate on an everyday basis. One stifling June day, wanting a breather I turned my back on the Forum. The horse-drawn vehicles, standing by the curb, offered *aranciata*, hot dogs, and ice cream. The vendor handed me a soft drink, the straw punched through the top of the container. Behind us, mounted on the wall of the Basilica di Massenzio, were the four great maps recording the progress of empire, ineluctably upwards. The story begins in the seventh century B.C. when Rome was a speck on the Palatine Hill. It ends at the zenith, the palmy days under Trajan. Mussolini, the vendor told me, had them put up the maps when he bulldozed his Via dei Fori Imperiali through this part of Rome. "After all," he said, thinking of Mussolini, "we didn't want an empire, we wanted a house."

Shimmed into the Forum, Santi Cosma e Damiano remembers two Arabian doctors, victims of Diocletian who had zealotry to spare. To enter the church, you walk up the ramp through the cloister. The dark leather doors, nail-studded, are often closed. Chances are, however, that the man in the kiosk will be peeling off tickets. The *presepio*, a Christmas crib, is open all year long. It has a room to itself, divided horizontally, half box set, half theater. If you aren't in Rome for Christmas, you can keep the day before it comes in Santi Cosma e Damiano.

Every year in December, miniature versions of the Holy Family, carved wood or plastic, go on sale in Piazza Navona. Romans like the whole story, not just the epiphany, so Jesus, Mary, and Joseph have their attendants, a peasant woman balancing a basket on her head, a boy with a frisking ewe, another boy with a flute and a billycock hat. Invariably, one of the Wise Men is black, and some of the shepherds play bagpipes. On Christmas Eve, their descendants come down from the Alban Hills to play the pipes on the steps of the Ara Coeli. I have my own *presepio*, purchased piece by piece from the vendors in Piazza Navona.

In Santi Cosma e Damiano, the lights go up on the other side of the proscenium arch. Men are bearing fardels, splitting wood, and bringing in the sheaves. Kettles hang from tripods over the fires, glowing as if they were real. Women bake bread, lifted out of real ovens. They card wool and rock the cradles. Donkeys loaded down with panniers are coming into town, dogs bark, cocks crow, pigs are squealing, and the camels in the distance are stately. On invisible wires against the night sky, angels descend, blowing trumpets. The sky is like the floor of heaven, sewn with stars.

The Christmas crib, an ark, holds five hundred animals and fifty houses for the men and women to live in. Some houses are grand, faced with white porticoes and white marble pillars, like the monument to Victor Emmanuel. King Herod, a villain, lives in one of these houses. In the manger, the ox and ass, leaning over the Bambino, caress Him with their breath.

The repletion, almost infinite, verges on Disney World. Cunning, also preposterous, the imitation is part of the charm. Packed in a shoe box, my toy soldiers are still in the attic. They have their bedrolls and Gatling guns, otherwise who would believe them? Outside the stockade, the redskins, whooping it up, carry tomahawks and shoot bows and arrows. I know how Gulliver felt, contemplating the Lilliputians, little versions of himself.

In Disney World, though, their art is only imposition, prestidigitator's art, compelling until you look beyond the sight line. The Magic Kingdom, seen from the front, declares its reality. Look at it from the side and you see where concrete blocks and two-by-fours are shoring it up. A Neapolitan, long dead, made the crib for Santi Cosma e Damiano. Enforcing priorities, also a point of view, he wasn't putting his art for real. His Nativity scene, the best of our humdrum business, is drawn to human scale, no cloud of fire, no voice from the whirlwind.

At the other end of the Via dei Fori Imperiali, the men who made the monument to Victor Emmanuel are saying that man is the measure. This doesn't mean human scale but elephantiasis, the old Roman virus. Dazzling in sunshine, the white Brescia marble is dust in the eyes. Overblown cartoons, the heroic figures on the façade melt like icing on a cake. Bedizened on the outside, the wedding cake is empty. My footfall echoes in the Risorgimento Museum. Finished in 1911, this arid pile predates the March on Rome by more than a decade. You can't fault Mussolini, who has enough sins at his door. But the same spirit that summoned him, not from the abyss, from the closet where old fripperies are bundled away, called up the monument to Victor Emmanuel. Before Fascism, it looks Fascist.

The Tiber at Ponte Milvio is oily green except where rocks, half submerged, break the current. There the water is white. A little arch like a croquet wicket spans the bridge on the Cassia side, a flagman standing before it. Traffic crosses by a single lane, one way only. Cars across the river wait for the flagman's signal, some honking their horns, evidently for the hell of it. At this end of the bridge, men with pneumatic drills, widening the approaches, are breaking up concrete on the Lungotevere. Garbage festoons the river bank like toilet paper after a ball game.

Devoting an excursion to this woebegone place is Giordano's *idea geniale*. A "brainstorm," it reflects his inflamed social conscience. If we enjoy ourselves today, tomorrow we have to poke in the dustbin. I would rather live in Cleveland than down by the Tiber, going north out of Rome. New apartment buildings faced with porous tufa stone stand behind the water. Not ugly, only nondescript, they take up space in Rome but aren't of it.

Scarabocchi scream from the walls of the buildings where left and right live together, awaiting a final knocking of heads. "*Libertà per i Compagni*," says the painted inscription, bristling with a hammer and sickle. "Reagan-BOIA" says another, proclaiming an equivalence, Reagan the Hangman. Crossed V's have partly canceled the invidious word. They stand for "*Viva*," as in "*Viva Il Duce*." We read on the walls how the MSI Lives, also: "*Semo Tutti Fascisti*." *Semo* is localese for *Siamo*. "We are all Fascists." Stenciled beneath this is the red, white, and green flame of the Meesee, MSI.

Where Ponte Milvio crosses the Tiber and the Via Flaminia changes its name, Constantine the Great and his rival for power had their bloody arbitrament. This was in 312 A.D. Maxentius, holding Rome, waited with his army behind the Aurelian Wall. I put him in Piazza del Popolo, where the Via Flaminia begins. Outside the gate, this section of the wall is called the Muro Torto, crooked wall. When the Goths attacked Rome, St. Peter, long dead, appeared on the ramparts to encourage the defenders. Since then, Romans, being pious, have left the Crooked Wall alone.

For Maxentius, staying put was the better part of valor. However, he read in the Sibylline books that on this day "the enemy of Rome should perish." Innocent of ambiguities, he left the wall and came out to fight. Constantine, having his piety too, marked his soldiers' shields with the monogram *Chi-Rho*, these interlocked letters forming the beginning of the word for Christ in Greek. They became his uncanny emblem or labarum, and in this sign he conquered. If *Vox populi* and *Vox Dei* had a part in what happened, no one can say. Italy, a ruin, didn't venture to speak, and God was on the side of the big battalions. Constantine led an army of one hundred thousand men, Britons, Gauls, and barbarians. Maxentius, who had the Praetorian Guard, squandered this advantage. He stood with his back to the Tiber, it being in spate. When the going got hot, there was no place to go. Dying by the sword or else in the water, he and his army disappeared from the earth.

They remember the famous victory in the Vatican Museum, a mixed bag thick and precious with the dust of time. Giordano, still sore, remembers the Vatican, like a bedraggled tour guide who has it by heart and wishes he didn't. In sleep, he says, the colored markers, pointing the crowd from one room to another, rise before his eyes. Ah, the Galleria delle Carte Geografiche (topographical maps of all the regions of Italy), the Galleria dei Candelabri. "*Ci sono tanti candelabri,*" says this tour guide morosely. Lots of candelabra.

The emperor waits for the tourist in the Sala di Constantino, where men are dying grotesquely by the Milvian Bridge. Inspired by the Cross in the sky, he hacks his way through fallen horses and a tangle of bodies. Looking at the writhing canvas, you can't tell Christian from pagan. Blood drenches them both. "Pig-sticking by the Tiber," says Giordano.

After the battle, the new master turned east. He liquidated his last rival on the shores of the Bosphorus at the City of Gold, then built his New Rome where the waters mingle and the land routes from three continents intersect. At first he meant to site this city on the plain of ancient Troy. Aeneas, leaving Troy, began the journey to Latium whose end was the founding of Rome. Or maybe this wasn't an ending. Old oracles said how someday Romans would go back again, "upstream" to the source. The propriety in this is a little chilling, like entropy, and Constantine changed his mind.

On a wall in the Vatican, in the Stanza dell' Incendio, "Troy" burns again. A real fire burned the Borgo in 847 A.D., almost destroying old St. Peter's. The painter, representing it, has seen how our endings are in our beginnings. In his painting, he harks back to the archetypal fire when Aeneas fled from Ilium and the Roman story began.

Creating the Second Rome, Constantine, a husbandman, grafted Christianity to the pagan stock. The grafting took and it didn't, and the new thing remembered the old. Like Ivan the Terrible, also Turk Suleiman, he murdered his son and heir. Blood, staining earth, fertilized his New Rome. A paste or cement, blood is in the foundation, like the bloody head dug up by Romans when they built their Temple of Jupiter on the Capitol Hill. Looking for a silver lining in this horrid apparition, soothsayers said it meant that Rome would be head of the world.

A connoisseur of art but not for art's sake, the emperor plundered the Greek world for statues. Some he defaced, knocking off Apollo's head and replacing this with his own pudgy likeness. His taste ran to big portrait statues, and he heaped them up by the hundreds in front of old Sancta Sophia. The world's biggest piece of porphyry, a monolith one hundred feet tall, made a pillar for one of these statues. From the top of this pillar, the image of Constantine looked over his dominion, meant to outlast time.

Constantine's Arch bisects Via di San Gregorio just below the Colosseum. The central archway and two side arches are flanked by detached columns and Corinthian "responds," half-piers bonded into the wall. Hollow like the Trojan Horse, the attic is reached by a stairway in the west pier. Mostly, this arch is other men's work, broken up and reassembled, a hodgepodge. The self-made man grudged the ancestors their glory. Trajan in particular made him look over his shoulder. Remembered in pious inscriptions, this emperor was "the weed on the walls." Ransacking the past, Constantine beautified his own triumphal arch with a frieze of Trajan's. He took the medallions from Hadrian, the reliefs on the attic from Marcus Aurelius. Where he didn't pillage, he made his art the servant of the state. Merging art in propaganda, Lenin, a long time after this, called it a cog or screw in the machine. The Arch of Constantine, instrumental art, shows you what this means. In reliefs above the smaller arches, you see the Man of God hectoring his people, winning in battle, or handing out largesse. Chiseled in stone by a cursory eye, the emperor isn't peculiar, only a type. Except for his costume, you wouldn't know him.

The huge basilica beside the Forum was Maxentius' legacy. This Constantine enlarged, erecting his own statue, forty feet high, in the apse. The coffered walls of the basilica, though broken, remain, and while the statue is gone they have the head in the Capitol museum. Like the shattered visage in Shelley's "Ozymandias," it says that the sculptor understood the Emperor's dropsical passion, still surviving.

Constantine had a granddaughter, Constantia. Outside Rome she built another basilica, off the Via Nomentana. This basilica is named for St. Agnes, one more victim of Diocletian's. Her tormentors stripped her naked before they killed her, but her hair, loosening and falling, covered her shame. Constantia, the good seed, has her resting place in the circular baptistery down a little path from the church. Against a white background, the mosaics on the vaulting resemble Nero's for his Golden House, beauty growing from horror. The floral arabesques make vines where fruit swells and flowers blossom. Greek amphorae decorate the vaulting, also cupids and songbirds. Latin *agnus* is "lamb," and every year in January on the day St. Agnes was martyred, two lambs hung with ribbons are blessed before her tomb.

Via Nomentana, running north and east from Rome, begins at the Porta Pia. Through this gate in the Aurelian Wall, the armies of united Italy entered Rome. The Pope ruled much of Italy for a thousand years before this. When the armies came in, he went out the back door. His claim to temporal power rested on a forgery, the Donation of Constantine, fabricated by priests. The emperor, said the priests, was cured of leprosy by Pope St. Sylvester. Old frescoes in Santi Quattro Coronati show him sitting in a tub, covered with spots like impetigo. Grateful for his cure, he gave Italy to the Church. On September 20, 1870, Italians resumed their birthright.

Quitting Ponte Milvio and its mingling of surly present and humpty-dumpty past, we walk back towards the city, following the

Tiber. "Langobards," modern Lombards with beards and shoulder-length hair held in place by elastic headbands, are playing tennis on the clay courts between the Lungotevere and the water. Some of these young men are swimming in the *piscina* built into the bank. At Ponte Duca d'Aosta, other young men, their knives out, load cannon, lob hand grenades, or feed belts of cartridges into machine guns. Some carry rifles with fixed bayonets. All are frozen in low relief, like the folk on the Grecian Urn, on the piers at either end of the bridge. On one of these piers, someone has chalked the words "*Roma Merda.*" Riding the sky, the dome of St. Peter's soars over the river.

Crossing the bridge, we come to the Foro Italico. Beached like a whale, the dead city remembers Mussolini who made it. After the War, Romans, pinched for house room, used this emptied-out place as a hostel. Staying there once, I drank thin sour wine and ate viscous macaroni. The toilets were holes in the floor.

A hundred-acre sprawl, the playing fields and sports palaces cover the old Campo della Farnesina. In their massive newness, they look ready for the boneyard, where the broken columns and fallen arches in the center of Rome look like outlasting time. The grandiose buildings, a version of Disney World, promise a lot but don't pay. This discrepant thing, says Giordano, is "fascist." He has an anecdote. Mussolini, on the island of Ponza, went without water and it made him angry. Why was there never any water in the tap? He said, "I've spent a pretty penny on getting the pipes laid in Ponza." Tactfully, they agreed that this was so. But the springs, they said, still ran into the sea.

A modern Nero building his Golden House, Mussolini appropriated the Campo for an exhibition that never came off. War broke out before he finished building. However, says Giordano, he was sure to win, so didn't stop. Strumming his harp, he raised the walls by magic, hoodwinking the people, but the magic was hocus-pocus. For bread he gave them a stone. "*Foro,*" says my friend, means different things in Italian, a public forum, also a hole. Italian peasants, close to starving as the war went on and on, drew in their belts to the last hole. " 'Mussolini's *foro*,' they called it."

The bogus magician, fooling others, fooled himself. His mind was a ragbag where ill-assorted couples made a pair. Like educated *fellaheen*, he was modern in this. Knowing a little Russian, he translated Kropotkin, a nonviolent man. Also he warmed to the sowers of violence. Young and penniless, an exile in Switzerland, his pockets were empty except for a cheap medallion of Marx.

Giordano, sneering, says how Mussolini called himself "profoundly religious." Until the day he died, he wore a scapular around his neck. "Much good it did him!" In Palazzo Venezia, the drawers of his desk were stuffed with amulets and charms. He practiced oneiromancy, divining the future by dreams. Friends were surprised when he told them what would happen by looking in the palms of their hands. In his deepest place a peasant, he worshiped dark gods. He feared the rays of the moon, and said how it was dangerous to let them shine on your face while you were sleeping. Where Turkish children wear the blue bead to protect them from the evil eye, he fended it off by touching his testicles. People watched him do this in public, putting his hand in his pocket.

But this "sawdust Caesar" knew his Machiavelli! "*Purtroppo*," says Giordano, unlucky for us. Like Constantine the opportunist, who saw how priests might be useful to a man on his way, he made his concordat with "the Bishop of Rome." (Giordano, like a Byzantine, won't recognize the Pope.) I think that Mussolini, maybe Constantine too, had his sincerity, a minor virtue. Irrational but not evil, not Hitler by a long shot, he was only empty, and the emptiness had to be filled.

A colossal obelisk, fifty-five feet tall and hewn from a single block of Carrara marble, dominates the outer square. Mussolini's name is engraved on the obelisk, below it in the center the Latin word DUX. The square, mostly empty except for scraps of newsprint, crumpled cartons, and broken bottles, is paved with tesserae, imitation Roman work. A drunk snores on the broken pavement, his face shielded by a copy of *Il Tempo*. Tanks, planes, and soldiers are featured in the mosaic, where young men play games or give the Fascist salute. Slogans admonish us: "*Molti Nemici Molto Onore*." Many Enemies, Much Honor.

Huge block letters set into the pavement repeat the word DUCE. Mesmeric when you say it over and over, it makes an ululating chant: Du-CHE-Du-CHE-Du-CHE-Du-CHE. Too young to remember, Giordano has his father, the left-wing Socialist, to tell him. At second hand, this living chronicle evokes for us both the cult of Mussolini. Italians, said Mussolini, needn't understand, only feel. He himself, when he followed his instincts, had never made mistakes, "but often when I have obeyed my reason." Inheriting the language of Dante, he emptied it of reason, showing how you could make it sound good but say nothing. Like margarine to butter, his no-speak was synthetic. After the March on Rome, when the king summoned him to power, he showed up for his audience wearing a black shirt, a bowler hat, and spats. Apologizing, he said, "I come from the battlefield." Florid and false, he was the mountebank, Signor Saltimbanco. However, Romans lent him their ears.

Says Giordano's papa, giving the devil his due: the man could work wonders. Like Garibaldi, he was "Saint and Hero! Mighty St. George!" People clipped his photo and hung it on the wall, sometimes above a votive candle. Out in the country, if he drank a glass of water they made off with the glass. If he hefted a pickax, something he liked to do to show his fellow feeling, also his hairy chest, they treasured this as a relic. Steering the ship of state, he lashed himself to the wheel. He wanted them to think so. In his office overlooking Piazza Venezia, lights blazed through the night. He wasn't in the office, however, but home in bed. Meanwhile, the ship went on the rocks.

The double row of stone monoliths, a promenade that wants

to overawe us, leads into the Foro. Inscriptions recall old battles and triumphs. They tell how Mussolini Founds the Fascist Party, Marches on Rome, Invades Abyssinia, Conquers Addis Ababa. One inscription compares him to the ruler of the gods: "*Duce Il Nostro Giove*." Another hails the ninth of May, Year Fourteen. On this day in the fourteenth year of the Fascist Era, Italy Finally Has Her Empire.

"The course of history," says Giordano scornfully, quoting Mussolini, "can be changed in a night." Throwing out the Christian calendar, Mussolini made a fresh start. He wanted Italians to take the world by the throat, the way they did in the old days. But they lacked the hard edge that goes with being single-minded. "Made flabby by art," was how he put it. When he sent his bombers to help Franco destroy the Spanish Republic, the world was horrified and this pleased him. He said it was better to horrify the world than charm it by playing the guitar. Importing the goose step from Germans, he called this the *passo romano*. It was how the legionaries used to march. Italians never got in step, though, preferring to sit by the side of the road. "Our good-for-nothing Italians," Mussolini called them, "this mediocre race."

At the end, they arrested him and put him in jail. From the Carabinieri's Podgora barracks, he looked out the windows at the huge white letters on the walls: CREDERE! OBBEDIRE! COMBATTERE! Giordano, puffing out his cheeks and pouting, does a convincing imitation of the Duce. "*Comunque*, he couldn't change the course of history." Giordano has a taste, not Italian, for abstractions. In the Foro Italico, the mocking slogans still sound mutely. Wanting them throttled, a lot of Italians think this gimcrack Forum ought to go into the lime kiln. However, some Italians know better.

When the radio brought the news that Mussolini had fallen, Romans, kissing each other, ran into the streets. Singing and dancing, they all became anti-Fascist. The paraphernalia of Fascism, a weed on the walls, disappeared overnight. On Via di San Gregorio below Constantine's Arch, anti-Fascists tore down the stone lictors that flanked the little waterfall built into the Caelian Hill. You can still see the silhouette where the lictors used to be. But the Foro Italico they spared. The garish fairy tale needing its conclusion, they brought in a laconic stonecutter to provide this. On the last block in the row, I read with a kind of dismay: "Falls From Power."

At the end, his make-believe kingdom falling about his ears, the Duce pulled himself together. He said or sang, "I leave life without recriminations, without hate, without pride. *Addio*." The composer was Verdi. As a boy in school, he declaimed an oration on the death of Verdi. Mussolini was sensitive, and everybody loves Verdi. But you hear the organ grinder in them both.

The warehouselike building behind the obelisk and on our left houses the Olympic swimming pool, fifty meters long. The diving tower in the building is ten meters high. At the back of the inner square, cascades of water play over an immense marble globe. Crossing this square, we come to the Stadio dei Marmi, named for its sixty marble statues. Bigger than the Colosseum, it seats one hundred thousand people. Refuse is piled beside the running track, where a solitary jogger goes his rounds. Monte della Farnesina, carpeted with trees, rises behind the stadium. High up on the hill, a statue of the Madonna has a bird's-eye view of Rome.

The heroic statues girdling the track, versions of Michelangelo's David, are dead white and heavily muscled. The men on the pedestals hold clubs like Hercules. They put the shot, throw the discus, heft a soccer ball, or lean on marble *fasces*. One carries a sword like a knight's sword. Some are naked with big penises, and some of the penises have been broken off. Many of these men wear fig leaves, however, like Michelangelo's nudes on the wall of the Sistine Chapel, draped by order of Pope Pius IV. The Pope, calling himself Pontifex Maximus, played at being an antique Roman. Romans glorified the body and he wanted to do this, but being modern and prudish couldn't carry it off.

Spooked by the bad place, Giordano wishes we hadn't come here. Mussolini, he says, like the ghost of Nero under the Colle Oppio, still walks up and down in the earth. In Rome, his speeches, tape-recorded, are selling like indulgences. If you believe Giordano, the devil is only biding his time.

I tell him he gives this devil more than his due. The Foro Italico, worth preserving, reminds you that the devil is an ass. Pricking up my ears, I listen for the Götterdämmerung-music, but don't hear it. Wonder and terror are missing in the Foro, and only banality remains. The mesomorphs on the pedestals are more embarrassing than scary. What we want, to complete the picture, is a sly little man in an electric-blue suit. Unlocking his valise, imitation leather, he takes out the dirty postcards and offers them for sale.

Contemptuous of "wogs" in general, my British-novelist friend admires Mussolini on the q.t. He cleaned up the canals, got the beggars off the streets, and wasn't just whistling "O Sole Mio." However, says this friend, mostly what you get in Rome is Figaro the barber. Everybody's comic Italian, he sings a lot and has the gift of gab. When not emoting, he sleeps.

Surprised by their "day of rest," I can't do what I meditate doing. The *riposo settimanale* may fall on a Tuesday or Wednesday, no telling. But knocking off, a way of life, doesn't need a notice over the lintel. Take Santa Maria Maggiore, for instance. In a locked grotto under the floor, they have an ancient Christmas crib, the work of Arnolfo di Cambio, a man of parts. I ask to see it. The priest in the sacristy, looking at his watch, says we are too close to lunchtime. Come back in the afternoon. I do this. The crib is only open in the morning, he says. *Scaccomatto*. Checkmate.

Over in Trastevere, Santa Cecilia shows the work and neglect of hands. The front garden is overgrown and the bay trees need trimming. Impudent fingers have deposited litter in the antique marble vase. But tree roses and chrysanthemums set off the façade, and the convent beside the church has a Last Judgment by Pietro Cavallini. He could paint souls. Christ, enthroned in a mandorla, is surrounded by angels, apostles, and saints, and not even Giotto matched the grave demeanor of the faces. Most of the fresco, obliterated by eighteenth-century monks secure in their own taste, is gone. What remains is half hidden behind the choir stalls and paneling. On Via del Babuino, a copy in a shop window teases my imagination. I want the real thing.

But the convent is closed. The nuns who live there are cloistered and don't welcome my visit. Holding the door just ajar, the young *sorella* tells me that I can't look at the fresco today. "*È una nostra clausura*," she says. This is their time for seclusion. Perhaps another time? Before the question is out, the door shuts on my foot. Phoning Rome Information, I ask for the number of this convent. Information can't find it. "*Ci sono tanti conventi,*" the operator tells me. "There are so many convents."

I set out *piedi* to explore the Caelian Hill. The Clivus Scauri, "a street ascending," is my way up. In this old Roman street, Pope St. Gregory lived. He said it was "foolishness" to value old things, the classics, for instance. Named for the Pope, the church at the foot of the street still has his episcopal throne. Once, when the church was empty, I tried this throne for size. A declivity spanned by brick arches, the Clivus ends in the piazza before the church of Sts. John and Paul. In vaults below ground, a painted room is decorated with *orantes*, prayerful figures on the wall supplicating the Creator. I mean to go down there and see for myself. Barring my way, the grilled gates of the portico are padlocked.

Possessing their city, Romans don't deserve it, or you can say that they get what they deserve. Rome is: *rumore* (noise), *scioperi* (strikes), dog shit on the sidewalk, a mammoth university where nobody teaches and all the classes are filled, crazy politics, somnolent priests, watered-down wine in mean trattorias that serve rubbery pasta and charge you the sky. In the opulent city, a beggar woman and her corrupted children snatch at my sleeve as I go up the steps to St. Peter's. There is snow on the Alban Hills but no heat in my pension, and the tiled floors, bare of rugs, are like the North Pole. In Piazza Venezia, *sfratti,* dispossessed Roman tenants, are camping out on the traffic island in the center of the square. The tent city empties in a hurry, however, charged by *carabinieri* with flailing batons.

"I'd rather be a pagan suckled in a creed outworn." This outburst is prompted by my visit to the *Santo Bambino*. A fat little idol stuck all over with jewels, he stands in a glass case in the sacristy of the Ara Coeli. The Altar of Heaven, this church on the Capitoline bears witness to false gods. The Tiburtine Sibyl, an ancient necromancer, shares the apse with the Emperor Augustus. At Christmas the Holy Child, carved from an olive tree that grew in the Garden of Olives, comes out of his case. Having his own transport, he "drives about to see the sick," said the English poet Clough. Like Santa Claus or Dear Abby, he gets a lot of mail. The unopened letters, piled at his feet, stay there until the sacristan burns them. Once the *Santo Bambino* upstaged Mussolini. Spellbinding from his balcony, Mussolini saw a limousine pushing through the crowd. Soldiers sprang to do something about this. They backed off helpless, however. The limousine held the *Santo Bambino*.

Hitler's henchman Goebbels, hearing that even Mussolini would never be able to make anything but Italians out of the Italians, thought this was "undoubtedly right." My misery, loving company, draws the line at Goebbels, and his point of view brings me up short. Clichés, always true, are only half true, and declarative sentences, lacking complication, are suspect. The stick-figure Italian, good-natured but good-for-nothing, needs a little flesh on his bones.

Rome, embodied chaos, is also gratuities, not a city you earn. However, you have to hold yourself ready. Italians have this talent, the uses of adversity. They learned it in their dark ages, after the decline and fall. The gain of sleep and dream, it isn't everyone's possession. Also it goes against the common wisdom, learned at my mother's knee. Italians, unlike me, don't just do something, they stand there. I am trying to get the knack of this but it doesn't come easy.

Playing up to the Roman emperor, his patron, Horace has a chesty line: *Fortiter, occupa portum.* "Be strong and gain the port." This Roman poet began the vogue of those ship-of-state poems, the despair of young students and the seedbed of their hypocrisies. "Sail on, sail on!" D'Annunzio, an excitable Italian poet, tried his hand at the genre but got it all mixed up with sex. "You, you, o ship of steel, straight, swift, flashing, lovely as a naked weapon, alive, quivering," etc. This is what happens when you gird up your loins. On my Roman side, "made flabby by art," I have been revising D'Annunzio and Horace, filleting their backbone. No longer straight and swift, D'Annunzio's torpedo boat runs in meanders. Not chesty but insipid, Horace is saying: *Leniter, occupa portum.* "Take it easy and gain the port."

Doney's on the Veneto is my house by the side of the road. Plane trees, palms, and grandiflora magnolia hint at the country, a Petit Trianon where Romans play at being bucolic. The Via Veneto is color-coordinated. Doney's blue awnings, keeping the sun off my head, match the blue of the tables. On the other side of the street, the awnings of the Café de Paris are orange. Carpano's, an elegant American bar, has yellow tables with green awnings. People who stay in the Cavalliere Hilton, outside the city on Monte Mario, are bused in here every morning and taken back in the late afternoon. The Hilton, an Italian Camelot, lies behind a defensive moat, Rome beating against it.

On a Sunday morning I sit outside Doney's café, Marcello Mastroianni looking idly at the passing parade. A cappuccino is at my elbow, in my lap the Sunday papers, bought at the kiosk over the road. The table, a little UN, comes bedecked with the flags of the nations. When I want a second cup of coffee, the waiter, hovering but not a pest, drops another ticket in the saucer. Having pocketed my lire, he tears the ticket across.

In this morning's papers, Mama Rosa is back on page one. She was Rosa Buzzini Quattrini, and twenty years ago she saw the Virgin in a pear tree. This happened in San Damiano, a little town near Piacenza. Blossoming out of season, the pear tree has become a national shrine. According to the *Tribune,* Mama Rosa's estate is worth four million dollars, mostly votive offerings. Her will, recently probated, names Pope John Paul as the heir. *L'Unità,* the Communist paper, is outraged. *L'Osservatore Romano,* the Vatican paper, wishes that Mama Rosa had thought of someone else. Cardinal Casaroli, the Vatican secretary of state, has just turned the inheritance down. In the dark ages, says *L'Unità,* its ironic editorial peppered with inverted commas, the Pope would have taken the money and run.

Il Messagero, tut-tutting, reports that slivers from the pear tree are selling briskly in shops on the Via della Conciliazione, only a stone's throw from St. Peter's. *Il Tempo,* tongue in cheek, compares the traffic in relics to the multiplying of the loaves and fishes. It has sent its reporter to Santa Prassede, Browning's church of St. Praxed's on the Esquiline Hill where the bishop ordered his tomb. In this church, they claim the pillar against which Christ was scourged. But the same pillar, says *Il Tempo,* is on view in Santa Croce. *Epoca,* in its census of miracles past and present, has struck a rich lode in Papa Celestino. This hermit-pope from the Abruzzi, a miracle worker, hung his cowl on a sunbeam. Unhappy in Rome, he heard God's voice at night, commanding him to lay down the tiara. That is what he did. However, says *Epoca,* it wasn't God who commanded him but the would-be pope Boniface, speaking through a pipe in the wall.

On the Veneto, a street of dreams, they all have their pipeline to heaven. Bread and wine are expensive but miracles come cheap. Couturiers on the side streets turn the water into wine. In the hours after sunset, the nineteenth-century buildings, pumpkins in the light of day, are fairy palaces in a magic kingdom. Neon, winking from the billboards, makes the rough places smooth. Glamorous in this half-light, the whores, like Cinderella, put on their magic slippers.

Rounding a pair of right-angled corners as it climbs the hill, the Veneto ends at the Porta Pinciana. Near Piazza Barberini, where it begins, the Capuchin church smells of great expectations. Wizard friars, building castles in Spain, live in this church of Santa Maria della Concezione. Like the Sibyls who were here before them, the friars have the trick of divination. They know the secrets of the lottery and can make a shrewd guess at a *terno*, the winning sequence of three numbers. Romans, credulous or wistful, believe this. Like most adepts, the friars, disclaiming occult power, are skeptics. I have heard one of them say, though, that if he had to make *terni* for everybody who came calling, he wouldn't have one left for himself.

The *lotto*, an ancient diversion, is the shortest Roman road from rags to riches. For a few lire, it offers six days of hope. Banning the lottery, the Pope threatened gamblers with the galleys or excommunication. Romans made light of this, failing to see the profit in saving your soul if you couldn't keep soul and body together. Ever a realist, the Pope changed his tune, taking the lottery under his protection.

Two hundred years ago, the weekly drawings were held on the Capitoline Hill, punctually at noon on Saturday when the cannon booms for *mezzogiorno*. A number of poor girls got tickets free gratis. Winning, they got a dowry, paid on their marriage day. Climbing the stairs Michelangelo built, a ladder to heaven, the *cittadini* kept their eyes on the velvet-draped platform. Some, holding a crucifix, let it nudge the lottery ticket. Marked on ivory balls, ninety numbers went into the silver urn on the platform. Five of these numbers were lucky. Later they used a glass barrel, stuffed with rolled-up papers. Suspended on its axis, it resembled Fortune's Wheel. An orphan boy, dressed in white, drew the numbers from the wheel. Like the boy in the Christmas crib, he wore a gray billycock hat. For this orphan, life's chances looked bleak. You never knew, however. The secular epiphany began with a blaring of trumpets. A purple-clad giant bawled out the combinations. From the crowd a soughing noise greeted the winning numbers, sometimes a cry of triumph.

In Rome from Monday through Saturday morning, hopeful punters queue up before the ticket windows. I buy my ticket at a sidewalk stall in front of Stazione Termini. One winning number makes a *simplum*, two an *ambo*, three a *terno*, etc. The *terno* is best.

Ascending the Veneto bound for the park, the traffic, a funeral procession, fills the street with mournful music. Directing from his podium, the white-helmeted policeman has slowed it to a crawl. In the 56 bus, the driver, shifting into neutral, unfolds his copy of *Il Messagero*. Eyeballing the traffic, the policeman raises white-gloved hands, then, with a flourish, lets them fall. This signals the start of the Oklahoma Land Rush. Around the corner they go, hell-bent for the Corso d'Italia. Slow off the mark, the bus driver makes up for this. ATAC is the acronym for public transport in Rome. Alarmed, I slop my coffee, watching the Vespa about to go under the wheels of the bus. "*Alli mortacci sua,*" says the man on the Vespa, shaking his fist. "Death on your family." In the street, however, the pedestrians are negligent. Practiced matadors ignoring the traffic, they shift a hip or move a shoulder.

Detaching itself from the traffic, the white Maserati pulls up to the curb. The license plate bears the letters S.M.O.M., for the Sovereign Military Order of Malta. In the center of the plate the heraldic shield has sixteen quarterings, denoting an Austrian Knight. Poking his head out the window, the Barone bids me a guttural good morning. Half Austrian, half Italian, the ancient misalliance, he speaks English like an Italian, Italian like a German. The Maltese passport he carries, courtesy of the Grand Master, is his hole card, he says, useful if the Communists take over.

An honorary commander of the Swiss Guard, he flies a little flag from the fender of the Maserati. When he goes to the Vatican, the guards at the gate, seeing this flag, stand to attention. The great and near great are among his acquaintance, and in the Roman Curia he knows half of them by name. The late pretender Umberto was a friend of many years. They say at Doney's tables that the Barone is a prime mover in the campaign to confer sainthood on Princess Grace of Monaco.

Her bottom planted firmly on the red leather seat, Gertrude sits behind the wheel, checking out the possibilities. Spotting a parking slot on Via Sardegna, she coasts along the curb and turns the corner. January and May, they thread the maze of tables, coming towards me. The Barone wears a double-breasted blue blazer with white bone buttons, white linen slacks, and black alligator pumps. His shirt, open at the neck, accommodates a silk foulard. An elderly copy of King Victor Emmanuel, the first of the name, he fingers his thick handlebar mustache, yellowish white like old ivory. Gertrude, a head taller, is all swish and silk. She has the high color of brunette German women and the soft tentative speech of the south. A Bavarian tart, she looks good enough to eat.

Appearances, as often, deceive, though. Where Gertrude is cold, the Barone is hot. Rome, a middle-class city, damps down his fires. When he wants to stoke the fires, he takes the car to Salerno, then crosses by boat to Capri. Like the Emperor Tiberius, a satyr for all seasons, he has a bolthole on Capri. His villa, bordered by an avenue of ancient evergreen oaks, is secluded behind a high wall. Caprese women, he says, dress differently from the women of Rome. "There the approaches to paradise are open."

Always on the boil, the Barone this Sunday morning threatens to ascend into heaven. A crony at the Vatican, where they know a sure thing when they see it, has given him a tip on the *lotto*. He can't wait to get his bet down, but this being Sunday the offices are closed. Like a numismatist, a gourmand at the table, or a drunkard with his drink, the Barone is a man obsessed. Gambling, next to venery, is his obsession. He bets on the dogs and horses, bike races, stock car races, cockfights when he can find one, also the soccer matches in Parioli. Mostly he backs Lazio, and what he loses every week, backing this local entry, would keep me in pocket for a year.

But the *lotto* is where he lives. Gertrude buys his tickets for him at the State Lottery Office on the Esquiline Hill, across from San Martino ai Monti. He sits in the car, consulting the auspices, then tells her what numbers to choose. On the walls of the church, the *scarabocchi* are auspices. "*Gesuiti sono falsi*" reads an inscription. "Jesuits Are False." This inflames the Barone. Toting up the letters, he arrives at his *terno*: 7-4-5. Mostly, however, he goes by the book, unless he has an *idea geniale*. Choosing the winning *terno* is a science, like oneiromancy, the science of dreams, or chiromancy, palm reading. His life is racy with omens, a head cold, a fender bender, the fall of the government. Each has its number. Dreams have their numbers. For this, he looks in his dream book, the *Libro dei Sogni*. Before Gertrude hove in view, there was Darlene, a salesgirl from Hammersmith. This romance cooled, the Barone in a dream discovering the lay of the land. Crossed in love, he said feelingly, "*Donne e buoi, dei paese tuoi.*" "Pick your women and oxen from your own province." Being resourceful, however, he took the age of the faithless Darlene and the month and day they parted. This made a *terno*. "When the bread and wine are gone," he says, "hunger and thirst will soon come back. With a ticket in my pocket, I am rich till Saturday."

The sun, post-meridian, heats the closed air underneath the umbrellas. Yawning, the Barone gets to his feet. Time, he says, for a *spuntino*. He suggests that we take this at a table indoors. What he calls a snack, however, would break the bank at Monte Carlo. Declining to join them, I head for the Piccadilly, an American-style cafeteria at the foot of the Veneto in Piazza Barberini. Standing tall before the embassy, the Marine guards are gnomons, red, white, and blue. On the other side of the street, at the corner of Via Ludovisi, the flower vendors have sold out their red roses and carnations and are packing up for siesta. The shop windows, mixing cheap and dear, offer crude cameos mass-produced in Naples, also the real intaglio thing. I can buy an ivoried copy of Michelangelo's David or the *Last Supper* in 3-D. The hand-crafted shoes in Magli's, made from the skin of an endangered species, fetch two hundred dollars a pair. Heaped up in the windows, the understated silk ties, tied in a four-in-hand, look like regimental ties from the Burlington Arcade. They wear these ties in the Banca Nazionale del Lavoro, across from the embassy annex. "*Lavoro*" is work, but the bank is closed for Sunday.

Wanting to indulge my taste for old bones, I turn off the street into Santa Maria. Inside, near the altar, St. Michael tramples the devil, and St. Francis, beside the nave, is ecstatic. In back of the altar and to the right, the stairs go down to the five chapels in the crypt, packed with bones. There are bones on the altars, on the vaulting, in niches cut in the walls, and even the lamp holders are bones. Clothed in robes and cowls, skeletons stand in the passageways. Some stretch out a bony arm. Four thousand Capuchin friars are down here, awaiting the resurrection and the life. Buried in soil imported from the Holy Land, the bony figures have broken their graves.

Friar Pacifico still haunts the passageways in Santa Maria della Concezione. In the last century he made his name a Roman byword, predicting the winning *terno* at the *tombolas* in the Villa Borghese. This version of the weekly *lotto*, restricted to the summer months, took place in the hippodrome where Giordano, a modern man, runs in the mornings. Cattle browsed on the grass, and once a year Prince Borghese, harvesting the park, made fifty thousand bundles of hay. Romans, filling the hippodrome, left the lame and paralytic to watch the empty houses. Some, being prudent, went first to the Ara Coeli and put their case to the *Santo Bambino*. The old church, his domicile, rises over the piazza where the velvet-covered platform used to hold the silver urn.

In the park, cards in hand, Romans pricked out the numbers. Friar Pacifico, smiling secretly, didn't do this. He was "the wizard" and had the numbers in his heart. Hearing how the crowd beat a path to his door, Pope Gregory took a hand in the game. An antediluvian, he prohibited the telegraph in his Papal States, saying how it might "work harm to religion." A killjoy, he wanted Romans to lay up treasures in heaven. Putting down the competition, he sent the wizard from Rome.

An admiring crowd brought Friar Pacifico on his way to the Porta del Popolo. Standing in the piazza outside the Crooked Wall, he delivered his swan song, reducing the crowd to tears. Solicitous of friends, he remembered the next drawing of the *lotto*, however. "*Addio,*" he said, and gave them the five winning numbers.

GIRL OF THE GOLDEN WEST

AT THE FOOT of "Cloudy Mountains," this is the "Polka," a California saloon in the days of the Gold Rush. The dimly lit interior, triangular-shaped, rises two stories. Calling "Hello! hello!" and "Whiskey!" the miners shake the room as they enter. Rough and ready customers, their emotions are all up front. They smoke, clink glasses, and shuffle the cards. Some, morose, remember the home folks in lands far away. One sings of his dog, *il mio cane*. Joe, a young miner, reads a letter that tells how his granny has died. "*Nonna se n'è andata!*" The man sitting beside me murmurs audibly, "*Brutte nuove!*" Bad news! Clicking their tongues, the English ladies behind him register disapproval. On the balcony, Larkens bursts into tears, wanting his mother. "*Vo' la mamma mia!*" The audience commiserates. "*Ah, poverino!*"

Seething with tears and violence, Puccini's *Girl of the Golden West* is a smash hit in Rome. For this open-air performance at the Baths of Caracalla, every seat has been gone for a week. "*Non c'è problema,*" says Monsignor Moran, not a problem for him. *A pezza novanta* or Roman V.I.P., he crooks a finger and people hurry to oblige. The black tunic and mantle haven't come off the peg and the patent leather shoes look like Gucci. Gulliver among the Lilliputians, Monsignor tips the scales at two thirty or forty. Beneath the biretta the close-cropped hair is gray, but the belly is flat where the leather belt cinches the tunic. A rosary hangs from the belt, and the tunic and mantle bear the heart-shaped emblem of his order, Discalced Clerics of the Holy Cross and Passion. "What is 'discalced'?" It means shoeless, he says.

We met for the first time just outside the gate in the Villa Celimontana. Nearby, on Via San Paolo della Croce, the Passionist Fathers have their Roman billet. Bordered by high walls, it stands over Nero's extravagant gardens, hateful to Tacitus. Through the grill in the *portone*, you can see a piece of the monastery garden. Writing a monograph on the smaller fountains of Rome, Monsignor provides his own illustrations. An artist's sketch pad in his lap, a canvas campstool beneath him, he was sketching the Navicella, a stone fountain shaped like a boat. Pope Leo X, who meant to enjoy the papacy, had them put the fountain there four hundred years ago. Down in EUR, says Monsignor, three little fountains bubbled from the ground when they chopped off the head of St. Paul. Does he believe this? I ask him. "I believe because it is impossible," he says. He likes to watch the rising of my Protestant gorge.

Footlights, screwed in the floor along the base of the triangle, separate the stage from the crowd. We sit on wooden tiers, like the temporary bleachers that ring the Hippodrome in the Villa Borghese. Stairs go up, stage left, to a balcony hung with animal skins and brightly dyed bedsheets, passing for Indian rugs. A stuffed bear's head is mounted above the door in the right-hand wall, and a sign tells us that this door opens on the "*Sala da ballo,*" a dance hall. Bottles and glasses shine dully on the bar that closes off the apex of the triangle. A large poster, crudely lettered, offers 5,000 *dollari* for the apprehension of Ramerrez, a desperado. The reward is posted by "Wells-Fargo." Resting on sawhorses, the green faro table makes an oblique angle with the footlights.

St. Paul of the Cross would have been at home in Puccini's "*Grande Selva California,*" says Monsignor. Wanting to participate in Our Lord's passion, he went into the desert, a retreat lasting forty days. This began his life's mission, "prospecting for souls." He mustered an army, postulants, novices, brothers, and priests. Some went out on the roads, serving the foreign missions in China and Bulgaria. When the Communists took over, the Fathers had to shorten their lines, a temporary adjustment, according to Monsignor. Against the flesh, this cunning soldier opposes the spirit. Have I seen the Pope on TV, paying his respects to Sts. Cyril and Methodius, "patron saints of Europe"? A thousand years ago, they converted the Slavs. Russian power in Europe being at its zenith, Pope John Paul means to confront it. "He isn't a Slav and political for nothing." St. Cyril, Monsignor tells me, is buried in Rome, above a Mithraic temple. "What Rome did for Mithras, Rome will do for Marx." On his tailored habit he wears a motto, *Jesu XPI Passio,* like the labarum the Emperor's soldiers wore on their shields at the Battle of the Milvian Bridge.

Slouched beside the faro table, Jack Rance, a sheriff, draws on his fat cigar. The lighted point, glowing, punctuates the gloom. In this black and white extravaganza, he presents the villain. Monsignor, amused, says we don't need a program to tell us. In Rome on special assignment, he lives in the mother-house on the Caelian Hill. At the Propagation of the Faith College, the students, attending his weekly lecture, call him Monsignor *Braccio di ferro,* Iron Arm. Skilled in canon law, he has Gratian's "Decretals" by heart. This medieval law book says how Rome, in matters legal, always gets the last word. "*Roma locuta, causa finita,*" says this broth of a man. "Rome has spoken, the question is settled." He can see a loophole where others see a blank wall. Some wealthy Americans are grateful for this. Divorce, he tells them, is out of the question, but annulments are possible where a marriage is technically flawed. *Defectus formae* is how he puts it. "Defects of form."

In the "Polka," lights brighten as the artificial daylight goes. Hung with scrim, the window at stage rear reveals a tree-covered valley, behind it snowy mountains, gold-tinted. While we watch, the sun sets and patches of stars appear in the night sky. Electrician's art, this elicits applause. "*Bellissimo!*"

An opera lover but fastidious, Monsignor isn't high on Puccini. Like "O Promise Me," he tugs at your heart strings. This evening at the Baths is a sop to my enfeebled modern taste. Fond of the old hymns and time-honored formulations, he wishes they had left the Latin in the Mass. Pope John XXIII, "Puccini in a tiara," was one of the Church's mistakes. Before the Passionists ordered him to Rome, Monsignor spent five years in Springfield, Mass., preparing copy for their weekly radio program, "The Hour of the Crucified." After Vatican II, however, they changed the name to "Crossroads," an ecumenical title. Wanting a larger audience, they livened up the program, introducing folk guitars.

On summer nights an opera house, the Terme di Caracalla is mostly empty by day. Plumy cypress and umbrella pines fence the six-acre ruin, disarticulated bones on the river flats behind the Caelian Hill. Where the ground has been cleared, it is surfaced with pea gravel or planted in grass. Hedges of boxwood demarcate the grassy areas, littered with toppled columns. As thick around as a man is tall, these granite monoliths are trees on the floor of a petrified forest. Brick structures like little kilns ventilate the work going on below ground. Tiny shards of green glass, the residue of soft-drink bottles, wink in the sun. Restoration inches forward, and chunks of mosaic, waiting their turn, are propped against the brick walls. Men in hard hats, erect on scaffolds, chip away at the brick.

Play for mortal stakes, opera finds its natural setting in Rome. Tourists in the audience outnumber Romans, but not by much. Many, bringing their children with them, have come ready for the long pull. In second-class railway cars, you see them slung with ropes of sausage, loaves of bread, a round of cheese, a fiasco of wine. This being opera, a civilized entertainment, they hide their smelly provisions in hampers. The children hold cardboard cartons moist with Pandoro, chewy cake like angel food cake. Rooks in their black habits and starched white wimples, a brood of little nuns and their Mother Superior have most of a row to themselves. Eyes popping, his mustache aquiver, the spitting image of fat Henry Armetta perches on the end of the row.

Shivering behind me in his polyester suit, the middle-aged Englishman fusses over his wife and two other ladies, aggressively maiden. One, her shoulders hunched, her mouse-colored hair coiled in a chignon, studies the libretto, in English and Italian. The pocket flash makes lanes of light in the darkness. Vendors, dressed in white smocks and carrying trays and insulated containers, move up and down the aisles. Indifferent to the action on stage, they cry "*Birra!*" and "Coca-Cola!" distracting the lady with the flashlight.

Gnawed by time's tooth, the Baths of Caracalla look good for another millennium. Working in brick and concrete, ancient Romans built to last. Their buildings appeared to deny this. Confectioner's work, the façade of the Baths dripped with fine stucco. In Blouet's reconstruction, the walls are lacy-thin. Poke them, however, and three inches down you came to the rock.

Spanning the central hall, the barrel vault, pierced by clerestory windows, rose a hundred feet above the pavement. This was the caldarium, a steam room. Where the opera stage, flanked by piers, ends at the footlights, once it made a floor for the room. Twenty feet high, the rectangular platform supported the ancient baths or "thermae." Underneath it, hypocausts stored heat from the furnaces, transmitting this to flues in the walls. When Romans wanted a lot of heat, they made their walls almost solid with flues, clay pipes a foot in diameter.

Next door in the tepidarium, the temperature was always lukewarm. The frigidarium on the other side was cold. They had their library in the frigidarium, also, says Monsignor, rooms for oiling and sanding the body. An athlete who played his football in the shadow of the Golden Dome, he likes to quote the Latin saying "*Mens sana in corpore sano,*" a sound mind in a sound body. Monsignor will never see forty again but wouldn't look out of place lining up at tight end.

The vault of the caldarium fell in a long time ago, and the arches that carried it are broken. Ornamented stucco covered the ceiling and the upper reaches of the walls. Below, the walls were faced with white and colored marble. Tritons, half man, half fish, swam in the black and white mosaic of the pavement. Stripped by medieval people, the walls show as brick work, buttressed by iron supports. Stunted shrubs, wild garlic, laurel, and oleander grow in the broken surfaces. But the darkness partly hides the work of time. Knit together beyond the sight line, the shattered walls on the north side, fourteen to sixteen feet wide, soar into the night, disappearing. Dwarfed by the immensity, the spectators below look naked in the glare of the arc lamps. Piranesi in his prison scenes, where the lines extend to infinity, offers a version of the Baths of Caracalla.

Murdered at twenty-nine in the year 217, the Emperor who built here had a love affair with death. His biographer Cassius Dio said he spent millions on exotic poisons, wanting to kill many men in different ways. Killing his brother Geta, he did this in their mother's sight. The victim, crying for help to the mother who bore him, was hanging on her neck when he died. An able soldier, famous for his massacres, the Emperor doted on the life of the camp. His portrait bust, surprisingly real, shows a bullet head, wrinkled forehead, and close-cropped curls. Caracalla is mustached. Curls valance the jaws and cleft chin. The thin line of mouth grimaces, the nose is strong and blunt. Darting eyes look suspicious beneath the angry line of eyebrow. Reigning six years, he left the army in mourning. The Senate, after his death, enrolled him among the gods.

Feeling for Larkens who wants to go home, the crowd in the "Polka" has chipped in to buy him a ticket. Grateful for this, Larkens smiles between his tears. "*Grazie, grazie, ragazzi!*" An emotional scene, it is interrupted without warning by snarling trumpets and bassoons. Sid, whose eyes are furtive, has been detected cheating. The cry is "*Al laccio!*" To the gallows! Soothing the savage breast, Minnie, a soprano, enters and takes down the Bible. "Wash me," she sings, "and I shall be whiter than snow." Hired by the soprano, a coterie of supporters comes in on cue, cheering enthusiastically. Cries of "*Bis! bis!*" bring Minnie to the footlights. The Girl of the Golden West, she has a heart of gold, also a frontierwoman's temper. Pulling a pistol from her bodice, she chastens the villainous Rance, an unwelcome suitor. *Una povera fanciulla,* only a little poor girl, Minnie has never been kissed. This is what she tells the tenor, and he and we believe her. He is Ramerrez in disguise, one of Nature's noblemen. As Act I winds down, Puccini gets a lot of mileage from the harp. Faintly dissonant, a C major chord dies in the ruined caldarium.

Festooned with flags, red, white, and green, the bar offers Cinzano, Campari and soda, Scotch whisky, and *Nastro Azzurro,* a "blue-ribbon" beer. Setting up for Act II, scene shifters on the curtainless stage mount frosted panes in the windows, hang draperies, and canopy Minnie's bed with flowered cretonne. On the deal table, they lay out tea and biscuits, cream cakes, and utensils. Longer than a night in Russia, the interval is noisy with their comings and goings. Pinching pennies, Italians sip the lukewarm beer, making it last. Tightfisted Uncle Sam, weighing profit and loss, is a fiction of theirs, created in their image and likeness. In the swarthy, wrinkled faces, the black eyes are inquisitive but hooded. Jolly on the outside, eager to please, Italians are all surface. What lies beneath is their secret. In a week of Sundays, they won't ever divulge it. Domiciled in Rome for a long time, Monsignor enjoys his hosts but advises discretion. Supers in the Puccini opera, they relish the salt taste of tears. Sometimes, however, they surprise you. In 1849, when French shells were falling in Piazza di Spagna, Romans, imperturbable, did their everyday thing. Up on the Gianicolo, Garibaldi and his men awaited the final assault. This came in the night, on June 29, the Feast of Sts. Peter and Paul. Not much caring to be gloomy, apocalyptic either, Romans lit votive candles in the windows of the houses. Crowding the dark streets, they fired off rockets. In the valley of the shadow, they wouldn't give up their festa. Later that night, some laid down their lives.

On stage, the sky has darkened and hissing strings announce a storm. The windowpanes, white with snow, define Minnie's cabin, a port in a storm. Draperies flutter, a fire blazes on the hearth. Flutes and English horns suggest the whistling of the wind, *di fuori.* Clinging to each other, Minnie and Ramerrez are lost in an earthquake of love. The Girl of the Golden West, kissed for the first time, clamors for more. Ramerrez presses his advantage. "*Spesso la mano, per avere il braccio.*" Give this man a hand and he'll want the whole arm. Around the corner, trouble is brewing. A volley of pistol shots tells us that the posse is outside the door. "*Sono un dannato!*" cries Ramerrez. "I am accursed!" A sacrificial victim, he plunges into the storm. Bassoons and trombones, trumpets and drums deplore this.

Silhouetted by the footlights, two men in the audience have got to their feet, butting each other like stags. Roars of "*Silenzio!*" mingle with derisive hooting. Attendants in uniform come to take the men away. An indignant couple, pushing past me, makes for the exit. Beneath the sign that says *Uscita,* outlined in red neon, young men in jeans and black naugahyde jackets smoke cigarets and chat with their friends. Bit players in a spaghetti Western, they aren't about to get out of the way. Imitating the hammer strokes on the celesta, an empty beer bottle, rolling down the steps, crashes against a metal stanchion, exploding. It being past midnight, the children in the audience have seen all they want. Letting their parents know this, they squall bloody murder but are silenced with a blow to the head.

"*Non puoi morire!*" Minnie sings in a rapture of distress. "You shall not die!" The audience, applauding frantically, calls for an encore. Some, carried away, repeat the imperious words *sotto voce.* The English ladies, beside themselves, look daggers and shush for attention.

Enveloping the stage, steam rises from the platform where the hypocaust heated the Baths. We are in a misty clearing in the "*Grande Selva California.*" Pursuers armed with knives and guns emerge from the mist, yelping like dogs on the track of their prey. One of the men, having plaited a noose, slings the rope over a branch. Between the trees, snow peaks glitter in the strengthening sun. Pushed and prodded from behind, Ramerrez enters, a captive, his face bloodied, the poncho torn. Still working a cigar, Rance, the vindictive sheriff, blows smoke in the face of his rival. A heavy, he loves to be cruel.

Death waiting to claim him, Ramerrez bursts into song. He sings of the girl he loves, *della donna che amo.* His aria, heart-wrenching, brings more cries of "*Bis! bis!*" We hear the aria again. As the hanging commences, agonized speculation fills the caldarium. Offstage a trumpet blast, like the William Tell music, electrifies the crowd. Minnie, riding a white horse, gallops on stage, her hair flying, a pistol held between her teeth. The crowd in the steam room goes wild.

The Girl of the Golden West, brandishing her pistol, faces down the mob. This man is hers, she tells them, "Mine from God!" Their lust for blood vanished like mist in the clearing, the miners weep softly. Where they were enemies, now they are friends. Exiting together, Minnie and Ramerrez sing a tearful duet. "Goodbye my sweet land, *addio mia California.*" Monsignor looks at his watch. It is past one in the morning.

Leaving the Baths, we cross the outer rectangle where the

Roman palestrae used to stand. The open courts, ringed by porticoes, were for boxing and wrestling. In the arena tigers, hippos, and rhinos gored each other on the sand. Art galleries and lecture halls catered to the sound mind in the sound body. Pedants lectured for a fee, rhetors argued, and poets recited. Endlessly tolerant, Caracalla accommodated cynics and sophists, Christians and Jews. An educated man, he had the best teachers his Syrian mother could hire. Conning the Greek playwrights, he got great swatches by heart. Euripides was his favorite.

Despoiled or sunk below ground, the lecture halls and arenas make a platform for the Ministry of Posts and Telecommunications. An international enclave, FAO squats on the eastern edge of the ruins. Taking thought for everything, ancient Romans never thought of a Food and Agriculture Organization. Spectral by moonlight, the white egg-crate buildings look as if the next *scirocco* will blow them away.

Leaving from its terminus in front of St. Paul's Basilica Outside the Walls, the 223 bus runs south and east to Tre Fontane, the Trappist monastery in the Campagna. Our driver, in no hurry, sucks on a cigaret in the lee of the bus. Having time on our hands, we walk the ancient basilica, big as all outdoors. "Stazione Termini," says Giordano, not impressed. In this chilly railroad station, the trains have come and gone, taking their passengers with them.

Gutted by fire in 1823, the basilica rose again from the ashes. Potentates around the world, not all of them Catholic, pitched in to rebuild it. The gorgeous facing on the altars at either end of the transept, malachite and lapis lazuli, came from Tsar Nicholas I. A pathetic ghost in Rome, Pietro Cavallini haunts the basilica. This medieval maker survives only in bits and pieces, a portent of things to come. One of these days I will get to see his *Last Judgment*, a piece of the whole, in the convent beside the church of St.

Cecilia. Sentimental restorers, putting the pieces together again, have refurbished the mosaics on the inner face of the arch. Scowling at us from a rose-colored heaven, the hairy Pantocrator is a look-alike for Giancarlo Giannini.

One of the seven basilicas, St. Paul's, a numinous place, has powerful magic. Under the pavement lies the martyred apostle, beheaded on the grounds of the old monastery a few kilometers away. In the First Rome, the quick and dead, sharing the city between them, are familiars, not antipathies. All Soul's Day, November 1, is a red-letter day. On this Feast of the Dead, Romans look inward. They go to their holy places, sanctified by heroes' blood, where soldiers guard the shrines of the *caduti*, honored dead. But any day in Rome is All Hallows. In some of their old churches, the skeleton of the holy person is laid out under glass for everyone to see. San Francesca Romana, beside the Forum, is one of these churches. The grinning skull in the casket, not rouged or chemically injected, is like and unlike the waxy corpse of the Founder in Red Square. Where the Roman saint, merest carrion, instructs us in last things, Muscovites wish them away.

Sheltering the bones of the apostle, the noble canopy remembers Arnolfo di Cambio. If they won't let you see his Christmas crib in Santa Maria Maggiore, you can pay him your respects in St. Paul's. Beneath the triumphal arch, the twelfth-century candlestick, writhing, seems alive. Two thousand years of history, framed in roundels, look down from the walls. Mosaic portraits of the Popes, they begin with St. Peter and stretch to the crack of doom. Where the fire stopped, the cloister begins. Papyrus, slender in the fountain, makes a Japanese screen. A sphinx crouches between the columns that support the arcade. Some of these columns, inlaid with cosmatesque work, twist and spiral like sticks of Christmas candy. Some have two shafts twined together. Bordering the grass plots, roses, in flower, accent the dark green of the leaves. The cloister, spared for a while longer, has a message, equivocal. The only permanent world, it tells us, is the world of things. Less addicted to things than me, Giordano, listening, isn't really tuned in.

In the sacristy nearby, we inspect the bronze door, removed from its hinges after the fire. Scorched but still intact, it came from Constantinople nine hundred years ago, a gift to Pope Gregory VII. He was the abbot Hildebrand, and his feet, he said, were kissed by all princes. Dreaming of a Christian imperium on earth, he faced down the German emperor in 1075. This Emperor Henry IV, coming to Canossa, knelt barefoot in the snow, craving the Pope's forgiveness. Dressed as a penitent in a coarse woolen garment, he waited three days before he got what he came for. The bronzecaster, a Greek, wanting us to remember him has left his name on the door. "I, Staurachios of Chios, made this work with my hands. You who read this, pray for me."

The bus driver lets us out in Via Laurentina, a modern highway going south between EUR and Quartiere Ardeatino. From the vendor beside the highway we buy an apple apiece, polished on the sleeve of his smock. Heaped with russet apples, the handbarrow, positioned cleverly, partly blocks the *portone* in the wall. The long tree-lined drive, quiet after much clamor, ends before a medieval gate, standing open. Regarding us or maybe not, the fantail pigeons in the eucalyptus trees are mournful, like cooing doves.

Dryads and hamadryads live in the wooded enclave, also shaggy satyrs. The sun making shapes and checkers, I see the foul goathead peering through the trees. In Rome, the Christian city, gods and presences proliferate, and these pagan survivors are welcome. Rebaptized, their names are different. Saturnus and Jupiter, going underground, reemerge as the Father and Son. The old gods of the latifundia, ancient Roman estates, still haunt in the Campagna, auspicious. One of these gods is called St. Cataldo. Romans, before threshing, pray to this pagan saint. If their ass is ailing, they summon St. Erasmo. Newly christened too, he remains adept in these matters. Their San Giorgio is old Perseus, slaying the dragon. Look beneath the lion's skin, and you see how Hercules the strong man and St. Christopher are one and the same.

Entertaining a hundred gods, the First Rome shows its difference from Constantinople and Moscow. Immortal cities, the Three Romes are psychologies too, pagan, monotheistic, and godless. Byzantines in the Second Rome, worshiping the One God, said how the Son of God, inferior, proceeded through the Father. Muslims, coming later, were a winnowing wind. In one of their mosques, a sancta sanctorum, the inscription from the Koran makes a manifesto. "Praise be to God who has no son or companion in His government." Moscow, the Third Rome, gives the gods their quietus. In this more rational polity, the government devolves on man.

Three little churches commemorate the three fountains that lamented the death of St. Paul. Bare bones going back a millennium and more, the unadorned portico of Sts. Vincent and Anastasius is denuded like the rock we stand on. Water, splashing in a stone sarcophagus, underlines the silence. Inside, massive columns, not pillars but piers like the elephant legs that hold up the Friday mosques of Islam, still carry the Romanesque arches. High above the nave, selenite windows, translucent, admit the light. Unlike the gorgeous ceiling of St. Paul's Basilica, the high roof, made of wood, dispenses with fretwork.

In the center of Rome not far from the Veneto, Santa Maria della Vittoria, Bernini's St. Teresa church, shows you the fretted thing, par excellence. More radiant than the sun of heaven, the great sunburst above the altar is never blotted by clouds. The coy sculpted figures almost dropping from the ceiling don't smell of carnality. A few motes of light, rationed, filter through the stained glass. In the womblike interior, drossy life, reconstituted, turns into something better. Facing this church across the Largo Susanna, Moses, not Michelangelo's but an imitator's Moses, glowers on his fountain. Grotesque and coarsely menacing like the head of Constantine in the Capitol Museum, he is flanked by roaring lions. The end of a great style, this naturalistic ensemble seemed absurd to Bernini and friends. You can see why they went indoors, turning the key on the world.

But vulgar naturalism is to baroque as baroque is to utter plainness. Put against the white "Congo" churches of New England, radical in their plainness, baroque architecture looks thin. Here in Tre Fontane, I begin to understand why my Protestant fathers, missing something vital, had to revolt to find it again.

Beside the ilex-shaded path where the fountains flowed two thousand years ago, the apostle laid down his head. The executioner's block, a stone column no higher than a kitchen stool, stands by itself in a corner of San Paolo alle Tre Fontane. My son, still a boy when he came here with me for the first time, claimed he saw gouts of blood on the column. A Roman survival, the polychrome mosaic in the middle of the floor represents the four seasons.

In the twelfth century, St. Bernard, a monk of Burgundy more Calvinist than Catholic, came to Rome for a visit. He didn't like it and said so, being an idol smasher in a city of idols, also an honest man. But he had done the Pope some service, and they offered him a relic. This was the head of San Cesareo, from which he extracted a tooth. In Rome, celebrating Mass, St. Bernard had a vision. He saw angels bringing souls up the ladder to heaven. On our left among the medlar trees is the church where he saw this, Santa Maria Scala Coeli, the Ladder of Heaven. Our middle earth and its business didn't much detain St. Bernard. Hating the mosaics and frescoes that glorified Roman churches, he preached against them when he got home. What did "all that" have to do with salvation?

Giordano is a throwback to the Abbot of Clairvaux, a comparison that wouldn't please either. Valiant for truth, he travels lightly, indifferent to creature comforts and pictures on the walls. A primitive Christian, "Protestant" and good, he wants to get rid of clutter, the dominion of things. Where St. Paul's Basilica makes his hackles rise, Giordano is at home in Tre Fontane.

In the last century, travelers to Rome, fearful of malaria,

skirted the ruined monastery. When the Trappists arrived in 1868, they put their house in order, draining the swamps and planting eucalyptus trees. People sick with malaria, a mysterious malady, said how the eucalyptus kept the germs at bay. From the sap the Fathers made a liqueur, on sale in the little gate-house built into the monastery wall. Like a lot of Romans, Giordano prizes this concoction, good for what ails him. An enlightened man, he goes to the doctor when he gets sick. Let the *scirocco* blow, however, and he wants his *roba dei frati,* "stuff of the Fathers." An all-purpose remedy, it beats the famous liqueur distilled by the Carthusians in their Charterhouse of Parma. Set out on the counter, the brightly colored bottles invite our inspection. I reach for my wallet but Giordano gets there first. "This one," he says, "is on me."

Romans, stingy with place names, boil down where they can. Leonardo da Vinci, their international airport, is called for the district "Fiumicino." Esposizione Universale di Roma, the modern city Mussolini built, abbreviates to EUR. To get to EUR, up the hill and west of Tre Fontane, we change for the 123 bus. Looking out the window, Giordano, a bespectacled Duce without his Shriner's fez, spreads both arms wide. "*Ecco,*" he says, "*la terza Roma.*"

This phrase was Mussolini's. To the Rome of the Caesars and the Rome of the Popes, built on the Seven Hills, he annexed his "Third Rome." It was going to extend over other hills, he told them, "along the banks of the sacred river, as far as the shores of the Tyrrhenian Sea." This boast, at any rate, he accomplished.

The bus brings us through canyons, steel and concrete. Unlike bedroom suburbs on the perimeter of American cities, they don't hug the ground but reach for the sun. Pueblo caves dot the cliff face. Cliff dwellers on their balconies lean over the balustrades or sit on aluminum lawn chairs. Growing in green metal boxes, geraniums, white and red, make a color contrast. More vivid than this, the improbable sky between the buildings is "cerulean," patented by Romantic poets like Shelley. Having been to EUR, Giordano, who has never been to California, doesn't have to go there.

Shades of pastel warm and soften the contours of the new apartment houses, a progressive kindergarten. The architecture, efficient but allowing for grace notes, says that modern isn't always anonymous or mean. Not an unbroken phalanx, the buildings arrange themselves in clusters, one different from the other. Each *rione* or neighborhood has its *pescheria*, a fish market, its *macelleria* or butcher's, a shop for poultry, a fruit stand, a coffee bar *all'angolo*, on the corner. Striding into the future, EUR looks brisk and cheerful. Istanbul, shambling towards the future, is Tobacco Road East, modern Moscow a Panopticon or prison. *Grazie*, Mussolini.

Only the new city is immaculately conceived. An airborne spore, it has existence without presence. I know other places like this city in the sun. Some of them benign, all are "*sossopra*," upside down with their roots in the air. As between Santa Monica, Fort Lauderdale, and EUR, there isn't a lot to choose. Down in Nashville, Tennessee, they have a full-scale Parthenon, complete in each particular. As good as new, it survives from some long-ago centennial honoring the city. Not pocked by time or acid rain, the limestone columns are straight and smooth as an ashplant. Turkish gunners have spared the metopes, and the Doric frieze between the triglyphs tells its story sans intermission. A perfect artifact standing by itself in a park outside the city, this Nashville Parthenon, needing Athens, is dead.

North of EUR, the Eternal City asserts its tie to heaven, like Hildebrand's failed Christian republic. Vindicated by failure, old Rome is earthbound. Held by a thousand filaments, it bellies and drags in the wind. Elsewhere the balloon, breaking loose from its moorings, soars into the stratosphere. Up there, the air is thin.

Back in Moscow, I see them sniffing this purified air. Beside the walls of the Kremlin, their bodies, turning blue, are stacked like cordwood.

Being self-contained, EUR has its churches, even a mosque. In the futuristic city, man rules the roost, however. This is different from old Rome, where man takes second place. On a scroll above the altar in Borromini's Sant' Ivo church, a Latin tag admonishes the people: "*Initium Sapientiae Timor Dominum.*" "The beginning of wisdom is the fear of the Lord." Nearby in Piazza Navona, they don't fear the Lord and most don't read Latin. But these Romans walk warily, knowing how in last things they aren't *prepotenti*. Prudence growing on me, I make this the beginning of wisdom.

Giordano, his tongue wagging, has another definition. He announces the religion of man. Where Jupiter Optimus Maximus used to preside on the Capitol, shaking the thunderbolt in his red right hand, Romans have a City Council, "men like you and me." Giordano adds, smiling, "Sometimes worse than you and me!" The smell of incense, climbing to heaven, offends him. "Anyway, the heavens are empty." Bowing the knee is servile, he thinks, a prehistoric reminiscence like going on all fours. He wants to empty out the churches, installing man in the tabernacle. I tell him his knobby knees are more supple when they bend.

Once, on a trip East, I got sick in the Arab Emirates. The little hospital on the eastern edge of the Arabian peninsula stood inland, near the Gulf. Getting up to sneak a pipe in the lounge beside the men's ward, I watched the young Bedouin going through his *sourates*, daily prayers prescribed by the Koran. Sleeping a lot myself, I can't swear that he was faithful to the five appointed times. He might have gone back to sleep, battered as he was in a car smash, when the muezzin called him in the hour before dawn. But whenever I was up, he was up, doing his devoir. First he took the tatty prayer rug from the formica-top table. This rug, unlike most, was representational, with the crescent moon and star in each of the corners, a mosque and minaret in the center. General Issue, it solaced devout patients on the ward. "My" patient, unrolling it, wound a turban on his head, then knelt, facing west, Mecca being behind us. His dry lips, forming syllables, made a sound like water drops coming fast from the tap. Otherwise, the bowing and scraping was pantomime.

Intent on her devotions, the young nun in St. Cecilia's, shutting the door on my foot, was like the young man in Dubai. Teasing out this unlikely connection is a yield of my travels in the present and past. Where the Christian God is personal, an old man with a beard, Allah is the Logos, Muslims being indifferent to the "human face divine." But in their deepest place, Rome and Mecca, antagonists and dissonant, speak for the same truth. Each says how we don't keep the universe alone.

Giordano discovers unity in diversity, too. What he sees doesn't please him, however. Superstition, sponsored by the black brood, "ministers of falsehood," is the common chord. "Garibaldi said that." Down here in EUR, I ask myself if this is true. Men in Moscow, superstitious, believe in their Dialectic. This doesn't resemble them to Mecca or Rome. On my "American" side, self-made, I am closer to Kraisky, the emancipated man, than I am to the Bedouin or the cloistered *sorella.* It isn't superstition or faith that unites them. The common chord is humility.

A Chirico landscape in the center of EUR, Viale Marconi recedes without ending. Lining the wide thoroughfare, the glass-fronted buildings, austerely perpendicular, look bigger than they are. This is deliberate, and comments on a secret struggle between the genius of yesterday and today. Near the Pantheon in Rome, the old Minerva church, calling itself Gothic, tries to play down the Gothic thing. Taking up a lot of room, it looks smaller than it is, and its grasp exceeds its reach. Piazza Minerva, in front of this church, has a whimsical elephant supporting an obelisk, the smallest in Rome.

In Piazza Marconi, men and women, homunculi, ascend the

steps of the Prehistoric and Ethnographic Museum. The Palace of Congresses, a self-glorifying import from Socialist Land, turns its fishy eye on the Museum of the Arts and Popular Traditions. Hanging from the façade, the red banner, stitched with gold letters, announces an exhibit: IL RISORGIMENTO APRILE-LUGLIO 1849. An illustrated poster, mounted on sandwich boards, stands to the right of the doors, above it a verse from Garibaldi's Hymn: *"Va fuori ch'è l'ora, Va fuori d'Italia, va fuori, o stranier."* "Stranger, begone from Italy, this is our hour."

The Garibaldini, more like brigands than soldiers, their bearded faces dusty, the shaggy hair uncombed, are pushing their way down the Corso. Supers in a romantic opera, they wear the conical Calabrian hat, gaudy with black ostrich feathers. Above them streams the black flag, ensign of the Italian Legion. Some of the legionaries carry lances and muskets, all are hung with daggers, more than they can use. Dramatic in their red tunics, the officers come first. Coming on behind them, the men wear dark blue. "Like the last scene of some absurd comedy," said Emilio Dandalo, the warrior historian of the Bersaglieri. He was there, says Giordano, when the Legion came to Rome. Later, this skeptical soldier changed his tune. Underneath the frippery, Italians showed him their stuff, *pietra dura,* hard as rock.

Inside the museum, the walls on the first floor are dense with photographs and etchings. Oil paintings and watercolors stand on easels in the corridors. Romantic poets, their eyes ardent or reproachful, look out of the old photos. The names are Masi, Mamelli, Ceccarini, Gaetano Bonnet. One of them is Polish, a man without a country. He wears the national cap with its four-cornered crown of red cloth. One, French and Republican, appeals against his country to a higher cause. Hot with youth and marked for death, most are Italian. Beautiful Angelo Masina, his cap at a rakish angle, flaunts the skull and crossed bones. He left his bones on the Gianicolo, whitening between the armies. Evidently a monarchist, not a republican, Luciano Manara displays the Cross of Savoy on his sword belt. Before he took the bullet that killed him, he said, "Am I to take nothing away from Rome?"

Not all these men are young, and some must have been villains, every army having its quota of such. P. Roselli, too old to be a poet, is a general who wants you to know this. Giacinto Bruzzesi, a colonel, bewhiskered and settled, looks like William Howard Taft. Ferocious beneath an outlandish hat, P. Pietramellara fills me with envy. On the fatal third of June, he made a desperate stand in the Villa Corsini. The broad brim and waving plumes of black-green cock's feathers denote the Bersaglieri, says Giordano. This regiment from Piedmont was elitist, however. Only officers got to wear the cock's feathers, the men having to settle for horsehair.

The corridors, like church on Sunday, have that rustling, uneasy sound, shushing for quiet. Fathers wtih their children pause in front of the photographs, telling over the names of the dead. Wanting to raise hell, a troop of school kids stifles the impulse. Their teacher, her beady eye on the sparrow, sees to this.

All by herself among these masculine heroes, the lone woman has no trouble making her presence felt. An easel painting shows her with her back to the mountains. We are looking at San Marino where Garibaldi, retreating, found a refuge. However, this Duce wasn't at his post the day the painter imagined his painting. Like chickens with their heads off, panicky soldiers are fleeing right and left. Descending from the mountains, the white coats move to the attack. A Puccini heroine indifferent to danger, the woman lashes these disorderly Italians with her tongue. Some, pulling themselves together, turn back to face the foe.

In her photographs, this woman is composed. Short, big-breasted, her straight black hair like an Indian's, she looks evenly at the camera, the dark eyes intent and unsmiling. The caption says, "Anita Garibaldi." Garibaldi in his memoirs tells how they met, gazing at each other, enraptured and silent. "At last I greeted her by saying, '*Tu devi esser mia*'—'You should be mine.' " Alexandre Dumas, a writer of fictions more likely than the truth, edited this memoir. In the museum they have a copy of the Brussels edition, also a letter from Garibaldi to Anita. Disregarding his wishes, she was on her way to join him in the beleaguered city, but he doesn't know this. "One hour of our life in Rome," he tells her, "is worth a century of ordinary existence."

The enemies are here, side by side with the friends. Pope Pius IX, "Pio Nono," rosy-lipped, young and handsome, wants to smile but remembers his place. The Warren G. Harding of the papacy, he had his good looks to recommend him. "*Ah! che bello!*" women said, half in love with their pastor. Succeeding Pope Gregory, the embattled foe of telegrams and railroads, he made a bad business worse. "After the policemen," says Giordano, "came the ladies." Antonelli the cardinal, a policeman, is all in black with red piping. He wears the red biretta and a single medal on his tunic. The strong face, lively with thought, is the face of an Inquisitor, one of the great Domenicans. "*Domenicani*," Giordano calls them, punning on the Italian for dog. "Hounds of God!" Where Pio Nono shrank from violence, this reprobate cardinal did the dirty work, he says.

Part of the dirty work, the ruined Villa Corsini, engraved by Carlo Werner, contrasts starkly with its rococo frame. The sides of the building, still standing, are pierced with big windows, their casements intact, but the front has fallen in, and among the shattered columns dead men are flung like rag dolls. A single volute, the crest of a wave, survives on the broken roof, above it a rack of clouds. Skinny umbrella pines look limp on the horizon. Still hung up on his Ship of State, D'Annunzio salutes the Villa Corsini, in verses attached to the frame: "Smoky prow of the Ship thrust forward into the tempest."

Against this haunted house, emblem of the Ruins of Rome from the beginning, Garibaldi threw wave upon wave of his men. Spurring them, he said incredible things: "I offer neither pay, nor quarters, nor provisions. I offer hunger, thirst, forced marches, battles and death." *Fame, sete, marcie forzate, battaglie e morte.* Not everybody admired this. One veteran, inured to the glamor of war, called him *piuttosto bizzarro*, rather quaint.

Across the corridor, the great man has a room to himself. Photographs and hectic paintings bring him from youth to old age. A boy in 1822, he goes down to the sea, the year Shelley sailed his last voyage. Almost thirty years later, after the retreat from Rome, he puts to sea again, making for Venice and freedom. He is standing in his *bragozzo*, surf beating against the hull. The feluccalike sail, reddish-orange, veers round above his head, and on the bow an allegorical figure blows a trumpet. Anita is with him, lying against the thwarts. She never made it to freedom but died in his arms, in the pine forest outside Ravenna.

They called him *Leone*, says Giordano. Flaring at the root, the strong straight nose gives him a lion's look. In the freckled face, burned by sun, the small eyes, deeply set, are ingenuous, the eyes of a hero. The mustache is heavy and the blond beard ends in two points. Short, bowlegged, and stocky, Garibaldi has an athlete's torso, pinched in at the waist. In some poses he wears a frock coat, inserting his right hand between the buttons, like Napoleon, in others he is dressed in the red shirt and baggy gray trousers. Knotted round the neck, the silk handkerchief is insouciant, but the horseman's saber in his left hand means business. The black sugarloaf hat has two black ostrich feathers, nodding to each other. Sometimes a poncho and a cartridge bag are slung over his shoulders. If the poncho is open, you see the knife at his belt.

Color by Technicolor, like the heroic canvases in Moscow's Tretyakov Gallery, *Garibaldi on Horseback* takes half a wall. His gold hair falling to the shoulders, he is followed by an orderly, Andrea Aguyar. This South American Negro, a comrade of old battles on the pampas, is bigger than Jack Johnson, once a black hope. A lasso hangs from his saddle. Wrapped in a blue poncho, the fierce-looking orderly wears a beret, red tunic, and blue trousers striped with green. A red streamer tips the long lance in his hand. Knocked over by a French shell on a Trastevere street, he died in the last days of the Republic. Aguyar's horse is black. Garibaldi, all in white, rides a white horse.

Considering this new St. George, Giordano is reverential but moves his chair to a distance. Garibaldi had no theory, summing up his doctrine in the single word "*Avanti!*" Putting instinct over reason, he snapped his fingers at mundane problems, vexing to you and me, taxation and finance, for instance. He thrilled them with slogans: "Here we shall make Italy or die!" The problems didn't go away, and the new Italy they made wasn't the Italy he dreamed of but the Italy of Fiat, *società anonima*.

Black and white drawings from the *Illustrated London News* show the old man on his island of Caprera, "awaiting a fresh call to arms." He is feeding his dog, swinging a mattock, or tending his donkeys, "Pio Nono" and "Antonelli." A little man of Calabria who happened to come from the North, he had a green thumb in the garden. This was lucky, says Giordano. He never heard the call to arms, and the revolution he expected was "put off on account of the rain." But he lived long enough to see what his new Republic was up to. Bankers, men of industry, and "Tagliatelle Socialists" ran the Republic. All got their snouts in the trough. Down south in Calabria, they left the poverty alone.

The grave on Caprera is like anybody's grave, surmounted by a pompous block of granite. He told them in his will to lay him on a funeral pyre in his red shirt, face upturned to the sun. He wanted to burn in the open air, like Shelley. "That is the right way." He said they would need a lot of wood for the fire. But they fiddled these instructions and gave him a proper funeral, not wanting common wood ash to mingle with the ashes of their Duce.

After the brassy triumphs, Garibaldi, "old and worn," wrote the story of his life. An English translation, introduced by a friend from Hampshire, lies open on the table, under a clear plastic tent. Silver clamps the size of thumbprints hold back the pages. Giordano, peering through his granny glasses, spells out the words:

"Where are those splendid horses? Where are the bulls, the antelopes, the ostriches which beautified and enlivened those pleasant hills?"

Outside the museum, the dying sun lights a fire in the glass blocks, Druid monoliths, that stand around the piazza. Remembering that this was farmland once, a concrete selion divides the furrows of traffic. Via Cristoforo Colombo, rising to a hilltop, bisects the city. Atop the hill, between Atlantic and Pacific streets, the Palazzo dello Sport exfoliates in concrete leaves. Geometric and cool, it is like the idea of a flower. In the shining center of EUR, *menefreghisti,* bad actors from Calabria who drop their litter on the sidewalk, aren't welcome.

The plush-lined instrument case lying open at his feet, a street musician is playing the viola part from *Harold in Italy.* Clapping the bellows and pulling out the stops, Berlioz in this symphony did his romantic best for Byron and Shelley, republican heroes. The fiddler on the corner doesn't have the drums or the yellowing horns, only his sweet viola, and the melody comes and goes, filtered through street cries and the irritable noises of traffic. You hear Byron in the melody. He said in *Childe Harold* how freedom's banner, torn but flying, still streamed like a thunderstorm against the wind. Fighting for freedom, this poet died at Missolonghi and is buried in England. Shelley, however, is buried in Rome. The stone above the grave has a Latin inscription: *Cor Cordium,* "Heart of Hearts."

On the rubbish dump beside the cemetery, Italians set up cannon in 1849. Monte Testaccio, an ancient mound of potsherds building over centuries like coral in the sea, rises forty-five meters above Via Caio Cestio. It made a good target for French gunners on Monte Verde. Zeroing in on the Italian position, some aimed their guns too high. The errant shells, exploding, fell unnoticed near Shelley's grave, beneath the Pyramid just in from the wall.

"A voice crying in the wilderness," says Monsignor Moran. That was the Catholic Theological Seminary out on North Harlem Avenue, home to East Indians, Hindus, and Jews. Graduating from Notre Dame with three letters in athletics and a Phi Beta Kappa key, Monsignor trained for the priesthood at CTS in Chicago. Deacon was the first step up the ladder. Rising to this, he did his "practicum," apprentice work, nearby in Norwood Park. At Resurrection Hospital, the trauma surgeons kept him busy, sometimes around the clock. Monsignor would like a nickel for every time he has administered the last rites of the Church. Race, color, and creed made no difference to him. Using his aspergillum like a garden hose, he sprinkled the holy water on anyone who came within range. "Baptize them all," he says, "and God will look after His own."

Running south of Norwood Park, the expressway runs west to O'Hare. Turning his back on the airport, however, Monsignor took the eastbound lane to Wrigley Field. In the old ballpark, its walls covered with ivy, the Chicago Cubs played languid baseball on sunny afternoons. Finishing last in the National League, they came first in the heart of Monsignor. Stan Hack, the third baseman, was batting .350. Back at CTS, the professor of hermeneutics wasn't hitting the size of his hat. To this day, says Monsignor, hermeneutics remains a closed book.

Baseball lingo is part of his working equipment. Distinguishing right from wrong, he imagines a strike zone, "hard to imagine, but there." When the two of us go at it, he is apt to quote Bill Klem. Calling balls and strikes, this old umpire said, "I don't call them as I see them, I call them as they are." A tractable man with his friends Tom, Dick, and Harry, Monsignor has his intractable side. On the matter of faith and morals, he digs in his heels. "Sentimental liberals," endlessly tractable, make his thumbs prick. "Something wicked this way comes."

The Risorgimento, when liberals got the upper hand, is his *radix malorum*, "the root of all evil." He calls it "the last of the barbarian invasions." Passing the Quirinal Palace in Rome, he signs himself with the sign of the cross. In 1871 King Victor Emmanuel stole this palace from the Pope, "Christ's Vicar on earth," making it the capital of united Italy. However, says Monsignor, Italy is "only a geographical expression." Garibaldi, born in Nice, spoke worse Italian than he does. In the streets of Naples, people shouted "Long Live Italy!" when the great man drew near, then asked each other what the word "Italy" meant.

The type of the assured man, Monsignor is palsied when he opens his red Michelin Guide. The people who make this Bible of good eating, handing out one, two, or three stars, speak *ex cathedra* like the Pope on his throne. Okay for faith and morals, this doesn't work when it comes to cuisine. Among top-class Roman restaurants, who can say which is better or best? Monsignor has his favorite restaurants, unranked but savored. Gratefully, he takes them one at a time. Today, he says, it is the turn of Scarpone. My time in Rome winding down, he proposes that I come as his guest.

Hailing a cab in Trastevere beside the Cestio bridge, we climb the twisting road called for Garibaldi. Villas and apartment buildings hide the steep hillsides, colored like money. Before Mussolini turned the city upside down, the Gianicolense quarter at the top of the hill was a wilderness, says Monsignor, "the Campagna without mosquitoes." On weekends, Romans came up from the city to the Villa Pamphili. Like men and women in the Manet painting, they spread out white linen and ate their picnic lunches in the shade of the evergreen oaks.

Some of these oaks were felled in 1849, "liberated" for the defense of the Republic. The old trees in the Villa Borghese had it worse. They went by the wagonload to make barricades. William Wetmore Story, a proper Bostonian, watched the barricades going up in Porta San Giovanni. Roman workmen, he said, were "too lazy to live," also "Bunker Hill ramparts were thicker." The enthusiasm he saw around him, not "of the right stuff," seemed to promise "a festa demonstration."

Our cabbie, instructed, puts us down on the terrace before

the Spanish church of San Pietro in Montorio, built for King Ferdinand and Queen Isabella. On a hillock beside the church, St. Peter was crucified. Anyway, Bramante thought so, and built a little temple on the spot. Intending to make a meal of it, Monsignor suggests that we walk the rest of the way, walking off our calories before we put them on. Also he wants me to admire the view. Across the red tiled roofs, we look over the Tiber to the Aventine Hill. Destroyed a thousand years ago, the palace of the Emperor Otto recomposes itself, its crenellated towers shivering in the haze of late morning. North of this looms the Palatine where Romulus drove his plough around the bounding lines of his little village, and the she-wolf, giving suck, saved the two brothers for Rome. Guiding my eye with his finger, Monsignor points out the Lateran in the far distance. Against the sky, the portico is thronged with its Christian militia.

Just west of us, Garibaldi directed the battle for Rome. Monsignor says he set up shop in Villa Spada behind the Aurelian Wall, placing cannon in the piney forest on the high ground near the church. Efficient against the Goths in Belisarius' time, the imperial walls couldn't stand up to cannon. Romans found this out in 1527, when Spaniards and German Lutherans broke into their city. After the Sack of Rome, the Popes built a new wall, protecting the west bank of the Tiber. Taking in the Vatican Hill, it extended from Castel Sant' Angelo in the north to Porta Portese on the south. The French, invading from Civitavecchia, made for the gates north and south of the Vatican. Outside the southern gate, Porta Cavalleggeri, rose the Janiculum Hill, its highest point looking over the wall. Garibaldi had his first headquarters there, in the Villa Corsini.

Defending the wall were the National Guards, the Carabinieri, and soldiers of the papal line, coming over to the Republic. Trasteverinos, armed with shotguns and spears, kept watch on the ramparts. One observer, says Monsignor, saw them carrying knives in their teeth. Brick and stone faced the ramparts, sloping backwards from the base. The bastions, outposts in the wall, stood on earthen platforms, cushioning the parks of artillery. From these bastions, Italian gunners traded cannon fire with the French. In the last days of June 1849, French shells blew in the roof of San Pietro in Montorio.

On the principle "Know your enemy," Monsignor is a student of modern Italy and her heroes: King Victor Emmanuel, the royal buffoon, Mazzini, a pedant whose watch stopped in 1848, Garibaldi, part prophet, part comedian. "You know the face of a lion? Is it not a foolish face? Is it not the face of Garibaldi?" Unexpectedly, Cavour, the sly opportunist who put this show on the road, gets Monsignor's reluctant admiration. "In practical politics," he says, "the impossible is immoral. Unlike the others, Cavour understood this."

Nino Bixio was one of the others, "a Hero." Angry with his insubordinate soldiers, Italian, he screamed at them: "I command here. I am everything. I am tsar, sultan, Pope." Where this careless revolutionary lumped the three together, "you and I," says Monsignor, "will want to discriminate." A clerical smoothie, he makes me part of his camarilla. To hear him tell it, the world gets on nicely without the tsar and sultan. Losing the papacy, though, it lost "the one great thing left." He is willing to say that the world was a better place when the Pope, a temporal sovereign, ruled his Papal States.

Behind us, the sober façade of San Pietro in Montorio hearses the bones of Black O'Neill. He was the Earl of Tyrone, like Garibaldi a guerrilla chief of genius. Leading the Irish in their struggle for freedom, he beat the English hollow at Yellow Ford on Blackwater. Afterwards, however, he came down from the hills, lured by notions of chivalry. He fought and lost a pitched battle, conducted by the rules. This happened in 1601, the year the Pope beheaded Beatrice Cenci. She has her last resting place in San Pietro too, near the grave of Black O'Neill.

Via Garibaldi, spiraling upwards, skirts the ossuary above

the church. "*Ai Caduti per Roma,*" says the inscription, remembering the fallen. "*Roma o Morte,*" Garibaldi told them. "Rome or Death." Monsignor, hearing fustian, makes a wry face. "Warmed-over antiquity, like Horatius at the Bridge." Near where Ponte Cestio joins Trastevere to the Tiber Island, a wooden bridge spanned the river, Livy's Pons Sublicius. At the Trastevere end, facing Lars Porsena and his Etruscans, stood "the dauntless three," Horatius at their head. I know about him, patriotic heroes being in, not offensive, when I was a boy. Regullus and Camillus were heroes of mine, also that Gaius Mutius who had as much courage to die as to kill. "It is our Roman way to do and suffer bravely," said this Mutius. Horatius was best of all, "the great soldier whom Rome's fortune gave to be her shield on that day of peril."

This is how Livy describes him, but we didn't read Livy. We read Lord Macaulay and his *Lays of Ancient Rome*. Up on the Janiculum where the Etruscan army menaced the Republic, I hear the lay of Horatius, and is it fustian or not?

And how can man die better
Than facing fearful odds,
For the ashes of his fathers,
And the temples of his Gods.

On our left beyond the monument, Pope Paul's Fontanone, a little Niagara, spills sheets of white water into the stone cistern, loot from some emperor's Forum. The Gate of San Pancrazio at the head of the road overlooks a web of streets, their names reminiscent: Angelo Masina, Giacomo Medici, Nicola Fabrizi, men of 1849. A quarter of a mile away, Garibaldi, standing on the high terrace of Villa Corsini, watched the French coming on. They wore their parade uniforms, white coats and gloves, heavy shakos on their heads. This was at the end of April, already hot. "Italians never fight," said their general. The French marched through an emptied countryside. On the walls of the houses, placards bore a text from their new Constitution: "France respects foreign nationalities. Her might will never be employed against the liberty of any people."

Letting the dead bury the dead, opulent villas on top of the hill address themselves to sweet idleness, *dolce far niente*. In the academy on Via Masina, epigraphers and classicists, mostly young Americans, aren't concerned with the proximate past. As we reach the summit, the cannon booms for *mezzogiorno*.

Some say that the Emperor Otto, cutting up his rival Crescentius in fours, displayed the parts on this Gate of St. Pancras, others that he hung the body on Monte Mario to the north. He was Ottone Terzo, "the wonder of the world," and he wanted to reform the world against the coming millennium, the thousandth year of the Christian era. Dreaming of a unified Italy, he wore the crimson and purple of a Roman Emperor. A seal of his was inscribed "*Renovatio Imperii Romani*." But he didn't renovate the Empire.

This Otto had his successors, Hildebrand, the architect of the Christian Republic, being one. Failing, he said, "I have loved righteousness and hated iniquity; therefore I die in exile." Monsignor thinks this makes a sequitur. Strong for the right, Arnold of Brescia roused the people of Rome against the Pope. He wanted to bring back the Roman Republic. In 1155, Pope Innocent got hold of him, burned his body, and threw the ashes in the Tiber.

Like everybody else, this republican hero has his street in Rome. Near Piazza del Popolo, it looks south and west to the street in Trastevere named for Cola di Rienzo. He called himself the Tribune Augustus. "Where are those good old Romans?" Cola liked to say. Invoking "Sacred Italy," this fourteenth-century Mazzini tried to put the pieces together again. The Roman mob cut off his head and burned him in the Mausoleum of Augustus. Wagner, Monsignor tells me, wrote an overture for Cola. However, he got the name wrong. Mussolini, a man for premonitions, got it right. "I am Cola di Rienzo," he said.

On the other side of the Porta San Pancrazio, two streets come together, one named for the gate, the other for the old Aurelian Wall. In the triangle between them the green space is kempt and ordered, almost English, like Hampstead Heath. This is the Villa Pamphili, named for a mansion that stood in the park. Villa Corsini, four hundred paces in from the gate, shared the park with Villa Pamphili. Between the grounds of these villas ran a little stream.

Tall, ornate, and alone on a hill, Villa Corsini made a landmark for Romans. Casa dei Quattro Venti, they called it, House of the Four Winds. Built of stone, it rose four stories, the first two hidden by a wall. A double staircase, climbing up the façade, opened on a balcony beneath the second-floor windows. You had to go up the staircase to enter the villa. Big pots holding orange trees lined the low walls on either side of the stairs. Men could crouch behind the orange trees, unseen but seeing.

Like someone's rustic garden, the park gates are surrounded with rockwork. I see embedded in the rock a cannonball the size of a grapefruit. Villa Corsini, up the drive, is only a ghostly presence, but Romans, clearing away the ruin, have built a triumphal arch where the villa used to stand. On this sunny afternoon, the park is crowded with soccer players, easy-going joggers, and kids on swings and slides. Some areas, cultivated, have rose bushes and patches of grape. A hundred years ago, vineyards and cornfields covered the green hillside, "Monte Verde." Lording it over the palm trees and *pinetti*, the evergreen oaks, famous for a long time, are still holding their own. Little men and handsome women, pulled along by big dogs, tug on the leashes. Having these dogs is a fetish in Rome. The corgi, a favorite dog in England, built close to the ground, doesn't have panache enough for Romans.

Thinking they could stroll into the city, the French soldiers made a mistake. Down the slope from the gardens of the Villa

Pamphili came three hundred students, volunteers for Rome, followed by the First Italian Legion. They met the French on Via Aurelia Antica, beneath the arches of the Pauline Aqueduct. As wild as dervishes they were, said a French officer, "clawing at us even with their hands." Sitting on his white horse, Garibaldi watched the fighting, then threw in reserves. "Onward with the bayonet, *bersaglieri!*" he said.

On this first day of the battle for Rome, the French lost five hundred men. Later, however, things went badly for the Romans. The French, wanting an armistice so they could recoup, got what they wanted, then broke their *parole*. In the early hours of Sunday, June 3, while Italians were sleeping, they seized the Villa Corsini, key to Rome. On Via Aurelia Antica outside the park, the plaque on the wall has a notice: *"Giacomo Veneziano Caduto 2 Luglio 1849."* The day after this Giacomo fell "for the defense of Rome," the French army entered the city.

Angling off to the left, Via di San Pancrazio is heavily trafficked. A parking lot, like a bombed-out site, serves the new apartment buildings. Across the street, harmonizing with this, a piece of ruin leans over the sidewalk. The ground-floor wall is still standing, and on the wall is a laurel wreath, dusty. "What is left of the Villa del Vascello," says Monsignor. While the siege lasted, General Medici held it for the Republic. *"Pochi contro moltissimi,"* reads the inscription. "Few against so many."

Inviting in its arbor planted with wisteria, zinnias, and lemon trees, Scarpone is Big Boot, the way "Fontanone" is Big Fountain and "Cupolone," St. Peter's, is Big Dome. The cover of the menu shows a charging soldier with fixed bayonet, also a single boot. Saying something like "Washington Slept Here," a legend in fancy script claims the patronage of Garibaldi. According to Monsignor, this claim has merit. The original Big Boot, nicknamed by the general, handed over his house in 1849, or maybe Romans took it. This was when the restaurant was Casa Giacometti. At the end of June, men of the *Unione* regiment held the house, enfiladed by

French fire and hemmed by their trenches. Garibaldi in a letter tells what Italians did here. Coping with a night attack, they "used the bayonet, killed a captain and three soldiers, made four prisoners and a number of wounded."

On the morning of June 3, Emilio Dandalo, weak from loss of blood, came to Casa Giacometti, looking for his brother. "It is too late now," said Luciano Manara. "I will be a brother to you." Emilio fainting in the arms of his colonel, Manara carried him away. Later these men exchanged roles, and Manara lay dying while Dandalo wept. "Does it grieve you so much that I die?" said Manara. He added, "It grieves me also."

"*Consiglia*," says Monsignor. Dispensing with the menu, he wants the waiter to advise us. The antipasto, like a colored photo in a coffee table book, is purple, silver, greenish gray, and orange. We eat: *aringhe*, herring; *funghi*, fried mushrooms, *grandi*, also *piccoli; melanzane*, eggplant; *cozze,* mussels; *carciofi*, artichokes; *cipolline*, little onions; *calamari*, squid. One bottle emptied, another appears. I push back my plate and reach for a pipe and tobacco. "*Mangia, mangia!*" says the waiter. "Eat!" He puts the pipe in my pocket.

This *cameriere* is a magician. He conjures up an enormous spigola, hooked through the gills. Fierce as a pike but native to salt water, the big fish is silvery gray with brown fins. We applaud politely. "*Preso stamattina*," says the waiter. "Caught this morning." Returning to the kitchen, he reappears bringing pieces of veal. Flavored with bay leaf and tightly rolled in prosciutto on a long wooden spit, this is *manganello*. Also he has veal *piccata*, rich with lemon sauce and butter, *scamorza*, a cheese dish, creamed rice and scampi, and *galletto novello*, a little rooster.

At the adjoining table, a French couple, man and wife, have pitched into their entree, crayfish *al cognac*. Between mouthfuls, their talk is of Rome, *ses églises, sa campagne, ses arbres, son peuple*. "All the shallow clarity of Descartes," says Monsignor. Against the deeper well of Rome, their neat discriminations, enunciated precisely, are only a drop in the bucket. "But a hundred years ago, they beat the Romans hollow."

This was revenge. Garibaldi, contemptuous, called the French "Gallic friars." They were modern men, however, indifferent to chivalry, where Italians, looking backwards, embraced a lost cause. When they were Romans, *mascula proles,* they warred on their Gallic neighbors to the north. They did this in the name of the future. Gauls, romantic and Celtic, stood for the past. Evoking a world of loss, *The Dying Gaul,* a marble sculpture in the Capitol Museum, says how the future has its price.

Defending their city, Italian soldiers carried a musket or rifle, fitted with the bayonet, maybe sixty rounds of ammo, a water bottle, a haversack, often empty. Most were young. Luciano Manara, already a veteran of the Lombard Bersaglieri, died at twenty-four, Enrico Dandalo at twenty-one, the same age as Mameli the poet. Morosini was a boy of seventeen. Urged not to let him go to the war, his mother said, "I give my country the best I have, my only and dearly loved son."

Salad, a change of pace, comes to the table, *insalatina capricciosa* for Monsignor, *puntarella,* tidy green strips mixed with anchovies, for me. Where the French tourists have gone on to dessert, a *Monte Bianco,* we cleanse our palate with cheese and fruit. *Pecorino romano,* the cheese is made from sheep's milk. Monsignor, sated, picks at this without interest. The waiter, taking note, brings *ovoline,* little white eggs. This is buffalo cheese. The fruit tray has *ananas,* fresh pineapple, mixed fruits of the season in a basket or *cestino, fragole a piacere,* strawberries to please. With the *caffè doppio,* Monsignor offers cigars.

The dining room, spacious, airy, and bright with cut flowers, is lighted by a high window, running fore and aft. Bougainvillea, in bloom, shows through this window, behind it the old boundary wall separating the grounds of the Villa Corsini from Casa Giacometti. Defending the wall were the French *tirailleurs,* sharpshooters. Also they held the wall in front of the villa, protected to the north by a deep lane, to the west by its natural moat. Garibaldi, shouting "Courage, my boys!" told them to storm this villa. Rome, he said, was "the dominant thought and inspiration of my whole life." This was "the Rome of the future—the Rome that I have never despaired of even when I was shipwrecked, dying, banished to the farthest depths of the American forests." On the third of June, he made his bid to claim Rome for the future.

Covered by small-arms fire from the Villa del Vascello at the foot of the Corsini hill, the young volunteers poured out of the narrow gate of St. Pancras. They ran up the drive between the high box hedges, uphill all the way. Crowds cheered them as they went, and a band played the *Marseillaise*. This was meant to shame the French, faithless republicans.

One human wave breaking, another took its place. Some men, reaching the villa, charged up the steps and got on to the balcony. They bayoneted the French defenders and threw them out the windows. But from the gardens of the Villa Pamphili, reinforcements moved up. Winning and losing, then winning again, the French always had the last word. This went on all morning, under a blistering sun.

Outside the Porta San Pancrazio, in a rectangle four hundred paces long by three hundred paces wide, a thousand Italians died, the best among them. Garibaldi, ruthless, wouldn't let them stop. "He had a special method of his own," said a friend. Using up his men, women too, he pressed the juice from the grapes and threw away the skins. However, he said, "I have never shrunk from helping any fellow creature in danger, even at the risk of my own life." Through the June days, risking his life, he led his redshirts, not caring to follow. Bullets and shrapnel tore his poncho and floppy hat. "I saw Garibaldi," wrote Emilio Dandalo, "spring forward with his drawn sword, shouting a popular hymn." At the end, crying "*Questa è l'ultima prova,*" "This is the last fight," he looked for death in the cannon's mouth but didn't find it. Nino Bixio, wounded, lived to fight again. He said fighting with Garibaldi was like living in "a world of poetry."

It was always now or never. When the Bersaglieri came up, Garibaldi sent two companies forward. Impatient, he didn't wait for artillery fire or musket fire to support them. Four hundred men of Lombardy charged the hill but never reached the villa. Kneeling in the open, they fired at the windows and the French behind the walls. Manara stood with them, watching them die, then gave orders for his bugler to sound retreat.

Garibaldi had a slogan, remembered from his days at sea: "*Bisogna approfittare dell'aura*"—"Make the most of the breeze." The French musket fire dying down, he saw his chance and took it. This opportunist had a yen for fine words. "We will conquer or die," he liked to tell Italians. On the third of June, however, Garibaldi kept decorum. Turning to the remnant, he said laconically, "I shall require twenty resolute men and an officer for a difficult undertaking." Emilio Dandalo, volunteering, stepped forward. "Go," said Garibaldi, "with twenty of your bravest, and take Villa Corsini at the point of the bayonet." Dandalo said, "I shall do my best." Dashing through the gate, the little force was decimated before it covered half the length of the drive. "I looked round me," said Dandalo. "We were alone." In a shower of bullets from the windows of the villa, the men stood "intrepid, silent, ready for any effort." Then their officer brought them back, six of the twenty.

Next came Masina and his Bolognese lancers. Cavalry soldiers, they wore red fezzes like Turks. In the last days, these cavaliers, dismounting, fought on foot in the pine woods near the grave of Black O'Neill. Crying "*Viva l'Italia!*" they used their lances like swords. Nearly all died. When the fighting ended, the ground was vivid with the pennons of their lances, still held in the hands of the dead. Galloping through the gate, they made it over the villa grounds and got up the steps. On their heels, Garibaldi led the tatters of his Legion. They pushed the French from the villa, where flames licked at the timbers and the floors were giving way. Heartened by success, Italian soldiers left the walls and stormed up the slope, with them a crowd of civilians. One more push, they thought, and all might be well. But the French, counterattacking, drove them off the hill. Garibaldi got back safely. Others weren't so lucky, among them Angelo Masina. "The leader of the *jeunesse dorée*," he died beneath the steps of the Villa Corsini. Later that summer, Italians recovered his bones.

Seeing his duty, Garibaldi went from Rome. Anita rode with him, dressed in the red shirt, her long hair coiled and hidden beneath a wide-brimmed hat. Where Mazzini wanted them to fight in the streets, dying for honor like O'Neill's romantic kerns, he meant to cherish Rome for the future. "Wherever we go," he told them, "there Rome will be." Romans said goodbye at the Lateran Gate. Calling softly "*addio*," they watched the long column disappear down the darkening road.

The French, having scotched the serpent, wanted to kill it. They hunted political refugees in Rome. Spies said that some refugees were hiding in the house of the American consul, Brown. Entering this house without a by-your-leave, the French were met on the stairs by the consul. Holding a sword in one hand, he held the Stars and Stripes in the other. The English poet Clough, in Rome when the French came in, saw "faces far more brutal than the worst Garibaldian." However, he said, "The bourgeoisie are very glad it is over."

Playing up to his role of *pezza novanta,* Monsignor has laid on a car and driver to return us to the Caelian Hill. We could catch the 62 bus at the foot of Via Gianicolo, but would have to get down in Piazza Venezia. This bus, turning north, runs to Porta Pia, where united Italy came to Rome twenty-one years after Garibaldi left it. Our private transport waits for us at the church of Sant' Onofrio, across the hill above Vatican City. The Passeggiata del Gianicolo takes us down the hill.

Busts line this promenade, one bearing the name Antonetta Columba. On the seventh of June, a musket ball, ricocheting, struck down a young soldier, here or hereabouts. Bursting into tears, an officer covered the body with kisses. The officer was Ponzio, the soldier was Columba, his wife.

In the little park beside the promenade, children ride electric bump cars and ponies. "*Ora e sempre,*" reads the inscription on a stone column, honoring the sons of Umbria who died on the Gianicolo. "Now and forever." Gigantic on his horse, Garibaldi, facing left, looks towards the Vatican, like Giordano Bruno in the Campo dei Fiori. Along Viale del Parco di Villa Corsini, the tree trunks, their bark peeling, are white and pistachio green. Filtering through the plane trees, the golden light is dusty with pollen.

Piazzale Anita Garibaldi stands above the lighthouse, a gift to Italians from the people of Argentina. At night the electric lantern shows the flag to the city, red, white, and green. Rome, spread out below us, is unlikely but graphic. Behind a wire fence, the playground in the piazzale belongs to a grade school. Pine needles, gummy with resin, carpet the playground where children, dressed in white smocks, are making the most of their recess. The smocks, says Monsignor, won't be white for much longer.

Aloft on the rearing horse, the woman has her hands full. She holds her baby in one arm, a pistol, cocked and raised, in the other. At the foot of the statue, a little Italian man walks an Irish wolfhound, almost as big as he is. "No! No! She isn't dead," Garibaldi protested, kneeling by his wife's body. "Look at me, Anita! Look at me! Speak to me! Oh, Anita, what have I lost!" Later, the authorities broke up the shallow grave. Anita wore no ornaments on her neck or fingers, said the police report, and the dark hair was dressed austerely, "*alla puritana.*" But the ears were pierced for earrings, and white flowers adorned the cambric burnoose.

CONSTANTINOPLE
(ISTANBUL)
HARBIYE
CUMHURIYET CAD.
Hilton Hotel
ASHI CAD.
TAKSIM SQUARE
To Jnonu Stadium
To Dolmabahche Palace
GOLDEN HORN
Pera Palas Hotel
ISTIKLAL
To EYUP
N
Tophane
Atatürk Bridge
Galata Tower
Kilitch Ali Pasha Mosque
BOSPHORUS
To USKUDAR
Fatih Chami (Mosque of the Conqueror)
FEVZI PASHA CAD.
Galata Bridge
Suleimaniye Mosque
Yeni Chami (Mosque)
Seraglio Point (Sarayburnu)
To Edirne Gate and EDIRNE
ATATURK BULVARI
Aqueduct of Valens
Spice Bazaar
Sirkeji Station
Topkapi Palace
University of Istanbul
Kapali Charshi (Covered Bazaar)
VATAN CAD.
Underground Cistern
To Yeshilkoy Airport
Hippodrome
To ANKARA
To BURSA
To IZMIR
SEA OF MARMARA